Zahera Harb is Senior Lecturer in Journali
and previously worked as a journalist in .... one is the author of
*Channels of Resistance in Lebanon: Liberation Propaganda, Hezbollah and
the Media* (2011) and co-editor (with Dina Matar) of *Narrating Conflict in
the Middle East: Discourse, Image and Communications Practices in Lebanon*
(2013), both published by I.B.Tauris.

'This book offers interesting perspectives on Western media depictions of the Middle East from a range of Arab countries. The fact that the volume includes chapters on Lebanon, Syria, Jordan, Iraq, Egypt and Palestine, predominantly by writers and scholars of Arab origins, makes a valuable contribution to existing literature on issues of media representation *from* and *of* the Arab world.'

– Dima Saber, Senior Research Fellow,
Birmingham Centre for Media and Cultural Research

£4.00

REPORTING
THE MIDDLE EAST
THE PRACTICE OF NEWS IN
THE TWENTY-FIRST CENTURY

EDITED BY ZAHERA HARB

I.B. TAURIS

LONDON · NEW YORK

Published in 2017 by
I.B.Tauris & Co. Ltd
London • New York
www.ibtauris.com

References to websites were correct at the time of writing.

International Media and Journalism Studies 3

ISBN (HB): 978 1 78453 271 0
ISBN (PB): 978 1 78453 272 7
eISBN: 978 1 78672 176 1
ePDF: 978 1 78673 176 0

A full CIP record for this book is available from the British Library
A full CIP record is available from the Library of Congress

Library of Congress Catalog Card Number: available

Printed and bound in Great Britain by T.J. International, Padstow, Cornwall

Contents

Contents

List of Illustrations

Acknowledgements

A few weeks after I arrived in the UK from Lebanon for my PhD, the 11 September atrocities took place. I soon realised that the Middle East and Arab world that I knew, grew up in and worked in as a journalist was different from the one I watched and read about in the American and British media. In 2004, the idea to put together a module on reporting the Middle East came about. Professor Terry Threadgold of the Cardiff School of Journalism and Professor Kevin Williams of Swansea University approved the module's rationale and listed it as a taught module in both the Cardiff School of Journalism and the MA Erasmus Mundus at Swansea. In 2007 I, with my 'Reporting the Middle East' module, moved to Nottingham University. From Nottingham I moved to the City, University of London Journalism Department where the 'Reporting the Middle East' module gained a more practical dimension. This book emerged from the module.

All thanks go to both Professors Threadgold and Williams who encouraged and supported me in sharing my own experiences and analysis as a journalist from Lebanon with journalism students. The module grew to include guest speakers – journalists and academics, who have worked in or on the region. Many of those who contributed to the module as guest speakers are featured in this book. My gratitude and thanks go to the book contributors for their willingness to participate in, and commitment to, this project. This book is of both an academic and non-academic nature. I want it to appeal to my journalism students first and foremost. I would like to thank all my 'Reporting the Middle East' students over the years. Many of them have made me proud of the journalism they have produced, remembering that history, context and semantics are three aspects they need to consider when reporting the Middle East.

Thanks go to my friends and colleagues in the UK and around the world, who hear and see me repeatedly and passionately speak and post regarding British and American media Orientalist tendencies, about coverage

Acknowledgements

inaccuracies and about how, in many instances, journalism values are lost when it comes to reporting the Middle East, Islam and the Arab world. Special thanks to Dina Matar for her continuous support as a friend and colleague. Many thanks to long-time friend Sadie Clifford who dedicated the time and energy to proofread this book and for her valuable editorial comments. Last, but not least, my thanks go to I.B.Tauris editor Joanna Godfrey for her support and patience.

List of Contributors

Mike Berry is Lecturer at the Cardiff School of Journalism. Mike is co-author of *More Bad News from Israel* (2011) and *Bad News from Israel* (2004). He also co-authored *Palestine–Israel: Competing Histories* (2006).

Birce Bora is a news producer for Al-Jazeera English, based in Doha. She was London correspondent at Turkey's flagship national daily newspaper *Hürriyet* for over three years before moving to Al-Jazeera. She holds a PhD in Journalism Studies from City, University of London. Her thesis examined the representation of Turkey in British broadsheets between 2007 and 2013.

Esmaeil Esfandiary is a PhD candidate in Communication at Georgia State University. His research focuses on mainstream media representations of Islam and Iran, Iran–US information and communication rivalry in the region, and dynamics of US–Iran relations and the role of media in that regard. His PhD thesis aims at drawing a comprehensive discursive map of American 'Iran experts' based on the range of discourses they construct regarding how to deal with Iran.

Shahab Esfandiary is Assistant Professor in Film Studies at Tehran's University of Arts and also a freelance documentary filmmaker. He is the author of *Iranian Cinema and Globalization* (2012) – based on his PhD thesis at the University of Nottingham – and has contributed to edited collections such as *De-Westernising Film Studies* (2012) and *Iranian Sacred Defence Cinema* (2012). He recently edited a collection of papers in Farsi also titled *Iranian Sacred Defence Cinema* (2016).

Omar Al-Ghazzi is Lecturer in Journalism Politics and Public Communication at Sheffield University. He completed his PhD at the University of Pennsylvania's Annenberg School for Communication. His work has appeared in *Popular Communication, International Journal of*

Communication, and *Media, Culture and Society*. A former Fulbright fellow, Al-Ghazzi holds a master's degree in International Communication from the American University in Washington, DC. He comes from a professional journalism and media analysis background and has previously worked for the BBC and the pan-Arab daily newspaper *Al-Hayat*.

Naila Hamdy is Associate Professor and Chair of the Journalism and Mass Communication department at the American University in Cairo. She has peer-reviewed articles published on various aspects of the journalism profession in Egypt and the impact of communication technologies and media development in the Arab region. Hamdy is also a former television journalist who has covered major news events for prominent international television stations.

Zahera Harb is Senior Lecturer in Journalism at City, University of London and previously worked as a journalist in Lebanon. She is the author of *Channels of Resistance in Lebanon: Liberation Propaganda, Hezbollah and the Media* (2011) and co-editor (with Dina Matar) of *Narrating Conflict in the Middle East: Discourse, Image and Communications Practices in Lebanon* (2013), both published by I.B.Tauris.

Dina Matar is Senior Lecturer and Head of the Media Centre at SOAS, University of London. Dina is the author of *What It Means to be Palestinian* (I.B.Tauris, 2010), and co-author of *The Hizbullah Phenomenon: Politics and Communication* (2014). She is co-editor of *Gaza as Metaphor* (2016) and *Narrating Conflict in the Middle East* (I.B.Tauris, 2013).

Fernando Resende is Senior Lecturer and Research Co-ordinator at Universidade Federal Fluminense in Rio de Janeiro. He holds a PhD from Universidade de São Paulo (USP). He was appointed as visiting scholar at SOAS, University of London and several other European universities. His research focuses on narratives of conflicts and diasporic movements; theory and philosophy of communication and journalism; comparative media and documentary studies; and critical cultural studies. He has published on Brazilian media coverage and representations (press and documentaries) of the 2003 invasion of Iraq and the Israeli–Palestinian conflict.

James Rodgers is Senior Lecturer in Journalism at City, University of London and former BBC Gaza correspondent. James is the author of *Headlines from the Holy Land: Reporting the Israeli–Palestinian Conflict* (2015), *No Road Home: Fighting for Land and Faith in Gaza* (2013), and *Reporting Conflict* (2012).

Haider Al-Safi was Head of Iraq Project, BBC Media Action; he holds a PhD in Journalism from City University, London. He reported, on post-2003 Iraq, as a freelance journalist for the *Independent*, Channel 4, ITV and the BBC. In 2009 he joined the BBC World Service as a broadcast journalist at the BBC Arabic Service.

Lina Sinjab is a journalist and writer who has covered the Middle East for over a decade. She is currently a BBC Middle East correspondent based in Beirut. She served as Arab Affairs editor at the BBC World Service in London. She has also served as World Affairs reporter covering the Syria peace talks in Geneva. Prior to that Sinjab was the BBC correspondent in Syria. In 2013 she won the International Media Cutting Edge Award for her coverage of the Syrian uprising. In the same year she produced and directed a film on Syrian women during the uprising, which was nominated for the One Media Award. She has also covered the uprisings in Libya and Yemen.

Introduction

Reporting the Middle East, the Arab World and Islam

Zahera Harb

The Middle East has been synonymous with conflict throughout the twentieth century and into the twenty-first. From the Arab–Israeli conflict to the Arab revolts, to the rise of fundamental religious groups, such as Al-Qaeda and the self-declared 'Islamic State' (IS, aka ISIS or Daesh), Western media coverage of the region has been mostly dominated by news of conflict.

Coverage of the Middle East region, in relation mainly to Islam and the Arab countries, has been deeply tainted with Orientalism that re-enforces negative stereotypes and connotations about the people of the East, mainly Arabs and Muslims. It gives way to Islamophobic sentiments in news discourse that engenders hate and fear against 'the Other'. Edward Said states in his book *Orientalism*, written in 1978:

> One of the important developments in nineteenth-century Orientalism was the distillation of essential ideas about the Orient – its sensuality, its tendency to despotism, its aberrant mentality, its habits of inaccuracy, its backwardness – into a separate unchallenged coherence; thus for a writer to use the word *Oriental* was a reference for the reader sufficient to identify a body of information about the Orient. (1978: 205, emphasis in original)

Very little has changed in the twenty-first century. Several chapters in this book argue that when some Anglo-American writers and journalists use the word 'Islam'/'Muslims' or 'Arabs' they are presenting their audiences with a set of negative perceptions that form a body of knowledge about more than a billion Muslims worldwide and more than 350 million Arabs spread over twenty-two countries. By referring to the extremist group as 'Islamic State' instead of Daesh or ISIS, hence giving the perpetrators the religious legitimacy they are claiming, they are inducing fear among their audiences of Islam and Muslims in general. For example, a headline in the *Scotsman* reads: 'Fears grow as Islamic State moves closer to Europe' (Bradley, 2015). This was a story about the beheading of twenty-one Egyptian Copts on the shores of Libya. The headline adopts the propaganda message ISIS had released with the video of the beheadings, which claimed that the West should fear their plans to 'conquer Rome'. The body of the article didn't seem to follow the implications carried in the headline, but rather quoted Egyptians saying that the threat is as much to Muslims as it is to Christians. Another article published in the *Daily Telegraph* on the same day carried similar connotations, with a headline that read 'Islamic State Planning to Use Libya as Gateway to Europe'. The article claimed that 'the jihadists hope to flood the North African state [Libya] with militiamen from Syria and Iraq, who will then sail across the Mediterranean posing as migrants on people trafficking vessels' (Sherlock and Freeman, 2015). These claims were attributed to what the writers referred to as 'plans seen by Quilliam, the British anti-extremist group'. Both articles send a message of fear of 'them' (Muslims and Arabs) as one homogenous group. Of an 'Other' that is mystic and barbaric.

Depicting Muslims negatively is not a new phenomenon. Edward Said's book *Covering Islam* (1997) is still a key reference on that matter in addition to the many scholars who followed suit, mainly the work of Elizabeth Poole (see Poole, 2002 and Poole and Richardson, 2006) and the research conducted by Kerry Moore, Paul Mason and Justin Lewis (2008). In his second edition of *Covering Islam* (1997), Edward Said wrote that much of what one reads and sees in the American media about Islam 'represents the aggression as coming from Islam because that is what "Islam" is'. He concludes that 'covering Islam is a one sided activity that obscures what "we" *do*, and highlights instead what Muslims and Arabs by their very flawed nature *are*' (Said, 1997).[1] He argued that in the minds of many Western journalists, writers and even scholars, 'Islam and Arabs are one and can be attacked interchangeably' (ibid).

Prior to that, in an essay Said wrote in the *New York Times* book review in 1976 on 'Arabs, Islam and the Dogmas of the West', he spoke of four dogmas through which the West sees the Orient. The third and fourth dogmas conceptualise the tendency towards inducing fear:

> A third Dogma is that the Orient is eternal, uniform, incapable of defining itself, therefore it is assumed that a highly general-ised and systematic vocabulary for describing the Orient from a Western standpoint is inevitable and even scientifically 'objec-tive'. A fourth Dogma is that the Orient is at bottom something either to be feared […] or to be controlled. (Said, 1976)

The fear factor of Islam and its followers, including all Arabs, rose notice-ably in the wake of the 11 September atrocities.

This pattern of coverage kept repeating itself. Neil Clark from the *Guardian* newspaper explained that the war on Iraq in 2003 induced what became known as 'Arabophobia'.

'It is not hard to find evidence of the increased pervasiveness of neo-con-induced Arabophobia in our media, whether intentional or not' (Clark, 2003). A British officer was quoted in the *Mail on Sunday* saying: 'I read T.E. Lawrence before I came here'. He added, 'A century ago he rec-ognised dishonesty was inherent in Arab society. Today is the same. They do nothing for love and nothing at all if they can help it.' That same T.E. Lawrence was quoted twelve years later in an article in the *Daily Telegraph* on the so-called Arab army fighting in Yemen, saying that Arabs have a difficulty defining who Arabs were (Telegraph View, 2015).

Lack of context, either deliberately or out of ignorance, is another feature that much Anglo-American reporting on the Middle East suffers from. The most apparent case is the Palestinian–Israeli conflict, discussed in detail by Mike Berry in Chapter 5 and James Rodgers in Chapter 7.

Journalistic texts are a product of a variety of cultural, social and political factors. Some Anglo-American journalists have a tendency to apply their own personal perceptions, re-emphasising stereotypes of the Orient. The rush to publish or broadcast makes them omit context. Lack of specialised knowledge makes it easier for many to retreat to preconceived perceptions and misunderstandings of the 'Other', in this case the people of the Middle East.

This takes us back to Edward Said's *Covering Islam*, when he argued that 'Sensationalism, crude xenophobia, and insensitive belligerence are the order of the day', with results on both sides of the imaginary line between "us" and "them" that are extremely unedifying' (Said, 1997).[2] With no intention to generalise, it could be argued that 'the order of the day' has not seen significant changes almost twenty years later.

This book aims to introduce and explore media coverage of the Middle East region mainly in Britain and the United States. Through studying the coverage of Middle East conflicts and beyond, readers will explore how media may be used to serve particular political agendas on a regional and international level. It also considers how the use of media can no longer be restricted to state or elite actors. In addition, by studying the coverage of the Middle East and the Arab world, readers will get clear examples of how news formats and practices may be defined and shaped differently by different nations.

This edited collection is intended to provide a practical, and theoretical, route for journalists and journalism students reporting on or from the region by addressing the political, cultural and other factors that shape journalism in conflict situations; allowing them to read and absorb media reportage on the Middle East in a critical manner; and assisting them in writing with some cultural sensitivity on the Middle East. The authors critically examine media texts on different countries in the Middle East, comparing different journalistic outputs and identifying the cultural and political interests that shape them.

This book includes both analysis through the prism of theory – including Orientalism, modernisation, framing, agenda-setting, news values and norms – and practical reflections presented by journalists who are either from the region or have covered the region's conflicts for British and American media. Journalist readers will have the opportunity to compare practice and think more deeply about it, with the aid of these ideas. Media academics and students interested in the Middle East will add to their bodies of knowledge about the issues, but with the addition of the fine-grained and vivid detail that only eyewitness reporting can bring.

The book consists of eleven contributions dedicated to analysing reporting on Syria, Jordan, Egypt, Lebanon, the Palestinian–Israeli conflict, Gaza, Turkey and Iran, and reflections on covering Iraq, Syria, Yemen and Saudi Arabia. The chapters on reporting Syria, Jordan, Lebanon, the Palestinian–Israeli conflict, Turkey and Iran assess the coverage through exploring and analysing specific case studies. The chapters on Gaza and Iraq, and reflections on covering the Middle East (with emphasis on Syria, Yemen and Saudi Arabia), bring in journalists' personal experiences and analysis, which make this collection also speak to professional journalists and non-academic readers in addition to student journalists and academics interested in the Middle East.

The volume also includes one chapter on the coverage of Palestine before the establishment of Israel in 1948 in the Brazilian press. The importance of such a chapter (despite the fact that it comes from a country outside the Anglo-Saxon media) lies in revealing the hegemonic power the British media discourse had on non-Western, non-Middle Eastern media at the time, a power that it still has.

Book Overview

In Chapter 1, Omar Al-Ghazzi uses a discursive approach to the analysis of controversial aspects of reporting Syria since its 2011 uprising. The chapter follows news stories about Syria that turned out to be false. It examines how these stories were produced by Anglo-American news media and how they elicited reactions from official Syrian media and lent credence to the communicative strategy of the Al-Assad regime. The chapter focuses on two contentious episodes in the Syria coverage: the case of 'A Gay Girl in Damascus' blog and the 'Syrian Boy Hero' short video. Both examples, in addition to others, reveal how the Syria coverage, since 2011, encompassed many of the challenges faced by contemporary journalism and its global flows, particularly in relation to tensions between news ideals of portraying reality versus truthful acknowledgements of the complexities of news representation.

Chapter 2 by Dina Matar discusses the coverage by the BBC and the *Guardian* newspaper of the kidnapping by ISIS militants of a Jordanian pilot in December 2014, his execution by immolation in early February

2015 and the Jordanian response to the murder, to open questions about reporting Jordan. Through engaging with the concept of 'first framing' and an examination of news sources, the chapter raises questions about the role of framing in promoting particular ways of seeing the world that, in this particular case, is constructed by local rather than global actors, thus challenging preconceptions of Western hegemonising frames. Though the case study is inadequate to propose any conclusive analysis of how Jordan is reported on any given day in the international news cycle, the analysis of the coverage highlights some problems related to directions of research on international news, perceptions about the flow of international news, the frames used to make sense of events and the dominance of particular frames in particular contexts. These problems, it suggests, demand comparative research into reporting the Middle East that takes into account a historically contextualised understanding of international news, which criteria govern news and its production and what factors should be taken into account when thinking of international news reporting in the digital age.

In Chapter 3, Naila Hamdy aims to explore Western media coverage of Egypt in the period following the 30 June mass protests up to the election of a president in 2014, by analysing US and UK elite newspaper reporting. Drawing on scholarship of framing and sourcing practices, a content analysis of four daily newspapers of record in both countries is conducted, presenting a clearer understanding of what features of Egypt and its political map are highlighted. The chapter explores how media may be used to serve particular political agendas at an international level. It also identifies an example of news practices that can be defined and shaped differently depending on the country.

In Chapter 4, Zahera Harb examines the coverage of three Lebanon stories that grabbed the attention of British newspapers and are not related directly to war. These stories are selected due to the negative reaction they received from many Lebanese readers, in both Lebanon and the diaspora. The chapter argues that Orientalism as a 'constructed system of knowledge' has been loosely incorporated into a form of news practice that tends to produce articles that are redundant, inaccurate, full of prejudice and amount to being deeply Orientalist, especially when it comes to gender reporting.

The first of the stories is an article published by the *Daily Telegraph* in July 2015 entitled 'War is a million miles away when the Lebanese begin to party'. The second is the British press coverage of the story of Lebanese TV talk-show host Rima Karaki cutting off an Islamist preacher while on air, for being impolite to her as his host. The third story is that of Joumana Haddad, the Lebanese poet, journalist and writer, who because of her controversial position on sexual freedom has been hailed by one article in the *Independent* as the Germaine Greer of the Arab world. The three stories mentioned above, and the selected coverage (five articles) related to them, were put to three high-profile Lebanese female journalists in a roundtable discussion organised by the author for the purpose of this chapter.

In Chapter 5, Mike Berry delves into assessing the coverage of the Israeli–Palestinian conflict, one of the world's most bitter and protracted wars. It is a conflict which has attracted an enormous degree of scrutiny from the international media. When set against the coverage accorded to other wars with far higher body counts, such as the conflicts in Syria, Darfur or the Democratic Republic of Congo, the sheer volume of reporting dedicated to the conflict appears disproportionate. This chapter concentrates primarily on research which examined the second Palestinian intifada (2000–2). Berry's research formed part of a series of studies that were undertaken by the Glasgow Media Group between 2000 and 2010, which also covered events such as the 2008–9 Gaza war and the attack on the Gaza flotilla in 2010 (Philo and Berry, 2004, 2011). These studies examined the whole of what they describe as the 'circuit of communication', which encompasses the production, content and reception of media messages. The chapter argues that lack of context is one of the most recurring features of the coverage in the British media. The chapter concludes by discussing the various pressures and constraints which structure the production of journalism and noting how their findings resonate with research conducted in the United States.

By understanding journalism as a discursive social practice, Fernando Resende in Chapter 6 reflects on the ways a Brazilian newspaper – *Folha da Manhã* (1936/46) – produces meaning about the Israel–Palestine conflict in the years that proceeded the establishment of the state of Israel in 1948. It anchors the conflict within its historical perspective and draws connections between power relations at the time, aiming at understanding the conflict as a journalistic event. The chapter also tracks the use of the term 'terrorism', and reflects on its use as a political tool. As the narrative analysis shows, the term is clearly attached by those in power to subjects that are of political interest to them. By doing so, it also discusses how journalism effectively takes part in processes by which political, cultural and discursive gestures and practices of inclusion and exclusion of subjects overlap.

In Chapter 7, based on the author's own experience as the BBC's correspondent in Gaza during the second intifada, or Palestinian uprising against Israel, and drawing on subsequent research, James Rodgers considers the nature and value of international, especially British, reporting from Gaza. It assesses the challenges which correspondents face. The chapter argues that international coverage of Gaza has had limited influence on the political and diplomatic situation relating to the territory. However, it also argues that Gaza's history, and the uncertainties in the wider Middle East, mean that good reporting from Gaza is more important than ever. International journalists have one great advantage over many others linked to the territory or affected by the situation there: their access. Because of the restrictions placed upon them, Israelis, Palestinians and even foreign diplomats have limited perspectives on the situation in the regions. International journalists, while not exactly free to come and go as they please, are offered a rarer and broader view. That being the case, access is one of the main aspects of Western reporting of Gaza which this chapter considers. The second is context. The third is the political attempts to influence journalism covering the conflict. The fourth is the impact which the coverage has on policy making.

In Chapter 8, Esmaeil Esfandiary and Shahab Esfandiary assess the coverage of the British newspaper the *Times* between July and December 2010 when they published more than 200 articles and reports on a single case: the apparently imminent stoning of a woman called Sakineh Ashtiani in Iran. The stoning never happened, but the media campaign gained global momentum. It took full advantage of all possible networks of influence, as well as new communication technology, to spread its message. The chapter aims to examine the discourses and narratives of this media campaign, in the context of wider political conflicts between 'the West' and Iran that include a war of narratives.

The chapter argues that the wars of narratives are inherently wars of moralities, and while both sides use systems of morality to justify and promote national interests and foreign policy initiatives, stories of human rights violations have always had a strategic value and function for 'the West' that, as is demonstrated in the present case, go far beyond condemning stoning or saving an individual's life. The analysis of the *Times'* media campaign demonstrates that moral themes are at the centre of the narratives. The chapter draws on Edward Said's observations in *Orientalism*, where 'Westerners' use the imagery of their own 'wicked past' to define an immoral, thus inferior 'Other'.

In Chapter 9, Birce Bora analyses Turkish representation in the British media using the concepts of othering and Orientalism, and tries to determine whether Westernised, secular and allegedly European Turkey is being included in the European 'Self', or whether it is still being othered and, as Said puts it, Orientalised as a result of its religion, cultural heritage and history. While arguing that Turkey is situated somewhere between 'the European Self' and the 'Oriental Other', this chapter seeks to understand how this unique position is affecting the way Turkey is being covered by the British media. The analysis is conducted on articles about Turkey published in four British broadsheets (*The Times, Daily Telegraph, Independent, Guardian*) and their sister Sunday papers (*The Sunday Times, The Sunday Telegraph, Independent on Sunday* and *Observer*) between 2007 and 2013. This analysis is focusing on media organisations based in a single country (Britain) rather than looking at the Western media in general because just like the Orient, the Occident is not a homogenous entity and it cannot be analysed as such. As a result of their specific cultural, historical, demographic and political identities and interests, countries such as France, Germany, the USA, Britain and Italy (and their media) all have different attitudes towards Turkey and the Turkish identity. Hence it is necessary, the chapter argues, to restrict any representation analysis to a specific country. It needs to be noted that this chapter is focusing on the representation of Turkey in the British media from 2007 to 2013, a period prior to the start of EU membership discussions and consequently a more aggressive representation of Turkey's EU membership ambitions.

Chapters 10 and 11 are reflections from two Arab journalists working on covering war-torn countries in the Middle East for British and American media. In Chapter 10, Iraqi journalist Haider Al-Safi uses his extensive experience covering Iraq for British and American media to provide us with an insider's look at the difficulties that journalists face when covering Iraq. His chapter is presented as a guide regarding what to do and not to do as a foreign journalist covering Iraq. The chapter presents readers with examples and stories, and the Iraq story's impact on the journalists covering it and the people that they are covering. Al-Safi emphasises the need for foreign journalists to understand and accept the importance of cultural difference when approaching a story in Iraq.

The final chapter is another reflection of a journalist's experience covering the Middle East. Lina Sinjab, BBC Middle East correspondent, shares her thoughts on what reporting on countries like Yemen, Syria and Saudi Arabia entails in order for journalists to present their stories effectively. She speaks from the viewpoint of an Arab female journalist covering these countries for an international organisation. She explores similarities and differences in countries run by dictatorships and monarchies trying to remain in power. Sinjab looks back reflectively at how the protest movements in these countries were perceived and handled. She speaks of how, as a journalist, she dealt with the flow of information from citizen journalists reporting the conflict in Syria, where they have become one of the main sources of information after both the government and rebel groups censored news coming out of that country.

Notes

1. Kindle edition. No page number included.
2. Kindle edition. No page number included.

References

Bradley, Jane (2015). 'Fears grow as Islamic State moves closer to Europe', *Scotsman*, 17 February. Available at: www.scotsman.com/news/world/fears-grow-as-islamic-state-moves-closer-to-europe-1-3692319 (accessed 2 April 2015).

Clark, Neil (2003). 'The return of Arabophobia', *Guardian*, 20 October. Available at: www.theguardian.com/world/2003/oct/20/iraq.comment (accessed 2 April 2015).

Moore, Kerry, Mason, Paul and Lewis, Justin (2008). 'Images of Islam in the UK: the representation of British Muslims in the national print news media

2000–2008'. Working paper. Cardiff University. Available at: http://jppsg.ac.uk/jomec/resources/08channel4-dispatches.pdf.

Philo, Greg and Berry, Mike (2004). *Bad News from Israel*. London: Pluto Press.

Philo, Greg and Berry, Mike (2011). *More Bad News from Israel*. London: Pluto Press.

Poole, Elizabeth (2002). *Reporting Islam: Media Representations of British Muslims*. London: I.B.Tauris.

Poole, Elizabeth and Richardson, John (eds) (2006). *Muslims in the News Media*. London: I.B.Tauris.

Said, Edward (1976). 'Arabs, Islam and the dogmas of the West', *New York Times*, 31 October, pp. 4–5; 35–7.

Said, Edward (1978). *Orientalism*. London: Penguin Books.

Said, Edward (1997). *Covering Islam*. Kindle ed. London: Vintage.

Sherlock, Ruth and Freeman, Colin (2015). 'Islamic State planning to use Libya as gateway to Europe', *Daily Telegraph*, 17 February. Available at: www.telegraph.co.uk/news/worldnews/islamic-state/11418966/Islamic-State-planning-to-use-Libya-as-gateway-to-Europe.html (accessed 3 April 2015).

Telegraph View (2015). 'The world needs a new Arab army', *Daily Telegraph*, 30 March. Available at: www.telegraph.co.uk/news/worldnews/middleeast/yemen/11503079/The-world-needs-a-new-Arab-army.html (accessed 2 April 2015).

1

On the Afterlife of False Syria Reporting

Omar Al-Ghazzi

As of June 2015, more than 220,000 people are estimated to have lost their lives in the Syrian uprising and the ensuing civil war. Hundreds of thousands more have been injured. About half of Syria's 23 million people are either internally displaced or living as refugees in other countries. Syrians have died under torture, by air bombings, including indiscriminate barrel bombs, in chemical weapons attacks, in suicide bombings and in sinking boats crossing the Mediterranean Sea. Ruled under the grip of the Baath Party since 1963 and the Al-Assad family since 1971, Syria in 2015 is considered one of the world's biggest humanitarian hotspots and refugee crises. The suffering of Syrians is unfortunately very real. And their struggles deserve the urgent and continuous attention of global news media.

However, the coverage of the Syria story in the last five years has shed doubts on the relation between reality, truthfulness and news in remarkable ways. Since the initial protests in Syria in March 2011, the Syrian regime banned foreign journalists from working in the country in its attempt to control the mediation of the popular rebellion. The nature of the initial protest movement, which often deployed clandestine tactics in the planning of collective action, also made activists the only witnesses. Activists shot amateur digital videos showcasing protests and regime atrocities. Networks of local and diaspora curators administered the flow of digital photos and videos from activists across Syria to global media. Rebel groups eventually developed their own media arms. For its part, the Syrian regime sought to take advantage of this complexity to undermine all amateur digital videos, many of which show crimes against humanity.[1]

In this chapter, I will discuss how false stories about Syria have reverberated across media contexts, particularly how they elicited reactions from official Syrian media that took advantage of them to defend and consolidate the position of the Al-Assad regime. I use contentious examples from the reporting of Syria, particularly those stories that turned out to be false. And I follow their afterlife and the ways they contributed to shaping the official Syrian media narrative. I highlight the importance of considering how news narratives, regardless of whether they are true or false, contribute to shaping events and influencing the choices of political players. While this is not a theoretical chapter, the empirical evidence it provides contributes to larger debates in journalism studies.

The politically significant reverberations of false Syria reports offer lessons that address the debate in journalism studies about the place of reality in the news. As Zelizer (2006) explains, while cultural studies approaches focus on the social construction of reality, emphasising that our understanding of the world is relative and mediated by various discourses, journalists treat facts, truth and reality as 'god-terms' in their profession, and use them as tropes to protect their privileged professional position to tell 'real' stories. My argument is that the recurrence of false reporting about Syria offers important lessons about how old discursive tropes mired in Orientalism and technological determinism are often intrinsic to news narratives. These pitfalls of contemporary journalism should not be dismissed as exceptional errors that have separated the news from reality. Rather, their discursive impact – their afterlife – should be recognised as part of our political reality, as it influences the choices of political players involved in Syria. The acknowledgement of this complexity is necessary, I argue, in order to enhance truth claims in news reporting. In what follows, I trace the pattern of reporting these false stories. In Anglo-American media, false stories were produced and often later dismissed as unrepresentative of journalistic norms. On Syrian official media, such stories served as a pillar of a strategy to cast doubt on media representations of the conflict and enable the dissemination of outlandish claims about a universal conspiracy against the country.

I focus on two contentious episodes in the Syria coverage. The first case is the 'A Gay Girl in Damascus' blog, which was a prominent news story in the summer of 2011. Purportedly written by a lesbian Syrian-American activist, who got arrested by the Syrian regime, the blog was later revealed to have been a fictional fabrication by a 'straight man in Scotland', US national Tom MacMaster (Kenner, 2011). The second case is known as the 'Syrian Boy Hero', a short video distributed online purportedly showing a Syrian boy escaping sniper bullets to rescue his sister. The video was shared by news media and was viewed 5 million times in a couple of days. It turned out to be a fictional video shot by a Norwegian filmmaker. Both cases were reported by news media, only to be retracted as false. These two examples, in addition to the emergence of what I refer to as the 'spokes-witness' media role in Syria, raise questions about photojournalistic authenticity and the slippage in the differentiation between activists and witnesses. They reveal how the Syria coverage of the past five years encompassed much of the challenges faced by contemporary journalism and its global flows.

A Gay Girl in Damascus

The 'A Gay Girl in Damascus' blog controversy is an important example of the problems of the Syria coverage. The fact that this news story about Syrian-American lesbian activist Amina Arraf is fictional does not mean that the reporting on her did not have 'real' impact on the discursive level and in the political world. The story of Amina reflected and reinforced broader cultural and political attitudes and beliefs, whether in Syria or in the West – not least about 'Arab and Islamic sexuality'. It follows a trend for 'transforming other people's struggles into self-serving morality plays' that leads to an 'alarmingly casual attitude towards the distinction between truth and lies' (O'Neil, 2011). The blog falls within the context of what Chouliaraki (2013) has called 'ironic solidarity' that explicitly situates the self at the heart of moral action and renders solidarity a 'contingent ethics that no longer aspires to a reflexive engagement with the political conditions of human vulnerability' (2013: 4). Rather, it exhibits an apathetic empathy with the suffering of others. The blog has also contributed to the Syrian regime's strategy of casting doubt over the authenticity of the protest movement, particularly in regards to its dependence on online media.

In May 2011, about two months after the outbreak of protests in a southern Syrian city over the arrest and torture of teenagers, Western media began to report on an English-language blog purportedly written by a lesbian Syrian-American activist, Amina Arraf Al-Omari. The blog was being updated regularly with memoire-style entries. They ranged from sensual poems about lesbian sexuality to commentary about the uprising in Syria. The blog was hyped up by Western news media. For example, in a report on 6 May 2011, the *Guardian*'s Katherine Marsh, 'a pseudonym for a journalist who lives in Damascus', declared that Amina is 'a heroine of the Syrian revolt'. Marsh added that Amina, 'female, gay and half-American [...] is capturing the imagination of the Syrian opposition with a blog that has shot to prominence as the protest movement struggles in the face of a brutal government crackdown'. Following the media attention, the blog gathered more followers and admirers, mostly from Western countries. On 6 June 2011, a post supposedly by Amina's cousin announced that she had been arrested. 'I have been on the telephone with both her parents and all that we can say right now is that she is missing. Her father is desperately trying to find out where she is and who has taken her,' the update stated.

The alleged arrest immediately became a main story on global news media as it captured the world's attention. Within a day, 15,000 people signed a petition on the Change.org website, calling on US authorities to work for the release of the blogger. The petition described Amina as a 'Sunni Muslim and openly gay woman' and 'an international symbol of the pro-democratic political movement' (Jacqueline M, 2011). Facebook groups and Twitter campaigns were also launched to rescue Amina. However, the blog and Amina's story also began to invite scepticism over their authenticity. The US State Department declared that it cannot verify that Amina Arraf is indeed an American citizen. It also turned out that the photo the blog had been using for Amina has been stolen from a Facebook account of a Croatian woman living in London. The Electronic Intifada website took the lead in investigating the blog. On 12 June 2011, Electronic Intifada found that a US address in Georgia used by Amina matched a property belonging to Tom MacMaster, a forty-year-old American masters student at Edinburgh University. That, in addition to other clues, corroborated that MacMaster is the author of the blog. Confronted by the *Washington Post*, MacMaster first denied the allegations saying: 'look, if I was the genius who had pulled this off, I would say, "Yeah," and write a book' (Flock and Bell, 2011).

However, on 12 June 2011, the blog was updated and MacMaster acknowledged his authorship identity. 'While the narrative voice may have been fictional, the facts on this blog are true and not misleading as to the situation on the ground,' he stated. MacMaster added that he hoped attention is directed towards the people of the Middle East and their struggles in this year of revolutions as much as it has been paid to his blog. He continued:

> The events there are being shaped by the people living them on a daily basis. I have only tried to illuminate them for a Western audience. This experience has sadly only confirmed my feelings regarding the often superficial coverage of the Middle East and the pervasiveness of new forms of liberal Orientalism.

Meanwhile, the Amina Arraf saga angered Middle East followers. Many pointed out that MacMaster's blog did much harm. It lent credence to Syrian regime narratives that news media are fabricating stories about Syria, endangered LGBT Syrians and undermined bloggers and citizen journalists as news sources (McCay, 2011). Others pointed to the nerve that MacMaster, as a white American married man pretending to be a Syrian lesbian woman, had in saying that reactions to his blog exhibited liberal Orientalism (Leo, 2011). As Mikdashi and Moumneh (2011) pointed out, the Amina character was a honey trap for Western liberals – 'the perfect half-white poster child of a brown revolution'. Indeed, Western media reports not only failed to question the blog's authenticity but also falsely reported that the blog is popular in Syria, while in fact its followers, and the media attention that it received, largely emanated from Western countries.

My use of this case is to stress that larger cultural and political discourses are an intrinsic part of journalistic narratives. To begin with, there is the obvious issue that Western media attention has honed in on the blog simply because it is English-language, which as Lynch et al. (2014) have suggested, is a large and persistent problem in Western journalistic coverage and academic analysis of the Arab uprisings' digital output. The contentious episode also exposes the privileging of a seemingly networked and technologically savvy individual as worthy of news media attention.

As Bollmer (2012) argues, 'disregarding the often tortuous negotiations of publicity and privacy necessary for the political action of marginal populations and identities, the demand to connect requires subjects to submit to a uniform ideal of openness'. Of course, the attention to this blog came within the context of the so-called Facebook and Twitter revolutions in Egypt and Tunisia. It is well known that the use of social media in political mobilisation against both countries' authoritarian regimes in early 2011 has been hailed by Western and Arab commentators, many of whom argued that new technologies empower activists and support their democratic aspirations.

Perhaps the most prevalent dimension within the Amina Arraf news saga was in relation to how news media inadvertently propagated narratives about sexuality and the Middle East. The news reporting of this story demonstrated intellectual historian Joseph Massad's (2007) Foucauldian critique of Western incitement to discourse about Arab sexuality as repressed and repressive. Most of the news reports about Amina lead with the 'extra information', meant to give background, that homosexuality is taboo in Syria. When Amina was supposedly abducted, it was reported that 'an outspoken lesbian blogger in Syria, where homosexuality is illegal, was reportedly snatched off the streets' (Sheridan, 2011). Another article explained that homosexuality in Syria is a 'strict taboo' and quoted from MacMaster's blog in which his Amina character said 'there are a lot more LGBT people here than one might think, even if we are less flamboyant than elsewhere' (Marsh, 2011). Thus, while Western coverage was expressing outrage over the Syrian regime's crackdown on activists, in this case a lesbian activist, it was also portraying the region as backward. While the language of news reports purports this information as if to contextualise news with a cultural background that already exists, it is also actually producing and renewing a discourse about the backwardness of the Arab world as evidenced by the region's homophobia. As Mikdashi and Moumneh (2011) contend, the situation of Arab gays and women is portrayed as a marker for backwardness and civilisation under the twinned discourses of 'tolerance' and 'Islamophobia'. Even when the inauthenticity of the Amina blog was exposed, Western news reports reached out to local gays and lesbians, who had voiced outrage over the Amina hoax, and presented their statements as authentic representations of sexual minorities.

The implication in the news reports was that, though Amina is fictional, the homophobic culture is genuinely real.

MacMaster eventually issued an apology. In addition to betraying the trust of many people, he also voiced regret by saying: 'I have distracted the world's attention from important issues of real people in real places. I have potentially compromised the safety of real people' (Leo, 2011). Major Western news media apologised and updated their erroneous news reports – pointing out the difficulty of reporting Syria given the regime ban on foreign reporters in the country. The 'Free Amina Arraf' petitions and Facebook groups were taken down. One of the campaigns' slogans, a quote from the blog, 'borders mean nothing when you have wings', lost its allure of inspiration when its author was no longer the rebellious lesbian in Damascus fighting an authoritarian regime. The phrase became the banal words of a straight white man fantasising about lesbian sensuality in the Middle East.

In Syria, it was the fabrication of the blog and the deception of the news that was reported. A report on the Syrian TV news channel, Addounia, owned by cousin of President Bashar Al-Assad, Rami Makhlouf, discussed the story. The report was uploaded on YouTube on 15 June under the headline, 'disentangling the threads of conspiracy'. The report portrayed the blog as part of a larger Western conspiracy, and used the gay identity of the fictional Amina to accuse actual Syrian activists of a homosexual agenda ('Lion Heart', 2011). The report stated that the blog 'made the sexually deviant (character) into a hero'. In a conspiratorial tone, the report referred to 'them', the conspirators behind the blog, as hoping that 'this story would be casually forgotten, like other campaigns that target Syria, as if it were a coincidence rather than a conspiracy'. It added that 'they' wanted Syrians to believe that 'it is a coincidence that the blog was launched weeks prior to the crisis in Syria'. The report then targeted Syrian activists, particularly those who often speak on Western media, and accused them of 'dreaming of a revolution of sexual deviancy'. It concluded that 'homosexuality is the common trait among more than one hero of the so-called Syrian revolution'. On 16 June, *Al-Watan* daily, also owned by Makhlouf, reported the story under the headline: 'The scandals of media fabrications continue. The *Guardian*: "the lesbian" figure in Syria is an American man's fabrication.' The article stated that the story of 'the lesbian blogger' has dominated

French, British and American newspapers and magazines. It added that the Amina character succeeded in mobilising lesbians around the world for her alleged cause up until the blog and the character were exposed as fictional. Amina was exposed 'for turning the world against Syria'. The editorial concluded: 'MacMaster's trick contributed to the anti-Syrian claims and lies that are being constantly fabricated about the kidnapping of bloggers and activists.'

In an interview with National Public Radio (NPR) on 14 June, MacMaster, the man behind the blog, apologised once again, expressing regret that 'quite a number of people are seeing my hoax as distracting from real news, real stories about Syria, and real concerns of real actual on the ground bloggers' (*Kojo Nnamdi Show*, 2011) His apology addressed the main accusation of those who attacked his hoax and emphasised the harm it may have caused. As the deceived administrators of Amina's Facebook fan page wrote, 'this foolish and cruel hoax has distracted from the real issue in Syria – that the Syrian people are sacrificing their lives for calling for an end to a regime' that silences, tortures and murders its people (Smith, 2011). Andy Carvin, of NPR, who was among those who took the lead in uncovering the inauthenticity of the blog, tweeted: 'if we could only calculate the sheer number of hours spent this week on #Amina, each one of which was an hour spent not on Syria itself' (Mccay, 2011).

As Carvin's tweet suggests, it is important to reflect on false reporting as a way to maintain journalism's authority and values. One way of doing that is in acknowledging that there is no absolute 'Syria itself' – a Syria that would present itself to journalists as unmediated reality. Stories like the fictional 'A Gay Girl in Damascus' have become intrinsic to the coverage of Syria. Rather than dismissing the story as an anomaly, it is important to tease out its Orientalist allure set in an imagined geography of 'romance, exotic beings, haunting memories and landscapes, remarkable experiences' (Said, 1978: 1). There is a reason news media believed the story of Amina, an English-speaking, technologically networked and sexually fearless Syrian-American. There is also a reason why Syrian official media sought to take advantage of the story about Western fantasies about Syria for their own political agenda. Of course, the story of Amina is not the only such contentious episode in reporting Syria.

Syrian Boys: The Heroes and Victims

In early November 2014, a purportedly amateur video showing a new horror in the Syrian war was uploaded on YouTube. It eventually also turned out to be fictional. The controversy it instigated focused on two issues: the failure of many news media to authenticate the video and also the intentions and implications of the film. The one-minute clip showed a Syrian boy targeted by sniper bullets. The boy appears to get shot and falls on the ground as if dead. However, within seconds we see the boy standing up and running. It becomes apparent that the boy, in a spectacular act of bravery, was playing dead in order to deceive the snipers so he can run to the rescue of a little girl, who was stuck behind a car in the middle of the road. Both children manage to run away and escape the bullets. The voices of Syrians allegedly witnessing this act of heroism expressed their shock and disbelief through their exalting cries of 'Allahu Akbar' (God is great).

Shot as a citizen journalist video with a shaky camera and a blurry quality, the 'Syrian Hero Boy' video was picked up and shared on YouTube and other social media by the Shaam News Network Channel, which is an important Syrian aggregator of amateur videos. The video became viral and was soon reported on and shared by human rights organisations and by Western and Arab journalists and news media. It got more than 5 million viewers in a few days. The video was described as 'amazing' and 'riveting' in the way its hero boy escapes bullets to rescue a girl (*Inquisitr News*, 2014). Some commentators assumed army soldiers were behind the shootings. An *International Business Times* article stated that the snipers in the video 'reportedly are said to be the government forces loyal to Syrian President Bashar al-Assad' (Varghese, 2014). Although most news media reports included the cautionary statement that they cannot independently verify the footage, the video was still assumed to be true. The *Telegraph*, for example, added that 'experts tell the paper they have no reason to doubt its authenticity', while the *International Business Times* 'went a step further spinning the statements to "experts told *The Telegraph* they have no doubts on the authenticity of the footage"' (Susli, 2014). Liz Sly, the *Washington Post*'s correspondent in Beirut, tweeted the video, saying 'Wow. Boy rescues girl from shooting in Syria. And the soldiers keep shooting. They're children.' Her comments prompted responses on Twitter stating that the video does not actually show whether the snipers were army soldiers or rebels.

On 14 November 2014, a Norwegian filmmaker, Lars Klevberg, announced that he directed the fictional film. According to the BBC, Klevberg wrote his film's script after watching news coverage of the conflict in Syria. The film received funding from the Norwegian Film Institute (NFI) and the Audio and Visual Fund from Arts Council Norway in October 2013. The NFI awarded the film about £26,500 for its production. It was staged in Malta on a set, where Hollywood action films such as *Troy* and *Gladiator* had been shot. The two children were professional Maltese child actors, while the Syrians playing the role of witnesses were actually refugees in Malta. The film did not go viral immediately. When it was initially uploaded on YouTube it did not get many views. So the filmmakers deleted it and reposted a new version with the word 'hero' added to the headline and then actively sent it to people on Twitter 'to start a conversation', as the director told the BBC (*BBC News*, 2014).

The film director and producers were, at first, defensive about their production and the way it was disseminated. 'The motivation behind the production and the internet release of the film was to spur debate (and) urge action on behalf of innocent children all over the world who are affected by war. We are pleased the film was shared widely', said Klevberg. He added that 'by publishing a clip that could appear to be authentic we hoped to take advantage of a tool that's often used in war; make a video that claims to be real' (cited in Tobal, 2014). The announcement that the film was fictional angered Syria followers, including journalists and human rights activists on the grounds of deception. Klevberg's statement, which was meant to clarify why the film was made, only ended up raising more questions. How does the pretence that the film is 'real' help spur a constructive debate about Syria or children at war? How did the film fit within the context of Syrian citizen journalist videos and the debates they spurred?

In fact, the video falls within a broader and much older habit of Western activists, filmmakers and journalists inserting themselves into the centre of the narratives of others. Klevberg claimed his intention was 'to see if the film would get attention and spur debate, first and foremost about children and war. We also wanted to see how the media would respond to such a video' (cited in Tobal, 2014). However, the impact of the video was to centre the debate on Klevberg himself, his intentions and choices. His intervention can be understood within a context of narcissistic empathy.

Klevberg was not the first filmmaker to produce citizen journalism-style videos. The British street artist and film director, Banksy, produced a short film in 2013 spoofing a video by Syrian rebels shooting down a military helicopter. As I have explained elsewhere (Al-Ghazzi, 2014), in Banksy's version rebels look up to the sky to spot their fallen target, which turns out to be the Disney flying elephant cartoon character, Dumbo! At the time, many criticised Banksy for what they considered a distasteful film that makes light of a brutal war. However, unlike Klevberg's, at least Banksy's film does not conceal its fictional character. Nevertheless, both films inadvertently deem Syrians invisible. In Klevberg's film, it is a telling detail that Syrian refugees, who had probably escaped Syria under traumatic circumstances, acted in subsidiary roles. Rather than highlighting their stories, the refugees were used as extras in the Norwegian filmmaker's imaginary account of how war may appear.

Fred Abrahams, a special advisor to Human Rights Watch, wrote that he was 'disgusted' that a video he assumed to be authentic was in fact a staged production. 'With access to Syria limited, videos and cell phone clips from local activists have been a crucial part of documenting crimes against civilians,' he said. Abrahams accused Klevberg of helping 'erode the public's trust in war reporting. Future videos and articles on atrocities may be summarily dismissed when the situation deserves exactly the opposite: critical attention and outrage' (Abrahams, 2014). One journalist angrily commented that 'the misery of children – and others – in Syria – is very real. There is no need to fictionalise it' (*BBC News*, 2014). News media that had reported the video corrected their stories. In an article reporting that the video was staged, the *Telegraph* said that it turned out to be 'too good to be true' (Crilly, 2014).

Echoing the reaction of MacMaster over his fake 'Gay Girl in Damascus' blog, Klevberg eventually retracted his initial defensive response and issued an apology over his 'Syrian Hero Boy' film, and deleted the video from YouTube. In a statement on 18 November 2014, the director and producers of the video stated that 'despite our humane and good intentions, we would like to sincerely apologize for releasing this film as real' (Goldstein, 2014). Though the director had stated before that he actively sought for the video to go viral, the statement added: 'we were overwhelmed by the attention the film received in such a short amount of time, on the web and media'. The statement reasoned that it was never the intention of the filmmakers to reduce the credibility of journalists and human rights workers who had shared their video as genuine.

Predictably, pro-regime Syrian media highlighted the controversy. The Syrian response shows that even though certain news stories are not 'real', they do reverberate and influence communicative strategies and claims about reality. The Syrian regime and its supporters have consistently used any evidence of erroneous reporting to cast doubt on all amateur digital documentation of the Syrian war because, especially at the out-set of the uprising, most digital videos showed acts of killing and torture perpetrated by the Syrian regime's soldiers and armed thugs. Although many of these videos were shot by torturers and killers and were arguably disseminated to terrify and deter Syrians from taking part in dissonant acts or armed rebellion, the Syrian official media denied the reality of these videos.

In the official daily, *Albaath*, an article entitled 'Western media and the mission of deception' by Abdelrahim Ahmad gave a scathing denunciation of Western media. I shall quote extensively from the article because I think it is representative of how the Syrian regime and its supporters interpreted the 'Syrian Hero Boy' controversy and linked it to other events in order to construct a narrative of distrust of the media in general, and particularly digital media. The *Albaath* article echoes the editorial line of other Syrian media about this story. Ahmad writes:

> Western media, which pride themselves with standards of free-dom, credibility, and professionalism, have propagated a fab-ricated film from social media [...] (Had the filmmakers not admitted that they made the film), it would have remained indisputable truth according to Western public opinion and hostile decision makers [...] Can this media stunt be innocent? Or is it complicit in the Western campaigns of misinformation and incitement against Syria? This incident shows that the basic tenants of media are continuously violated when the matter is related to Middle East politics. The reader still remembers the

Western fabricated stories that target our region and our peoples, such as the lie of the twenty-first century about the Iraqi weapons of mass destruction, to the lie about the Syrian army using chemical weapons, and now the lie that the West is actually fighting *Daish* (the Arabic acronym for the Islamic State organisation).

Ahmad concludes that Western media should cease to accuse Syrian national media of deviating from objective and professional standards and calls on them to curb their pride over their alleged independence and credibility, which are 'mere slogans upheld in order to conceal overdependence on Western decision makers'. Again this example shows how false stories take a life of their own and become linked to larger political issues in support of particular political discourses.

Humanitarian cases that may not be explicitly related to the Syrian war and political conflict also got mired in controversies. For example, in February 2014, a picture of a Syrian refugee boy crossing the desert on foot into Jordan went viral. The photo is a close-up of the four-year-old walking as he struggles to carry a large plastic bag. The picture gives the impression that the boy was alone. Like a lesbian in a Muslim country and the hero boy dodging bullets, this boy was reported to have a story of survival against all odds. The image was tweeted by United Nations staff with the caption 'Here 4-year-old Marwan, who was temporarily separated from his family.' The image was retweeted by CNN international anchor Hala Gorani with the caption 'UN staff found 4-year-old Marwan crossing desert alone after being separated from family fleeing #Syria' (Sherwood and Malik, 2014). The picture and the four-year-old's unlikely story of crossing the desert alone were reported and shared by news media. However, it turned out the boy was not alone as he was straggling behind and trying to keep up with a larger group of refugees. The head of the United Nations refugee agency UNHCR in Jordan, Andrew Harper, clarified that the boy was reunited with his mother within ten minutes of the original picture (Sherwood and Malik, 2014). The coverage of the photo shifted from the story of Syrian refugees to a story about photojournalistic authentication.

Again, Syrian media reported the error. Under the headline 'Reports on lost Syrian boy in the desert are sheer media lies', a Syrian news agency

SANA report stated the boy was simply 'traveling to Jordan with his family' (SANA, 2014). It rhetorically asked, why 'media campaigns insist on propagating lies about Syria to incite public opinion without checking the truth and the credibility of the information'. Supporters of the Syrian regime took to Twitter and Facebook to share the correction of the photo as a means to discredit international media. The plight of Marwan struggling to keep up with his family as he was indeed crossing a desert was no longer the story. As Morris (2014) wrote, 'the fact that the boy was never alone doesn't make Marwan's story, or the stories of the more than 1 million other children who have been forced to flee their home country, any less heartbreaking'. She added that the lack of a viral photo does not change the severity of the suffering of Syria's refugee children.

This case once again demonstrates the complicated relation between reality and journalists. The discussions about reality that the photo generated have focused on its authenticity rather than the refugee crisis in Syria. This case indicates the continuing importance of the discursive anchoring of news photos. The refugee picture was not manipulated but the description of what was happening was not accurate. The news value of the photo seemed to be that the boy was alone. The picture of the boy alone within an empty desert background is striking. It seems to tell an unlikely story of survival against all the odds. It is difficult to imagine that a photo of refugees crossing the desert as a group would have gone viral at all without the extra twist that introduces the popular narrative trope of individual and unlikely survival. Thus, both the controversy in the global coverage and the Syrian accusations of deliberate Western media fabrications have highlighted the sensationalism within the conversation on the plight of Syria's more than 12 million displaced, the figure estimated by the United Nations (UNHCR, 2015).

On Activists and Witnesses in Western and Arab Coverage

Clearly, official Syrian media took advantage of any controversy about outside misinformation, by accusing foreign journalism of running a political campaign against the country. In fact, Syrian officials have been claiming since 2011 that the country is fighting and resisting a 'universal war' against it. Syrian media have dedicated whole programmes and news sections to debunk what they refer to as a foreign hostile media deception campaign. Syrian media strategy changed from a complete denial of the protests in 2011 into calling all protestors and dissidents 'armed groups and terrorists'. The claims made by Syrian media were often outlandish, such as accusing Qatar's Al-Jazeera news channel of constructing whole sets and models representing Syrian cities. According to Syrian TV, the purpose is to shoot, with the help of American, French and Israeli directors, fictional scenes purportedly showing protests in Syria in order to justify a US and NATO future military campaign ('Addounia', 2011). Repeatedly, arrested activists have been forced to 'confess' on television that they were trained by hostile Western and Arab countries to fabricate videos of protests and revolt.

While the official Syrian media's mobilisation in support of the Al-Assad regime and the army is obvious, the bias of other channels can be more subtle. The Syria story has been a particularly difficult test for Arab news media that built a reputation for journalistic authority. For example, the support of the Qatari Al-Jazeera and the Saudi Al-Arabiya Arabic-language news networks for the Syrian opposition is well known. As Al-Qassemi (2012) has pointed out, 'in their bid to support the Syrian rebels' cause, these media giants have lowered their journalistic standards, abandoned rudimentary fact-checks, and relied on anonymous callers and unverified videos in place of solid reporting'. One of the main manifestations of this editorial policy is the generous airtime that Syrian activists have been given in newscasts to relay, as witnesses and citizen journalists, what is happening in Syria. 'It is not uncommon' to tune in to either Al-Jazeera or Al-Arabiya 'and find that the first 20 minutes of a newscast consists of Syrian activists' (Al-Qassemi, 2012), who are allowed to describe the situation on the ground without other means of verification. Since the beginning of the Syrian uprising in March 2011, the Qatari Al-Jazeera has also been known to give voice to the Muslim Brotherhood and Salafi factions at the expense of secular and civil protestors. Several Al-Jazeera reporters quit over accusations of the channel's bias. Echoing the case of Al-Jazeera, the Lebanese daily *Al-Akhbar*, which was seen as an important leftist and socially liberal news outlet, faced accusations of bias in favour of the Syrian regime, also leading a number of its journalists to resign (see Blumenthal, 2012).

It may be easy to dismiss the struggles of Arab media as reflective of journalism in non-democratic contexts and in countries with limited freedom of expression. However, there is evidence that Western media attention to Syria has generally paralleled the focus of decision makers. While initially the focus was on pro-democracy activists and the brutality of the Syrian regime, as of 2014 the news is largely dominated by the terrorism angle, particularly in relation to the Islamic State organisation. As Chouliaraki (2015) has argued, even at the outset of the 2011 Arab uprisings, Western news media, such as the BBC, presented digital witnessing within wider geopolitical frames. Considering how, in contrast to the Syrian case, Libyan witnesses were reported as requiring humanitarian warfare, Chouliaraki concludes that 'the capacity of citizen voice to make a difference depends upon the geopolitical interests and alliances that global news institutions sustain' (2015: 118). These dynamics do not seem lost on Syrian activists.

Activists have been at the forefront of Western reporting as well. One prominent example is the rise of 23-year-old Syrian-British activist Danny Abdul Dayem, who was in the restive central city of Homs in 2012. Abdul Dayem, a native English speaker in Homs, soon became what I am calling a 'spokes-witness', an ordinary person given the task of witnessing a series of events and incidents by media networks. Referred to by the US press as 'the voice of Homs', Abdul Dayem appeared regularly on Arab and Western television news networks to narrate what was happening. In most of his witness appearances, he reiterated the rebels' demand for international support – calling for a no-fly zone and Western military intervention to oust the regime of Bashar Al-Assad. Other Syrian activist-witnesses in Homs were caught embellishing the setting of one video testimony by burning an out-of-frame tyre to produce smoke for dramatic effect. As a Channel 4 report showed, they did not need to embellish because in the very same report close bombardment is clearly audible (Giglio, 2012). The point is that these activists understandably have a political agenda and are not objective witnesses of a reality out there. While many have been killed, others continue to risk their lives in a war zone to get their story out. After all, it was to Homs that world attention turned following the death of *Sunday Times* reporter Marie Colvin and French photographer Remi Ochlik after a shell hit a makeshift media centre in February 2012.

As for official Syrian media, the reporting has been a mix of denial of responsibility and a further discrediting of the opposition. In August 2012, Syrian TV interviewed a young man who 'confessed' that he 'manufactured false news and fabricated stories while presenting them as reality' (RTV, 2012). The man said he used to call Arab and Western TV networks falsely claiming to be in Homs. Pro-Al-Assad news outlets, such as the Lebanese *Al-Akhbar* daily, also criticised the Western news reliance on Syrian activists to insinuate that Western reporting of Homs is as fictional as Hollywood films (Narwani, 2012) in implicit attempts to dismiss as false all amateur videos that implicate the Syrian army in the torture and killing of civilians.

Conclusion

The Syria story has presented journalists with a set of different challenges to their position as narrators of reality. Of course, some of the problematic coverage that I have discussed would have been less prevalent had journalists been allowed into Syria. However, even when journalists are on location, it does not mean that reality is unproblematically mediated. For example, the journalist who dubbed the 'Gay Girl in Damascus' as a Syrian revolutionary heroine was in fact in Damascus at the time. Another example is a report by the *Independent*'s journalist Patrick Cockburn from Damascus, in which he wrote that foreign media reporting of the Syrian conflict is inaccurate and misleading. He said that after travelling in Syria 'it is possible to show how far media reports differ markedly what is really happening'. To illustrate his point, he said there was an explosion near his hotel and that his being there showed that 'there can be no replacement for unbiased eyewitness reporting'. He reported that a random rebel shelling hit a 'Shia hospital' – situated in 'the Christian quarter' of Old Damascus. I am not sure what Damascene hospital Cockburn is referring to but I find it strange to designate religious affiliations to hospitals and assume these labels are self-explanatory. In a way, this is a call to underscore that the words that journalists (or academics for that matter) choose contribute to larger discourses about a certain place and also that there is not a singular 'there', where, in this case, the authentic Syrian reality unfolds.

I am not implying that since reality is too complex, there is no point in journalists writing narratives that seek to represent real events or to also learn from mistakes. Rather, I am emphasising that in order to strive towards truthful portrayals, journalistic narratives may benefit from avoiding confident authenticity claims about capturing an unmediated reality; and from further acknowledging that words and tropes have a discursive history entrenched in political struggle. As Chouliaraki argues, journalism construes events from particular standpoints 'at the moment that it claims to simply represent them' (2015: 109). These particular standpoints are often shaped by the geopolitical contexts in which they happen. There are other considerations that often influence journalistic writing, such as Orientalist allusions, narrative tropes about unlikely heroism, sentimentalised attitudes about the political impact of new technology, narcissistic accounts of empathy and the conflation of activist and witness roles. These problematics not only determine how stories are covered but also what stories are covered in the first place. While these pitfalls of journalistic narration may engender false stories, they should not be dismissed as obstacles to some unmediated reporting of reality. News, whether true or false, is part of our globalised reality. And regardless of truthfulness, news narratives have consequences in shaping and understanding our world. They have an afterlife. My use of the Syrian context is to stress that journalistic accounts can be more truthful through further recognition of the impossibility of authentically representing reality.

Note

1. A presentation by political scientist Lisa Wedeen (November 2014) at the Middle East Studies Association meeting in Washington, DC in 2014 about the Al-Assad regime's strategy to create an environment of uncertainty and doubt over online content was helpful for my analysis.

References

Abrahams, Freda (2014). 'Dispatches: hoax harms children in war', Human Rights Watch, 15 November. Available at: www.hrw.org/news/2014/11/15/dispatches-hoax-harms-children-war (accessed 1 July 2015).

'Addounia' (2011). 'Television addounia', YouTube, 9 September. Available at: www.youtube.com/watch?v=rGZgZpL3gNI (accessed 1 July 2015).

Ahmad, Abdul Rahim (2014). 'Al-I'lam al-gharbi', *Albaath*, 19 November. Available at: http://goo.gl/YSyC5D (accessed 1 July 2015).

BBC News (2014). '#BBCTrending: open letter condemns fake "Syria hero boy: film', 17 November. Available at: www.bbc.com/news/blogs-trending-30087389 (accessed 1 July 2015).

BBC News (2015). '#BBCTrending: Syrian "hero boy" video faked by Norwegian director', 14 November. Available at: www.bbc.com/news/blogs-trending-30057401 (accessed 1 July 2015).

Bell, Melissa and Flock, E. (2011). 'A gay girl in Damascus comes clean', *The Washington Times*, 12 June. Available at: http://goo.gl/Y1tzYv (accessed 30 June 2015).

Blumenthal, Max (2012). 'The right to resist is universal: a farewell to Al-Akhbar and Assad's apologists', Max Blumenthal blog, 20 June. Available at: http://goo.gl/4KmsCy (accessed 27 October 2015).

Bollmer, Grant (2012) 'Demanding connectivity: the performance of "True" identity and the politics of social media', *JOMEC Journal*. Available at: https://publications.cardiffuniversitypress.org/index.php/JOMEC/article/view/289/299 (accessed 30 June 2015).

Chouliaraki, Lilie (2013). *The Ironic Spectator: Solidarity in the Age of Post-Humanitarianism*. Oxford: John Wiley and Sons.

Chouliaraki, Lilie (2013). 'Re-mediation, inter-mediation, trans-mediation: the cosmopolitan trajectories of convergent journalism', *Journalism Studies*, 14(2), 267–83.

Chouliaraki, Lilie (2015). 'Digital witnessing in war journalism: the case of post-Arab Spring conflicts', *Popular Communication*, 13(2), 105–19.

Cockburn, Patrick (2013). 'Foreign media portrayals of the conflict in Syria are dangerously inaccurate', *Independent*, 30 June. Available at: www.independent.co.uk/voices/comment/foreign-media-portrayals-of-the-conflict-in-syria-are-dangerously-inaccurate-8679937.html (accessed 1 July 2015).

Crilly, Rob (2014). 'Syria "hero boy" video is too good to be true', *Telegraph*, 14 November. Available at: http://goo.gl/nsfAzu (accessed 1 July 2015).

Al-Ghazzi, Omar (2014). '"Citizen journalism" in the Syrian uprising: problematizing Western narratives in a local context', *Communication Theory*, 24(4), 435–54.

Giglio, Mike (2012). 'Syrian rebels caught embellishing on tape', *Daily Beast*. Available at: www.thedailybeast.com/articles/2012/03/27/syrian-rebels-caught-embellishing-on-tape.html (accessed 1 July 2015).

Goldstein, Sasha (2014). 'Norwegian filmmakers apologize for fake "Syria boy hero" video', *New York Daily News*. Available at: http://goo.gl/Cb2Qwe (accessed 27 October 2015).

Inquisitr News (2014). 'Syrian hero boy rescues girl while under sniper attack, amazing video', 12 November. Available at: www.inquisitr.com/1604293/syrian-hero-boy-rescues-girl-while-under-sniper-attack-amazing-video/ (accessed 1 July, 2015).

Jacqueline M (2011). 'Release abducted Syrian-American blogger Amina Arraf ("A Gay Girl in Damascus")'. Available at: www.change.org/p/release-abducted-syrian-american-blogger-amina-arraf-a-gay-girl-in-damascus (accessed 30 June 2015).

Kenner, David (2011). 'Straight guy in Scotland', *Foreign Policy*, 14 June. Available at: http://foreignpolicy.com/2011/06/14/straight-guy-in-scotland/ (accessed 1 July 2015).

Kojo Nnamdi Show, The (2011). 'The meaning of the "Gay Girl in Damascus"', 14 June. Available at: http://thekojonnamdishow.org/shows/2011–06–14/meaning-gay-girl-damascus (accessed 1 July 2015).

Leo, Alex (2011). 'What we can learn from the "Gay Girl in Damascus" hoax', *Reuters Blogs*, 13 June. Available at: http://blogs.reuters.com/mediafile/2011/06/13/a-gay-girl-in-damascus-hoax/ (accessed 30 June 2015).

'Lion Heart', Man hiya Amina Arraf (2011). YouTube, 15 June. Available at: https://goo.gl/OMjqyu (accessed 30 June 2015).

Lynch, Marc, Freelon, Deen, and Aday, Sean (2014). 'Syria's socially mediated civil war', *United States Institute of Peace*, 91(1), 1–35.

Marsh, Katherine (2011). 'A Gay Girl in Damascus becomes a heroine of the Syrian revolt', *Guardian*, 6 May. Available at: www.theguardian.com/world/2011/may/06/gay-girl-damascus-syria-blog (accessed 30 June 2015).

Massad, Joseph A. (2007). *Desiring Arabs*. Chicago: University of Chicago Press.

McCay, Nemo (2011). 'Lesbian blogger hoaxes harm the credibility of news gatherers', *Frontiers Media*, 15 June. Available at: www.frontiersmedia.com/frontiers-blog/2011/06/14/lesbian-blogger-hoaxes-harm-the-credibility-o/ (accessed 30 June 2015).

Mikdashi, Mikdashi. and Moumneh, Rasha. (2011). 'Gays, Islamists, and the Arab Spring: what would a Revolutionary do', *Jadaliyya*, 11 June. Available at: www.jadaliyya.com/pages/index/1836/ (accessed 30 June 2015).

Morris, Loveday (2014). 'That 4-year-old Syrian refugee wasn't alone, but his story is still heartbreaking', *The Washington Post*, 18 February. Available at: http://goo.gl/Wpngpo (accessed 1 July 2015).

Narwani, Sharmine (2012). 'Hollywood in Homs and Idlib?', *Al-Akhbar English*, 13 March. Available at: http://english.al-akhbar.com/blogs/sandbox/hollywood-homs-and-idlib (accessed 1 July 2015).

O'Neill, Brendan (2011). 'Why so many hacks fell for the "gay girl in Syria"', *Spiked*, 15 June. Available at: http://goo.gl/tGUORC (accessed 30 June 2015).

Al-Qassemi, Sultan (2012). 'Breaking the Arab news', *Foreign Policy*, 2 August. Available at: http://foreignpolicy.com/2012/08/02/breaking-the-arab-news/ (accessed 1 July 2015).

RTV (2012). 'Nashit muta'mil sabiqan', 3 August. Available at: www.rtv.gov.sy/ index.php/www.syriasteps.com?d=21&id=99936 (accessed 30 June 2015).

Said, Edward (1978). *Orientalism*. New York: Vintage.

SANA (2014). 'Al-Umam al-mutahida', 19 February. Available at: www.dampress.net/ index.php?page=show_det&category_id=6&id=39689 (accessed 1 July 2015).

Sheridan, Michael (2011). '"Gay Girl in Damascus" blogger abducted in Syria: report', *NY Daily News*, 8 June. Available at: http://goo.gl/p5yLjy (accessed 1 July 2015).

Sherwood, Harriet and Malik, Shiv (2014). 'Image of Syrian boy in desert triggers sympathy – and then a backlash', *Guardian*, 18 February. Available at: http:// goo.gl/Rio9t8 (accessed 1 July 2015).

Smith, Sydney (2011). 'Gay Girl in Damascus hoax, should news outlets correct stories?', *iMediaEthics*. Available at: http://goo.gl/43WfWx (accessed 1 July 2015).

Susli, Maram, (2014) 'When fake videos go viral: what the fake Syria sniper boy video tells us about "media experts"', Global Research, 28 November. Available at: http://goo.gl/LwrFqI (accessed 1 July, 2015).

Tobal, Katherine J. (2014). 'Mainstream media makes mistake: Syrian boy rescue film revealed as fake', *Collective-Evolution*, 19 November. Available at: http://goo.gl/OvGwio (accessed 1 July 2015).

UNHCR (2015). 'UNHCR: total number of Syrian refugees exceeds four million for first time', 15 July. Available at: www.unhcr.org/559d67d46.html (accessed 27 October 2015).

Varghese, Johnlee. (2014). 'Syria: "Hero" 8-year-old boy saves younger sister from sniper fire, risking own life', ibtimes.co.in, 11 November. Available at: www. ibtimes.co.in/syria-hero-8-year-old-boy-saves-younger-sister-sniper-fire-risking-own-life-video-613671 (accessed 1 July 2015).

Zelizer, B. (2006). 'When facts, truth, and reality are God-terms: on journalism's uneasy place in cultural studies', *Communication and Critical/Cultural Studies*, 1(1), 100–19.

Zelizer, B. (2007). 'On "having been there": "eyewitnessing" as a journalistic key word', *Critical Studies in Media Communication*, 24(5), 408–28.

2

First Framing and News

Lessons from Reporting Jordan in Crises

Dina Matar

International news of the Middle East takes up a fair share of the day-to-day news agendas of Western mainstream[1] news organisations. This is not surprising given the strategic relations major Western powers, such as the USA, the UK, France and Germany, have had with the diverse countries making up the region and the long history of colonial and military interventions. While on any given day the international news agenda is replete with reports and news from Iraq, Syria, Palestine, Israel, Egypt, Saudi Arabia and Iran, there are very few stories about Jordan, which shares borders with all of them and which has been involved directly or by proxy in many of the conflicts in the region. Jordan's involvement goes back to 1948, when Israel was created and the Palestinians lost a significant portion of their homeland and were made homeless, with about 450,000 taking refuge in Jordan. In recent years, Jordan has provided support for Western military intervention in Iraq, and more recently Syria. It has also been the host of the largest number of war refugees fleeing various regional conflicts, including Palestinians forced out of their homes in 1948, refugees from Iraq and, more recently, refugees fleeing the Syrian conflict to the north.

However, Jordan topped the international news agenda between January and February 2015 as reports emerged that ISIS militants had executed by immolation a captured Jordanian pilot who was taking part in air strikes against the extremist group in Syria. Within a few hours of the announcement that the pilot had been confirmed dead, Jordan executed two Islamist jihadists it had held in prison for their alleged involvement in a bomb attack in Amman, despite its earlier announcement that it was prepared to release one of those executed in return for the pilot, in response to an ISIS demand. World and media attention turned to the country amid messages of international support for Jordan and the pilot's family, and condemnation of the new form of ISIS brutality. As some Jordanians took to the streets in support of the regime's move to execute the prisoners and the tough Jordanian position on dealing with 'terror', the Jordanian armed forces announced they would intensify their bombing campaign, as part of an allied force, against ISIS targets in Syria. The media coverage of the death of the pilot and the events that followed focused on regime narratives about the unfolding events and the 'national' response to the crisis, the tribal make-up of Jordanian society, Jordan's role in the global fight against terror and the unity of the Jordanian people against existential threats the kingdom might be facing or subjected to. Broadly speaking, the narrative in the Jordanian media appeared to be homogenous in its purpose and themes, presenting the reaction to the murder as a legitimate and national action in defence of Jordan's sovereignty and its national interests, while publishing statements of support for the government and the family of the pilot (BBC, 2015a). There were no dissenters, meaning there were no visible or audible voices of opposition to the Jordanian moves, confirming that the Jordanian regime had made clear to the media that it would not tolerate any attempt to cross the specific red lines it had set around public speech and political opposition since the capture of the pilot. These red lines were set by the kingdom's attorney general, who announced that the publication or republication of ISIS-sourced news could result in prosecution, which coincided with the release of a military communiqué by the Jordanian armed forces calling on local media to not publish any information that harms national security.

The killing of the pilot and the reaction to it made Jordan the top news item in the international news media agenda, with professionals, experts and policy advisors taking turns assessing what effect Jordan's response would have on the country, its tribal make-up, loyalty to the Hashemite rulers and whether Jordan's increasing involvement in the fight against

ISIS would spell a change in the regional battle with them. The hyper-media discourse and coverage relating to this particular event, and reactions to it in Jordan and outside, seemed to reiterate and project an image of a country united behind its 'moderate' leaders as well as its progressive 'politically engaged' royal family members. There was no sustained local critique of the kingdom's actions or the war on ISIS in the local media, whether in the mainstream or even in the more critical online venues (Abu-Rish, 2015).

The media discourse in Jordan, and its allies, is not surprising considering Jordan is an authoritarian state that has maintained a tight grip on the local media through a politics of control of public debate that includes various punitive measures and practices on those who offer alternative views. However, what is interesting is that the same narratives and frames also found their way to the international news agendas. Indeed, in the UK, as this chapter will show, the reporting of Jordan broadly followed the same storyline, with the dominant narratives repeating the Jordanian regime's line that fighting ISIS was part of the international campaign to wage war on terror, thus serving to provide legitimacy to the regime at a time when regional protest movements had challenged authoritarian rule in different ways, while also perpetuating long-held myths and narratives about the country and its people. These myths and narratives often portray the kingdom as one of the remaining bastions of modernity, stability and moderation in the region, tend to gloss over aspects of Jordanian society and politics and, more importantly, repeat Jordanian officials' own narratives about the country and themselves. With this background in mind, I provide a snapshot of Jordan to put this chapter in context, and then give a brief overview of international news theories pertinent to this discussion. I conclude with analysis of the BBC online and *Guardian* coverage, and some remarks about new directions in international news theory and research.

Background

Jordan is a relatively new country which, until 1918, was under Ottoman rule. In 1921 it became an independent constitutional state under British rule, and remained so until 1946, when it gained full independence as the Hashemite Kingdom of Jordan. The country is rich in human capital, but poor in natural resources. It occupies an area of over 90,000 km^2 with a population of just over 6 million, nearly half of them living in the capital, Amman, and over half of them of Palestinian origin. Jordan shares borders with Syria to the north, Iraq to the east, Saudi Arabia to the south and Israel and the occupied West Bank to the west, and, as such, remains deeply implicated in regional politics and turmoil.

Jordan is a constitutional monarchy ruled by the Hashemites, who are said to be descendants of the prophet Mohammed, a narrative that has been repeated in Jordan's discourse about itself and which is consistently reiterated in the local media. The king holds ultimate power as he is authorised to approve amendments to the constitution, declare war, command the armed forces and dissolve parliament. Constitutional amendments were made after protests swept across parts of the Arab world in early 2011, including limiting the king's ability to postpone elections indefinitely. However, his powers remain intact, as the king still appoints and dismisses the prime minister and the upper house of parliament, particularly during moments of crisis.

The kingdom's current ruler, King Abdullah, came to the throne in 1999, succeeding his father, King Hussein, who had been well known in the West, thanks to media coverage, as a 'moderate' king with Western tastes (his second wife and mother to the current King Abdullah, Queen Mona, was British) and a deep desire to push his country towards Western-style modernity. Abdullah inherited a country that was politically stable, as Jordan had signed a peace treaty with Israel five years earlier and had succeeded, under his father, to fend off threats from several Arab regimes while forging close relationships with them. When he succeeded the throne, King Abdullah II attempted to launch a number of political reform initiatives, but all efforts to open up the political system were thwarted by a resilient class of political elites and bureaucrats who feared that such efforts would move the country away from a decades-old 'rentier' system to a merit-based one. One example of the gradual and serious reform efforts by the king was the Jordanian National Agenda, a blueprint for political, economic and social reform that was developed in 2005 by an inclusive committee of personalities from political parties, parliament, media, civil society, the private sector and the government, who represented a wide spectrum of political, economic and social ideologies. This group

36

did not rely on rhetorical statements, but suggested specific programmes with timelines, performance indicators and links to the budget (Muasher, 2011). In the political reform field, the agenda proposed new laws to open up elections, prevent discrimination against women, encourage freedom of the press and address other issues – all with the goal of gradually building a system of checks and balances in the country and moving from the old, rentier system that privileged a small elite class to one where success was based on skill. It is precisely because of this goal that the effort was shot down by an entrenched political and bureaucratic establishment.

Like other state-building nations in the Arab world, Jordan had been keen on building its media systems and environment to support its national projects and state institutions. In the years since independence, it developed its state media, particularly the press, radio and television, and used it to promote its vision and narrative of itself, as a country well on the road to modernity led by a moderate king and a consensual society. Despite the arrival of new communication technologies and their uptake by a majority of the population, television remains the mass medium par excellence, reaching virtually all Jordanian households. However, in recent years, new independent stations such as Roya TV and Nourmina TV have also become competitive alternatives to the government-owned Jordan Radio and Television Corporation (JRTV). Since early 2006, internet services have also offered Jordanians alternative platforms for news. With internet penetration standing at 23 per cent, AmmanNews.com.jo was developed as one of the first news websites in the country, introducing a new trend in media consumption. Since then, hundreds of other news websites have emerged, providing Jordanians with alternative news and information. As of August 2012, there were some 2.2 million Facebook users and 59,726 active Twitter users (Sweis and Baslan, 2013).

While the availability of and access to the internet has profoundly affected the regime's capacity to control public spaces, the news media continue to face severe restrictions on free speech. Assessments of media freedom in Jordan have shown a drop in performance, with Freedom House's ranking falling from 'Partly Free' in 2009 to 'Not Free' in 2010. Jordan also ranked 120th out of 178 countries in the Reporters Without Borders' 'Worldwide Press Freedom' table for 2010. Media freedom has declined mainly due to additional restrictions in the press and publication laws, restrictions on internet freedom, surveillance, and indirect pressure on certain journalists and editors (Freedom House, 2013; IPI, 2014; Reporters Without Borders, 2010). As such, the lack of press freedom, authoritarian media legislation, lack of professionalism and self-censorship continue to hinder the development of free media systems. In fact, although recent survey data suggest this has declined somewhat following the Arab Spring, some 86 per cent of journalists still admit to practicing self-censorship.

The Jordanian government continues to play a strong role in regulating the spread and flow of information through the 2007 press and publications law, which continues to allow the government – through the state court – indirectly to block the publication of any printed materials it deems offensive. It also allows courts to block publication of any printed material and withdraw media licences, but limits the government's ability to shut down printing presses. The Right to Information Act (Law No. 47 of 2007) was heralded by the government as a move to safeguard the right of Jordanian citizens to any information they seek. However, this law was severely hampered by the existence of the State Secrets Law (Provisional Law No. 50 of 1971), which prohibits the free flow of government information to the public and remains in effect today (Freedom House, 2013). The proliferation of a vast number of media outlets, both virtually and physically, throughout the country has nonetheless persisted despite attempts to regulate their activity. Jordanian bloggers and independent e-zines have established themselves firmly and show no sign of abating or disappearing. The steady growth of such media is highly encouraging and demonstrates the power and value of public expression and the importance of freely flowing information. This has happened, however, despite the government's directives, not because of them.

First Framing, Sources and International News

The most influential paradigms related to international news production emerged in the 1970s and 1980s at the height of the Cold War. Despite technological changes and the expansion in the digital modes and forms of international news since then, few major or substantial studies on international news and its production have emerged, which means that our understanding of international news remains stuck in these dated paradigms. Broadly speaking, these paradigms as well as debates in media and journalism studies have been concerned with the Euro-centrism of the news-reporting agenda, the dominance of mainstream Western news agencies in international news and the continued treatment of the Global South as the 'Other' in mainstream Western media discourses.

These debates, as well as the theoretical paradigms that followed and that specifically examined the politics of representation/misrepresentation, bias and objectivity, audiences and their power as well as structural imbalances between the North and the South, have been challenged by the expanding news media ecology worldwide, new media platforms and the emergence of citizen journalism. However, and despite these changes, research on international news continues to come to the same, increasingly monotonous yet necessary, conclusion – that international news coverage does not offer a deep understanding of complex other places and other histories, and that the language used remains stuck in Euro-centric practices and paradigms that privilege, as Noam Chomsky has suggested, the voice of the powerful, or played a role in misrepresenting Arabs and Muslims, as Edward Said (1979; 1997) has argued, and in recreating exceptionalist discourses about the Orient in general, and Islam in particular. In summing up the debates, Patterson and Sreberny (2004: 8–9) note that when news 'becomes integrated into local news channels it produces a common structure: a media map that is ethnocentric and narrow. In any country's media on any given day can be found a small set of common stories that are reported with virtually identical pictures or words'.

Van Ginneken (1998: 113–14) takes the argument further, suggesting that the domination of news reporting by the major international news media organisations has meant that these outfits are able to produce the 'first framing' of important world events and themes. He writes that the 'major world news agencies [...] have a quasi-monopoly in providing prime definitions of breaking news in the world periphery. Even if they are not actually the first on the spot, they are usually the first to inform the rest of the world.' What is important about first framing is not the fact that one agency manages to report something before the other, but how first frames can come to represent, or explain, complex issues, and how first frames, as discursive tools, can become normalised and taken for granted through their repetition and use. It is in such ways that first frames can impose particular ways of seeing or not seeing the 'Other', making sense of complex issues through making associations that are easily understood, as will be discussed later regarding the frames used to cover the above-mentioned Jordanian event.

The literature on framing theory is vast and there is no need to cover it in detail here, but broadly speaking frames are discursive tools journalists use to make sense of events, in the process making them the central organising ideas that provide meaning to an unfolding strip of events. Or, as Entman (1993: 6–7) suggests,

> News frames are constructed from and embodied in the key words, metaphors, concepts, symbols, and visual images emphasized in a news narrative. Since the narrative finally consists of nothing more than words and pictures, frames can be detected by probing for particular words and visual images that consistently appear in a narrative and convey thematically consonant meaning across media and time.

In international news reporting, frames can be the most important, and efficient, tools journalists can use to transmit the most important aspects of a complex issue and make them accessible and understandable to the lay population, thus allowing journalists to classify information and package it for efficient relay to audiences (see Gitlin, 1980). During crisis, Norris et al. (2003) suggest, framing prioritises some facts, images or developments over others, thereby unconsciously supporting a particular interpretation of events. As they note, it follows that 'terrorist events are commonly understood through news "frames" that simplify, prioritise, and structure the narrative flow of events' (Norris et al., 2003: 10). Judith Butler takes the argument about frames in a more critical direction, suggesting in her acclaimed book *Frames of War* (2009) that frames not only organise the visual experiences (of the audiences), but also the general specific ontologies of the subject – so much so that the subjects are constituted through norms which, in their reiteration, produce and shift the terms through which subjects are recognised. However, as she notes, frames that seek to contain, convey and determine what is seen also depend upon conditions of reproducibility in order to succeed. Such approaches to framing do not take into account the agency of journalists or audiences; these are important to consider, but are outside the scope of this chapter.

Given that only a very small amount of what we call international news is, in fact, composed of original news material (meaning material that has not already appeared elsewhere), and that most of what we call international news is a reproduction of 'other news' elsewhere, then the questions one needs to ask are: who produces the frames in the first place, what are their intentions and does the reuse of already existing material always produce something new or different, or does it just reproduce the original frame created in the place where news originated? A related question would ask about the criteria behind the reuse of already existing news material. In their important study about news values, which remains relevant today, Galtung and Ruge (1965) argued that international news is determined by a set of news values, which may differ from country to country, and which may result in a selective image of the world that is linked to geopolitical considerations.

Scholars working on the theory of agenda-setting in news – which states that while media may not tell you what to think, it does tell you what to think about – have suggested that the reuse of original material is determined by international themes and considerations, while scholars exploring the concept of gatekeeping have pointed to the various ways news producers use filters to decide which news should become available to their audiences. Finally, work on sourcing has also provided some clues as to which stories are used or reused. In this scholarship, studies have been concerned with addressing the relationship between journalists and sources as a way to consider broader questions about power and autonomy within national contexts, and a consensus has emerged that sourcing practices derive from a symbiotic and consensual process in which both parties – journalists and their sources – have much to gain from making news. As such, as Barbie Zelizer (2004) writes, the source–reporter link was seen as a series of bargaining or exchange interchanges between political reporters and governmental personnel.

While most of the original studies on sourcing have been carried out in the USA, similar patterns of source–reporter interactions were detected in other contexts. Thomas Patterson (1998) showed how different journalists across national boundaries displayed varying degrees of independence from their sourcing practices, reaching the conclusion that Western journalists, depending on which country they come from, played different roles in their relationships with sources. Studies of other parts of the world showed different patterns in different countries, with, for example, British journalists seen to be more passive and neutral in their sourcing patterns, while Italian journalists acted as advocates for their sources. In Latin America, sources tended to use journalists to put forward their own political views more aggressively than in other regions (Waisbord, 2000), while in Japan formal associations of journalists determined which sources reporters could access (Feldman, 1993). Broadly speaking, scholarship on sourcing practices offset the naive notion that the power of journalists was limitless, positioning journalists within an identifiable set of interactions with peoples in other parts of the world and positioning journalism within the contexts of other institutions, rather than being seen as separate from them. Paying attention to sourcing is important because it involves making decisions on who is included or excluded, and draws attention to how sources ascribe meaning to events, shaping public perception and understanding. With this summary in mind, I turn to the coverage of the events surrounding the execution of the Jordanian pilot, before making some concluding remarks about assumptions related to reporting countries like Jordan.

Reporting Jordan

As discussed in the introductory section, the death of the Jordanian fighter pilot and its aftermath was covered worldwide and topped the international news agenda for a few days. Given the scope and theoretical impetus of this chapter, I focus here on the dominant frames that the BBC and *Guardian* used in covering the event from 29 January to 11 February 2015.

Broadly speaking, two main frames emerged in the analysis: the first frame was the consensual nature of Jordanian society (or the unity of the citizens behind their leaders), and the second focused on the leading political role of the Jordanian royal family in the events. The first frame was evident in the language and images used to portray the national unity of Jordan, and tended to represent Jordanians as consensual and acritical subjects, or as a homogenous national community supporting their government's action, thus silencing or making invisible some critical voices that have questioned the nation's readiness for a long-term war of attrition with unintended consequences (e.g. Obeidat, 2015). There was little context or background provided in the news reports accessed for this chapter, though some stories referred to the tribal make-up of Jordan and worries about whether the regime would be able to receive the support of all tribes behind its action. This said, the coverage of the tribal make-up was limited to reports discussing the possibility of a rift in the national consensus, referring mostly to the immense power of the tribes in particular regions of Jordan before the killing of the pilot, and the ways all of Jordan came together following his death.

The frame of national unity was emphasised in most of the articles, thus giving priority to the 'national' need to maintain unity in the face of threats. This, of course, would be the frame the Jordanian regime would want to be highlighted and maintained in order to be able to carry out its objectives and to continue to support the US-led campaign against ISIS. This frame comes across clearly in a BBC report on 6 February 2015 which carried the lede: 'Thousands have rallied in Jordan's capital Amman in support of their government's military response to the killing of a Jordanian fighter pilot by Islamic State (IS) militants.' The frame of Jordan's unity was also clear in another story which carried the headline 'The brutal killing that hardened Jordan's hearts against IS' (BBC, 2015d), clearly suggesting that all of Jordan's people were united behind the regime.

The *Guardian*, too, played up the frame of national unity, consistently running stories that reflected Jordan's unity following the killing of the Jordanian pilot. This theme was also repeated in an editorial published during the period studied for this chapter entitled 'The *Guardian* view on Islamic State's attempt to disrupt the links between the monarchy and Jordan's tribe' (*Guardian*, 2015), and which clearly focused on the fact that citizens and the monarchy had been united and that ISIS was posing a threat to this unity, which would be a position espoused and promoted by the regime.

A related frame was evident in the use of language that seemed to imply that all of Jordan was behind the response and reaction in revenge for the killing. Indeed, the words 'response' and 'revenge' were consistently used and often in conjunction with the actions of Jordan, thus giving the impression of a collective outrage from Jordan (aiding the unity frame), as well as demonstrating that Jordan was discontent with not responding.

As such, the framing showed the kingdom as a reactive and leading partner of the US-led coalition against ISIS, emphasising its important role in the attacks. Further evidence of the consensual aspect of Jordanian society comes across clearly in the use of phrases such as 'Jordan speaking' or how 'Jordan feels' and other similar phrases – giving the impression the nation is fully united. Furthermore, the words retaliation and response are consistently used in describing Jordan's action against ISIS, making it clear firstly that Jordan is being active and secondly its actions are as a response to ISIS. It is noticeable that the language used is less strong than in the *Guardian*, which tended to use more aggressive language to describe Jordan's response.

Another major frame that emerges in both the BBC's and the *Guardian's* coverage is the focus on the political and leading role of the Jordanian ruling royal family, also serving to legitimise the country's actions and legitimise its stance. The analysis showed that the BBC paid more attention to coverage of the Hashemite rulers, their actions and statements, with almost every other article in the period covered mentioning King Abdullah or his wife Queen Raina at some point. In many of these articles, the royal couple were presented as active and concerned leaders who go out to the streets to join their public. Queen Rania was represented as a concerned political leader as well as a mother and wife caring for her subjects. For example, in a report by the BBC on 6 February 2015, the headline reads 'Queen Rania joins thousands at Amman rally' (Muir, 2015), and the report focused on her paying respects to the wife of the slain pilot while also making statements about the illegitimate actions of ISIS. The focus on Queen Rania is not out of the ordinary given the general attention in worldwide media to celebrity leaders, but the focus on the Queen Rania not only helps make associations with the British royal family, but also serves to show her as a modern and moderate political actor advancing the cause of women and promoting the view of Jordan as a modern Islamic country. King Abdullah, too, is portrayed as a determined political actor involved in important issues facing the kingdom. A BBC article on 6 February 2015, under the headline 'Is Jordan's Abdullah really a warrior king?' (BBC, 2015b), noted that the news cycle highlighted the king's hands-on military background (he was educated in the UK). The *Guardian*, too, focuses on the royal family, such as in an article on 4 February 2015 under the headline 'Jordan's King Abdullah vows "relentless" war against ISIS' (Black, 2015).

Much of the BBC reporting, and to a lesser extent the *Guardian*'s, suggests that there was little or no original news, meaning that the reporting had appeared elsewhere first, such as in the official Jordanian media, while offering little understanding of complex other places and other histories. As such, the concept of first framing, which van Ginneken introduced to reflect on the dominance of the Western media in news reporting, has originated elsewhere. In fact, the frames, in this case, were Jordanian frames that made their way into Western media, raising questions about the centre–periphery argument that has dominated discussions of international news and their appropriation in different contexts. However, what is important about first framing is not the fact that one agency manages to report something before the other, or who controls the flow of information and knowledge, but how first frames can come to represent, or explain, complex issues, and how first frames, as discursive tools, can become normalised and taken for granted through their reappropriation and use elsewhere.

Furthermore, many of the BBC articles were highly reliant on straight quotes from Jordanian officials, suggesting the narrative had already been framed according to the official Jordanian viewpoint. For example, a report on 6 February 2015, under the headline 'Islamic State crisis: UAE sends F-16 squadron to Jordan' uses official Jordanian sources for the material, reflecting the hierarchical organisational nature of news (BBC, 2015c). The reliance on elite and official sourcing opens up debates about the relationship between politics and media, not only within national boundaries, but across them as well. Importantly, the use of official sources raises important ethical questions about who speaks and who is made visible in the mainstream media, and who remains silenced.

Conclusion

Episodic coverage, or event-driven coverage of particular places, often does not give us a comprehensive picture of those places or the people living in them. In fact, episodic coverage tends to give us partial images and discourses of various contexts, thus underlining the importance of frames and sourcing in making sense of events, particularly during wars and crises. As discussed at the beginning of this chapter, Jordan rarely features in the top international news stories regarding the Middle East. And, as shown in the analysis of the coverage of one event, our understanding of Jordan through mainstream media coverage remains restricted due to the use of dominant frames that can become normalised and taken for granted, and that can impose particular ways of seeing the Other.

While this chapter and the evidence provided do not give us a concrete picture of how Jordan is reported in normal news cycles, nor does it engage with the question as to why Western journalists tend to reiterate first framings that originate in local contexts and that reflect local interests. What the discussion does provide is an account that challenges the accepted vision of the hegemony of Western news frames in international news. However, such a claim also needs to take into consideration the fact that the reproducibility of first framing depends on the conditions of production, the agency of different journalists as well as structural and material factors of news production, which are questions that this chapter does not address.

Irrespective of these limitations, it is hoped that the discussion opens questions as to how we need to address reporting countries like Jordan, which often do not appear in the mainstream news, and what we need to ask in new research on international news. New research needs to revisit questions regarding what international news is and which criteria govern news reporting and dissemination in the digital age, and ask about the geopolitical significance of frames, particularly when these frames become normalised discursive practices that tend to impose a hegemonic representational order that, through repetition and association, generates particular ways of seeing or not seeing the world and the 'Other'. Importantly, these frames play a role in legitimising systems of power, such as the Jordanian one, while silencing dissenting voices. It is in this sense that they become part of the broader global geopolitics of power.

Finally, the examples discussed above, though few, suggest that only a small amount of what we call international news is, in fact, composed of original news material (meaning material that has not already appeared elsewhere). Given the fact that the number of foreign journalists is being reduced and that new forms of journalism (citizen journalism) are emerging, what seems to be needed is a critical re-engagement with journalism as a practice and profession, and also a critical rethinking of the major paradigms that have shaped our understanding of the field and its relevance in contemporary societies. For the purpose of this book, reporting Jordan provides a small, but hopefully useful, intervention towards a critique of practices and assumptions that have long been shaped by dominant perspectives about distant Others.[2]

Notes

1. By mainstream I mean those media outfits that reach the majority of audiences and are seen to set the public agenda. The BBC in the UK is a good example.
2. I would like to thank Charlie Garnett for his help in researching this chapter.

References

Abu-Rish, Ziad (2015). 'Manufacturing silence: on Jordan's ISIS war, Arab authoritarianism and US Empire', *Jadaliyyah*, 14 February. Available at: www.jadaliyya.com/pages/index/20856/manufacturing-silence_on-jordans-isis-war-arab-aut (accessed 18 August 2015).

BBC (2015a). 'Islamic State crisis: thousands rally in Jordan', 6 February. Available at: www.bbc.co.uk/news/world-middle-east-31158919 (accessed 18 August 2015).

BBC (2015b). 'Is Jordan's Abdullah really a warrior-king?', 6 February. Available at: www.bbc.co.uk/news/magazine-31161971 (accessed 18 August 2015).

BBC (2015c). 'Islamic State crisis: UAE sends F-16 squadron to Jordan', 7 February. Available at: www.bbc.co.uk/news/world-middle-east-31202878 (accessed 18 August 2015).

BBC (2015d). 'The brutal killing that hardened Jordan's hearts against ISIS', 8 February. Available at: www.bbc.co.uk/news/magazine-31161971 (accessed 18 August 2015).

Black, Ian (2015). 'Jordan's King Abdullah vows "relentless" war against ISIS', *Guardian*, 4 February. Available at: www.theguardian.com/world/2015/feb/04/jordan-king-abdullah-war-isis-pilot (accessed 18 August 2015).

Butler, Judith (2009). *Frames of War: When is Life Grievable?* London and New York: Verso.

Entman, Robert M. (1993). 'Framing: toward clarification of a fractured paradigm', *Journal of Communication*, 43(4), 51–8.

Feldman, Ofer (1993). *Politics and News Media in Japan*. Ann Arbor: University of Michigan Press.

Freedom House (2013). 'Jordan', Available at: https://freedomhouse.org/report/freedom-press/2013/jordan#.VdOHxfTIJME (accessed 18 August 2015).

Galtung, Johan and Ruge, Mari H. (1965). 'The structure of foreign news: the presentation of the Congo, Cuba and Cyprus crises in four Norwegian newspapers', *Journal of Peace Research*, 2(1), 64–90.

Gitlin, Todd (1980). *The Whole World is Watching*. Berkeley, CA: University of California Press.

Guardian (2015). 'The *Guardian* view on Islamic State's attempt to disrupt the links between the monarchy and Jordan's tribes', 4 February. Available at: www.theguardian.com/commentisfree/2015/feb/04/guardian-view-islamic-state-attempt-disrupt-links-monarchy-jordan-tribes (accessed 18 August 2015).

IPI (International Press Institute) (2014). *IPI Report: Press Freedom in Jordan*, 28 May. Available at: www.freemedia.at/fileadmin/resources/application/JORDAN_REPORT_FINAL.pdf (accessed 18 August 2015).

Muasher, Marwan (2011). 'A decade of struggling reforms in Jordan: the resilience of the rentier system', The Carnegie Papers, May. Available at: http://carnegieendowment.org/files/jordan_reform.pdf (accessed 18 August 2015).

Muir, Jim (2015). 'Jordan IS: Queen Rania joins thousands at Amman rally', BBC, 6 February. Available at: www.bbc.co.uk/news/world-middle-east-31171149 (accessed 18 August 2015).

Norris, Pippa, Kern, Montague and Just, Marion (eds) (2003). *Framing Terrorism: The News Media, the Government and the Public*. London: Routledge.

Obeidat, Sara (2015). 'Air strikes no way to honour slain Jordanian Pilot', Al-Jazeera, 6 February. Available at: www.aljazeera.com/indepth/opinion/2015/02/air-strikes-honour-slain-jordanian-pilot-150206072528748.html (accessed 18 August 2015).

Patterson, Chris and Sreberny, Annabelle (eds) (2004). *International News in the 21st century*. London: John Libby.

Patterson, Thomas (1998). 'Political roles of the journalist', in Doris Graber, Denis McQuail and Pippa Norris (eds), *The Politics of News, the News of Politics*. Washington, DC: CQ Press.

Reporters Without Borders (2010). *Press Freedom Index 2010*. Available at: http://en.rsf.org/press-freedom-index-2010,1034.html (accessed 18 August 2015).

Said, Edward W. (1979). *Orientalism*. New York: Vintage.

Said, Edward W. (1997). *Covering Islam: How the Media and Experts Determine How We See the Rest of the World*. London: Vintage.

Sweis, Rana F. and Baslan, Dina (2013). *Mapping Digital Media: Jordan*. Open Society Foundations, 10 October. Available at: www.opensocietyfoundations.org/sites/default/files/mapping-digital-media-jordan-20131121.pdf (accessed 18 August 2015).

Van Ginneken, Jaap (1998). *Understanding Global News*. London: Sage.
Waisbord, Silvio (2000). *Watchdog Journalism in South America*. New York: Columbia University Press.
Zelizer, Barbie (2004). *Taking Journalism Seriously*. New York: Sage.

3

Reporting Egypt

A Framing Analysis of the Coverage of the 30 June Mass Protests and Beyond

Naila Hamdy

Narrating the story of Egypt's political changes took precedence in the Western media from the moment that mass protests took place in Tahrir Square on 25 January 2011 and for some time afterwards. Egypt's revolution was a comfortable news story to tell. The revolution was peaceful, it was popular, it was youthful and it glamorised internet savvyness and seemed a tad secular (Bady, 2012).

After the riveting events, the dictator was ousted, the regime collapsed and news reporters followed Egyptians as they embraced their freedom, changed their constitution, prepared for parliamentary elections and, arguably most significantly, went to the polling stations to vote at their first multi-candidate presidential elections.

Tahrir square become a symbol of a wave of pro-democracy protests that hit the Middle East and was termed the Arab Spring by Western media. The Egypt story had a clear ending when, in June 2012, Egypt announced its first democratically elected president. If you were analysing Egypt's transformations through the Tahrir lens at least, then the revolution was complete (Bady, 2012).

Surprisingly, exactly one year later the spontaneous mass protests of the Tamarod movement against the elected Muslim Brotherhood president on 30 June 2013, and the subsequent military intervention on 3 July, shattered the simplistic frame (De Smet, 2014). The Tamarod movement, whose name means 'revolt' in Arabic, is a grassroots protest movement that claimed it collected over 22 million signatures for a petition calling for the president to step down (BBC, 2013).

The Western media quickly labelled the military takeover a coup, rarely stopping to understand the unfolding process. But in the eyes of the anti-Morsi mass protestors, the power-hungry Muslim Brotherhood had hijacked the revolution, and this was a popular second revolt. The army was perceived to be an instrument of popular power, the only force that could rid the nation of the Brotherhood, put the democratic process back on track and save the revolution (De Smet, 2014).

Western media was criticised vehemently both by the protest supporters and local media, as their focus was on the military intervention rather than the mass protests, and accused of underplaying the importance of the 30 June protests and portraying a 'polarisation' message of balanced opposing rallies (Shaalan, 2013).

In fact, this mistrust of Western media coverage was exacerbated because Egyptians felt that the 'Tahrir lens' was no longer in use. Protests demanding the ousting of Morsi were simply not covered with the same approach as protests against Mubarak in 2011. Anger towards Western media became entangled with anti-Western feelings and served to feverishly mobilise and fuel strong nationalistic sentiments (Tadros, 2013).

Morsi's year in office did not meet the expectations of many Egyptians. It was marked by controversial decrees and political and economic instability. Press and media freedoms were constrained, and serious encroachments on the independence of the judiciary occurred. In the months that followed his election Morsi did not respect any basic tenets of democratic rule (Ozdemir and Haddad, 2013), yet much of this picture was omitted from the news coverage.

Egyptians were faced with a new government that had in a short period broken major promises. Egyptians emerged in solidarity to protest against the new president and regime because they were fed up with the blatant disregard of human rights and constitutional freedoms. To add insult to injury, the economy had been badly handled and Morsi failed to address protestors' concerns (Pierce, 2014).

On the other hand, Morsi did have his supporters, whose view was that the Tamarod movement and ensuing protests were just a tool to derail the democratic process and pave the way for a counter-revolution. They felt betrayed by the West for not sufficiently defending the idea of reinstating their leader, but they did indeed receive the lion's share of attention from Western press, while the anti-Morsi camp received minimal attention that was disproportionate considering the size of their protests (Tadros, 2013).

Later in the summer, Western media focused on the method by which Egyptian security forces raided the pro-Morsi camps of protestors after the failure of initiatives to end a six-week sit-in, and the killing of at least 800–1,000 people (Human Rights Watch, 2014). It was conventional news values that required coverage of an event of such magnitude and violence, but in Egypt local media; public opinion was swayed against Western media and criticised it for its lack of understanding of the Egypt context.

Selective reporting on human rights violations during such a turbulent year has been noted as a deliberate misrepresentation of the truth. The backlash against the Muslim Brotherhood on the streets of Egypt has been condemned, as have security clampdowns, which have been frequently ruthless. However, the Western press has ignored human rights abuses committed by the Muslim Brotherhood and their sympathisers. There has also been minimal coverage of retaliations against revolutionary youth or the Copts (Tadros, 2013).

This perceived slant in the coverage was also a concern to Egyptians because of the reliance of the country on foreign aid from the USA and its Western allies. And indeed there is some evidence that news media may influence the foreign policy making process to some degree. In addition, if the military ousting is accepted as a coup d'état then under US law the US administration must cut off $1.5 billion of aid to Egypt.

The failure of the Western media to recognise the validity of the 30 June protests and the strong support of the military intervention is just one example of the media's skewed representation of the Egypt story. Although a strong body of literature exists on both framing and US and UK foreign news, and a number of studies focused on the coverage of the 2011 Arab Spring and Egypt, nonetheless there is a dearth of studies that have paid attention to Egypt beyond the first round of uprisings.

This chapter seeks to fill the gap and provide insight into how the mass protests of 30 June, the ousting of the elected Muslim Brotherhood president, the raid of the pro-Morsi camps and events leading to the election of a new president were framed by elite US and UK newspapers.

The Framing of News

Framing theory is based on the idea that the presentation of an event or an issue can have different angles, and that the media can change an opinion or opinions by the way that presentation is constructed. This 'framing effect' is defined as the shift that occurs when changes (often subtle) in the presentation can significantly change public opinion (Chong and Druckman, 2007). The concept implies that it is a dynamic communication process that consists of a build-up of phases: frame-building, frame-setting and individual and societal consequences of framing (D'Angelo, 2002; De Vreese, 2005; Scheufele, 2000).

Framing can have a significant impact on individuals and society at large. Studies suggest that, to date, audiences with little exception have only limited inoculation against framing effects (Chong and Druckman, 2007). Thus, if on an individual level frames can effect a person's attitude, then on a societal level frames can affect processes such as political socialisation and collective actions (De Vreese, 2005).

Taking the case of Egypt's political events, such an impact on public opinion in the US and/or the UK may influence foreign policy towards the country, although the veracity and scope of that influence has been the subject of controversy. Nevertheless, in this context news framing in particular is important, as audiences most likely have no experience with the events in Egypt, and therefore depend on the media to keep them informed (Entman, 1991).

In fact, research in the field of communication has shown that media can and do frame events in multiple ways, and therefore influence public perception of those events (Entman, 1991; Scheufele, 1999; 2000). Entman (1993) found that media can select an event or idea, and portray reality according to their own perspective in such a way that promotes their own definition of the problem and causal interpretation. In addition, the frame can make a moral evaluation of the situation and offer a recommendation or solution.

Scholars continue to study frames not just to identify how an event is framed but also how it may influence public opinion because of the way audiences react to media's construction of reality (Chong and Druckman, 2007).

News framing often occurs because journalists depend on news values when reporting events. De Vreese (2005) suggests in his synthesis of previous research that the different types of news frames that have been used by newsmakers can be generalised to a general typology that is either 'issue-specific frames' and only pertinent to a particular event or topic, or 'generic frames' that transcend thematic limitations but can be identifiable in relation to different topics. In his analysis, he finds that 'frame-building' is influenced both by internal journalism factors that determine how journalists frame issues, and external factors such as the interaction between journalists and elites and the interaction between journalists and social movements.

Semetko and Valkenburg (2000) found that frames could be inductive in that they begin with roughly defined preconceptions that drive the content frames, or deductive where pre-defined frames appear frequently. Commonly used themes include emphasising the conflict, the emotional aspect of the story and the economic consequences (Entman, 1993; Severin and Tankards, 2001), promoting a problem definition, causal interpretation and moral evaluation (Entman, 1993), and thus influencing the debates and the structure of political outcomes.

News frames commonly identified in previous studies do include the conflict frame, attribution of responsibility, human interest, economic consequences and moral evaluation (De Vreese, 2005; Hamdy and Gomaa, 2012; Semetko and Valkenburg, 2000). In addition, Semetko and Valkenburg (2000) theorised that attribution of responsibility was often associated with the government rather than with individuals and groups in the type of episodic coverage of events that is common in news production, in opposition to findings in previous literature.

It is also noteworthy to recognise that frames can be created both intentionally and unintentionally. Arguably, journalists should be considered 'sponsors of frames' (Gamson, 1998). Both intentional and unintentional frames can be present to provide context to the information presented, but intentional frames can also serve the agenda of the source.

In addition, frames can be identified by what they include, but they can also be identified by what they choose to ignore (Entman, 1993) – in essence, using and omitting frames are both tools for articulating ideological messages.

The 2011 Egyptian revolution was a focus of foreign news reporting, portrayed through the Tahrir lens as a democracy movement and often using familiar news frames (Fornaciari, 2011). When Egyptians rose up against their newly elected president on 30 June 2013, foreign news reporting of the crisis in Egypt was strongly criticised by Egyptians. They were afraid of what the impact of this reporting on global public opinion would be (Tadros, 2013). This chapter aims to study that coverage using framing theory to understand how respected US and UK newspapers framed that period in Egyptian history.

Sourcing of News

In this chapter, framing theory is used to provide a foundation for understanding how US and UK newspapers covered events in Egypt. Adding an analysis of sources used by these newspaper journalists will identify those given a voice in the construction of the Egypt news story. Not to be ignored in this formula is the relationship between sources and journalists, which Gans (1979: 116) explained, 'resembles a dance, for sources seek access to journalists, and journalists seek access to sources. But ultimately, it is the journalists who choose whom they will dance with.'

Carpenter (2007) identified sources by analysing both direct and indirect sourcing through looking at verbs of attribution, adding an important layer to the framing category. Attribution provides authority and credibility to a news story and constitutes a fundamental portion of a news medium's vision of reality. In that context, the exercise of identifying source attributions helps the researcher examine how the news frame may have been influenced by the source during the 'frame-building' process.

Rationale for Selecting Newspapers

Prior work in academic and popular literatures serves as a good starting point for identifying representative Western media to be used in this study. Many scholars have identified the *New York Times* (Gamson and Modigliani, 1987; Kiousis, 2004) as a key gatekeeper in news coverage in the USA. The *Washington Post* is also considered a key member of the elite newspapers in the USA (Gamson and Modigliani, 1987). In the case of British newspapers, the *Daily Telegraph* and the *Guardian* are both considered elite newspapers that are likely to have impact on public opinion. In fact, these are precisely the news outlets that produce the set of 'culturally available frames' in elite discourse (Gamson and Modigliani 1987: 144) that are used by journalists in their coverage (Chong and Druckman, 2007; Carpenter, 2007).

So why do journalists use frames? Entman (2007) noted that frames are created to introduce or raise the importance of certain ideas. By highlighting the salience of that idea journalists can activate schemes that encourage readers to think in one direction or another. Indeed it may be to reduce the complexity of an issue and to make it understandable, but frames also function as a persuasive device that helps individuals recall interpretations of certain ideas or issues and also shapes exactly what those individuals will recall (Scheufele, 1999). Chong and Druckman (2007) also noted that much of the public debate involves the use of frames that are intended by opinion leaders to influence policy preferences by establishing the meaning and interpretation of issues. This leads us to deduce that framing is purposefully used to influence.

Additionally, the average circulation of all four newspapers remains high in each of their countries. Examples of US newspapers included the *New York Times* (1.8 million copies) and the *Washington Post* (473,000 copies) (Alliance for Audited Media, 2013). Examples from the UK included the *Daily Telegraph* (479,290 copies) and the *Guardian* (174,941 copies). There has been a decline in the circulation of newspapers worldwide, nonetheless these figures represent top newspapers and do not include digital versions (Jackson, 2015).

This chapter analyses how these US and UK newspapers have framed political events in Egypt and outlines the themes that emerged in the coverage. It also analyses the differences between the coverage of US and UK newspapers and the proposed solutions. It also argues that sourcing does influence the framing used to describe events.

Sample of Analysis

A content analysis of news articles published in the *New York Times*, the *Washington Post*, the *Telegraph* and the *Guardian* covering events in Egypt between 30 June 2013 and 30 June 2014 was conducted in order to understand how these elite newspapers framed controversial political changes in Egypt. During this period, mass protests against Islamist President Morsi took place. These protests were followed by a military intervention to depose the president, and eventually led to the election of former army General Abdel Fattah El-Sisi as the new president of Egypt.

McQuail (2000) states that this method of analysis produces a statistical summary of the larger picture, and thus allows for a reduction of vast amounts of information to a viable size. A sample of articles from the four newspapers was collected through the LexisNexis and Proquest databases. To select articles, the researcher used the keyword 'Egypt' to search for related articles, but since this provided a very large number of articles the researcher instead used the constructed week method (Luke et al., 2011). From the selected time period, seven constructed week samples were drawn for each newspaper because Luke et al. (2011) found that a minimum of six constructed weeks was sufficient and that this is an efficient method to use. The sample included sixty-seven articles from the *New York Times*, fifty articles from the *Washington Post*, twenty-nine articles from the *Telegraph* and twenty-four articles from the *Guardian*. The unit of analysis used was the single article. Only articles that consisted of news coverage or related to foreign policy news were included in the sample. Editorials and opinion columns were also included in the sample. All other articles were excluded.

Measurements of Frames

The study used a statistical method of factor analysis to discern the regularity by which frames were used. The analysis yielded a factor solution in which the framing questions clustered into five frames; human interest, economic consequences, morality prescription, government responsibility and solution to the conflict.

Factor 1: *The Human Interest Frame* identifies the news stories that provide a human angle to an issue. It also employs methods of writing that can generate feelings of outrage, compassion and/or sympathy. It also emphasises how the individual and groups are affected by the issue.

Factor 2: *The Economic Frame* verifies the use of financial losses/and or gains in the future. It also mentions the costs of the expenses involved. Economic consequences are also identified.

Factor 3: *The Morality Frame* shows that the story does contain a moral message. It refers to moral tenets. It also refers to specific societal prescription on how to behave. Morality included ethical values beyond religion such as tenets of democracy during coding.

Factor 4: *The Attribution of Responsibility* factors only two items: whether the government can alleviate the problem and the level of government responsibility. For that reason, Factor 4 should be viewed in this study as attributing responsibility to all the governments, including the Muslim Brotherhood government, and the military-backed interim government.

Factor 5: *The Solution to Conflict Frame.* This factor includes several items: whether the story suggests a solution, whether that solution requires urgent action and who is responsible for the problem. One item has been excluded from the analysis due to its low value, which is whether one individual or group is responsible for the conflict. This factor also addresses whether one party reproaches another and whether the story refers to more than one side of the issue, and finally if it refers to winners and losers. In essence this frame attempts to identify the problem, suggests its solution and projects an end to the problem by implying a winner or loser. It is for this reason that this frame is viewed as the solution to conflict frame.

Frame Visibility

The average of numbers was calculated to extract further analysis and identify the visibility of the five frames. The calculated means showed that the four newspapers under observation in this study had extensive coverage of Egyptian news, particularly during peak political upheavals. The study also indicated that familiar frames have been used to construct the news stories during those times. The least commonly used frame has been the morality frame. However, the human interest frame was used by all four newspapers: the *New York Times* scored the highest mean while the *Daily Telegraph* used this frame the least. The *New York Times* and the *Washington Post* have used the economic consequences frame extensively, and the results show that they surpassed the two UK newspapers in usage. The attribution of responsibility frame is present in all four newspapers but there was not an obvious difference in the mean scores among them. Finally, the conflict frame has proved to be a popular tool for journalists who are intentionally or unintentionally biased when telling a news story. All four newspapers used this frame extensively. However, the *New York Times* was the least dependent on this frame in portraying the Egypt news situation.

Diagnosis of Reasons

Ten main themes emerged from the content analysis as causes for the political unrest in Egypt. The Egyptian government, the judiciary, the military, the Muslim Brotherhood, the military-backed government, the military judiciary, the US administration, the political divisions and violence, the undemocratic atmosphere and the secular opposition.

During the time being studied, Egypt witnessed a few days when the Muslim Brotherhood was in government. Several articles in the sample referred to that particular government even after 3 July when the military ousted the former president. In fact, some articles indicated that the main diagnosis of the problem was the Muslim Brotherhood government. The term military-backed government was used to refer to the government that came under the presidency of interim president Adly Mansour that lasted from 3 of July to June 2014 because he was appointed by the military for eleven months in-between elections.

In this sample, the articles that find the military and judiciary jointly accountable for the unrest are referring to military trials. Frames used by the *Daily Telegraph* diagnosed several reasons for the political situation in Egypt. The military received the lion's share of 25 per cent while the judiciary, the Muslim Brotherhood and military-backed government received 12.5 per cent each. This was followed by 10.4 per cent for the government. The military trials, the divisiveness and the undemocratic atmosphere each received 2.1 per cent of the coverage.

In the case of the *Guardian* the blame fell mainly on the Muslim Brotherhood (23.8 per cent) and the military (21.4 per cent). The military-backed government and military trials accounted for 11.9 per cent each. The judiciary was diagnosed 7.1 per cent of the time as the reason for political troubles and the government 4.8 per cent.

The *New York Times* found the military to be the reason for political conditions in 22.3 per cent of the articles. The government received 14.9 per cent and the judiciary 12.8 per cent. The Muslim Brotherhood, the military-backed government and the military trials were each used in 4.3 per cent of the sample articles. The *New York Times* also found the US administration to be responsible 4.3 per cent of the time. The divisiveness between Islamists and secularists accounted for 1.1 per cent of the reasons.

The *Washington Post* mainly found that the military judiciary (14.3 per cent) and the US administration (12.9 per cent) was responsible for the political unrest. The government and the military government were the reasons 11.4 per cent of the time. The judiciary was blamed 8.6 per cent of the time and the military and divisiveness 7.1 per cent. The *Washington Post* found the Muslim Brotherhood to be the reason 5.7 per cent of the time and the general undemocratic atmosphere 1.4 per cent. The *Washington Post* was unusual in finding the secular opposition to be the reason for Egypt's troubles in 4.3 per cent of the articles sampled.

Suggested Solutions

Few articles prescribed solutions or clearly suggested them. The most common suggestion was a political solution. The *Daily Telegraph* suggested a political solution in 12.5 per cent of the articles and the *Guardian* used this suggestion in 28.6 per cent; the *New York Times* in 12.8 per cent and the *Washington Post* in 14.3 per cent. Some coverage called openly for reconciliation between the government and the Muslim Brotherhood. The *Daily Telegraph* (6.3 per cent), *New York Times* (8.5 per cent) and *Washington*

Post (5.7 per cent) suggested this solution. The *Guardian* did not use this suggestion at all.

Unlike the US newspapers, the *Daily Telegraph* (2.1 per cent) and the *Guardian* (2.2 per cent) suggested that the USA use their diplomatic weight to seek solutions. The *Daily Telegraph* suggested (4.2 per cent) that the USA pressure Egypt to solve the problem, while the *Washington Post* (1.4 per cent) suggested that the USA support Egypt at this time. Other suggestions included withdrawing US aid, in the *Daily Telegraph* (1.1 per cent), *New York Times* (1.1 per cent) and *Washington Post* (1.4 per cent).

Source Attribution

The content analysis also identified the sources and quotes used in the articles published during the period under investigation. The main sources identified belonged to government officials, members of the Muslim Brotherhood, experts, military figures, opposition political party members and recognised revolutionary activists.

An observation of the sources used in the articles under study shows that the *Daily Telegraph* used government officials for 41.7 per cent of the quotes in their reporting. Another 31 per cent were quotes from experts in the field. Another 12.5 per cent were quotes attributed to members of the Muslim Brotherhood. Egyptian military figures or spokespersons were quoted 6.3 per cent of the time, while opposition party members were quoted in 4.2 per cent of instances. In this study opposition parties did not include the Muslim Brotherhood, who were counted separately. The articles did not quote any revolutionary youth or activists.

The *Guardian* articles cited government officials in 23.2 per cent of the quotes and members of the Muslim Brotherhood in 28.6 per cent. Experts gave 19 per cent of the quotes and opposition party speakers 4.8 per cent. The military and activists were not quoted at all.

The *New York Times* used quotes from government officials in 48.6 per cent of the sources and 37.2 per cent were from experts in the field. The Muslim Brotherhood was quoted 20.2 per cent of the time and military sources were used as frequently as opposition party members; 10.6 per cent each of the quotes. Revolutionary activists' sources were quoted in 11.7 per cent of the sample.

The *Washington Post* depended on sources from the government and experts for the larger portion of the quotes. Government officials were quoted in 48.6 per cent of the sample quotations and experts were quoted in 47.1 per cent. Opposition party members were quoted 14.3 per cent of the time while revolutionary activists and military quotes were used in 8.6 per cent of instances.

In this study, the term 'government officials' refers mostly to government officials from the interim government. 'Muslim Brotherhood members' refers to spokespersons or members directly affiliated to the organisation. 'Experts' refers to experts in the field, often members of think tanks (policy or research institutes) who are not officially identified by their ideological associations. 'Military figures' refers to members of the Egyptian military, whether a spokesperson or a general. Opposition party members include all political parties excluding the Muslim Brotherhood. 'Activists' refers to recognised revolutionary youth or activists who had become known during the 2011 revolution. All quotes were included in the sample whether direct or indirect and whether a result of an interview, television airing or official website statement. The category of 'other sources' refers to anonymous quotes and quotes from unnamed pro- and anti-Morsi protestors mostly from rallies and protests.

Reverting to Familiar Frames

When protests against the ousted President Morsi erupted on 30 June and the military intervened to oust him on 3 July, journalists were challenged to report on the changes that were taking place in Egypt.

Discussing how Western media framed Egyptian politics shows that the familiar frames identified in the literature review dominated the coverage. In the broad question asked of how the US and UK newspapers frame events in Egypt and what themes emerged in that coverage, it appears that the frames identified are the same ones used by journalists to tell the story no matter what it is (Semetko and Valkenburg, 2000).

Analysed data showed that the frame categories of human interest, economic consequences, morality prescription, responsibility frame and conflict frame were once again employed, confirming the Semetko and Valkenburg (2000) theory. Human-interest angles were used when trying to show the victimisation of Muslim Brotherhood supporters but never to describe the moderate Muslims, secular groups or Christian Copts (Tadros, 2013). The economic consequences frame centred on the massive amount of financial and military aid given to Egypt by the USA and America's ability to use that as leverage on Egypt.

Morality prescription mostly supported the argument that since the USA and UK have foreign policies rooted in democratic ideals, they should not support the ousting of an elected president. With the exception of one article in the sample studied there was no indication that Egyptians must choose their leaders and their political systems in the method that they found right and suitable.

Attribution of responsibility fell on the government but mostly suggesting that the government did not act alone. Instead, it was down to responsibility that combined with the military and/or the judicial system. The news articles analysed were predominantly episodic, focusing on the event of that moment. This trend was also connected to the use of the attribution of responsibility that identified the government as mainly responsible for the problem. This too confirms Semetko and Valkenburg's (2000) hypothesis.

The well-known conflict frame emerged as the most dominant theme in the coverage. Frequently used by journalists to emphasise a situation and attract reader's interest, the conflict frame was used in the same manner to cover Egypt. It reduced the complexity of the Egyptian scene to a picture of two camps.

The solution to the problem was framed as reconciliation with the Muslim Brotherhood and at times hinted towards the reinstatement of the ousted president. Political solutions were encouraged, although strategic and political outcomes were not clearly spelled out. Not surprisingly, after the ousting of Morsi violence erupted across Egypt as his supporters protested the move against their elected president, but the framing neglected and unrepresented the reasons of those who threw him out. In the year of his presidency he violated almost every principle of elective government (Pierce, 2014), a point that was generally ignored in these articles.

The analysis also showed that the four newspapers covered Egypt extensively, indicating the heightened interested in Egyptian affairs since the 2011 revolution. It also verified that familiar frames were used to construct the story. However, there was a difference between these newspapers. For instance, although the human-interest frame was used, the *New York Times* used this frame the most frequently, while the *Daily Telegraph* used it the least.

The US newspapers' use of the economic frame surpassed the UK newspapers, given the fact that the sum given by the USA in military and financial aid is far higher than that from Europe. The responsibility frame was present in all four newspapers and no significant difference was apparent in its visibility or frequency of use. Given that the conflict frame is a popular tool with which to tell a story, all four used this frame considerably. However, the *New York Times* used it the least. The least commonly used frame was the morality frame, but when it was used it was mostly to prescribe democratic values as a moral principal. Additionally the analysis confirmed that journalists did focus on the economic and conflict frames.

The challenge brought by 30 June caused journalists to revert to the use of familiar frames, and they stopped viewing Egypt through the Tahrir lens. They could no longer frame Egypt from a romanticised angle so instead they revived well-known frames.

The *Daily Telegraph* assigned blame mostly to the military, followed by the judiciary, the Muslim Brotherhood (these articles were published during the Raba'a sit-in when articles referred to the harbouring of weapons) and the military-backed government. The *Guardian* diagnosed the reason for the problem as the Muslim Brotherhood followed by the military. They also found the problem to be related to actions of the government, military trials and the judiciary.

Unlike the UK newspapers, the *New York Times* pointed to the military as the problem. This was followed by blaming the government and judiciary. However, the US newspapers also point to the US administration for its weak stand on the ousting of Morsi and consequent change in politics. The *Washington Post* found the reason to be the military trials followed by the US administration, and was the only newspaper to find the secular opposition to be the reason for the political instability. In this case the reason was because they allied with the army against the Muslim Brotherhood.

Several articles also warned of, or inferred that, a civil war would break out at any moment. For instance, a *Washington Post* article from 20 August 2013 compared the situation in Egypt and Syria.

Although framing theory posits that journalists also offer a solution to the problem it is notable that the majority of articles did not suggest a specific solution. Political solutions were suggested but few gave specific directions as to how to achieve these solutions. Nonetheless, the *Daily Telegraph* articles suggested political solutions, reconciliation with the Muslim Brotherhood and US pressure through the withdrawal of aid. The *Guardian* stuck with the vague political solution prescription. Meanwhile, the US newspapers added the reconciliation and withdrawal of US aid concepts to their reports. However, all articles studied for this content analysis veered away from clearly identifying solutions or pointing out barriers to the implementation of those solutions.

The study findings also revealed that the sources most relied upon for quotations were associated with three characteristics: government or official sources, affiliation with the Muslim Brotherhood and experts who were frequently accused of having Islamist leanings. This indicates that on the dance floor (in reference to Gans, 1979) the political actors are inviting the journalists to dance, and the journalists are choosing to dance with the Muslim Brotherhood. This is part of the frame-building process that eventually gives the news story its angle.

Unexpectedly, the study did not identify large differences between UK and US newspapers. Differences emerged in quantity and content. American newspapers covered the Egypt story more frequently than their UK counterparts. They also used the economic frame more frequently. In contrast to the UK journalists, the US journalists blamed the policy of the US administration in a large number of the articles. Finally, when it came to sourcing, American newspapers, and specifically the *New York Times,* quote anonymous sources, which were nearly exclusively from the Muslim Brotherhood at a time when they could no longer speak openly, while the UK newspapers did not use anonymous sources at all.

Conclusion

By understanding how newspapers frame and source we can better explain phenomena related to how journalists construct information.

This research adds to framing theory by demonstrating the relationship between newspaper framing and source type, showing that the news media are most comfortable using predictable frames to tell their stories and that they make an intentional choice when they use a source. Source selection can influence and affect framing.

The main premise of framing theory is that an issue can be viewed from multiple angles and can be formed in a manner that can have varying implications. Framing can reorient the way people think about an issue (Chong and Druckman, 2007) by using the same old familiar frames.

By omitting a frame that may have explained the 30 June uprising, the coverage of all four newspapers lacked the full context of the political situation in Egypt.

References

Alliance for Audited Media (2013). 'Top 25 US newspapers for March 13', 30 April. Available at: http://auditedmedia.com/news/blog/top-25-us-newspapers-for-march-2013.aspx (accessed 27 January 2014).

Bady, Aaron (2012). 'Spectators to revolution: Western audiences and the Arab Spring's rhetorical consistency', *Cinema Journal*, 52(1), 137–42.

BBC (2013). 'Profile: Egypt's Tamarod protest movement', 1 July. Available at: www.bbc.com/news/world-middle-east-23131953 (accessed 3 May 2015).

Carpenter, Serena (2007). 'U.S. elite and non-elite newspaper's portrayal of the Iraq War: a comparison of frames and source use', *Journalism & Mass Communication Quarterly*, 84(4), 761–76.

Chong, Dennis and Druckman, James N. (2007). 'Framing theory', *Annual Review of Political Science* 10, 103–26.

D'Angelo, Paul (2002). 'News framing as a multi-paradigmatic research program: a response to Entman', *Journal of Communication* 52, 870–88.

De Smet, Brecht (2014). 'Revolution and counter-revolution in Egypt', *Science & Society*, 78(1), 11–40.

De Vreese, Claes (2005). 'News framing: theory and typology', *Information Design Journal + Document Design* 13(10), 51–62. Available at: http://msap-unlam.ac.id/download/bahan__bacaan/New%20Framing.pdf (accessed 2 January 2014).

Entman, Robert M. (1991). 'Framing US coverage of international news: contrasts in narratives of the KAL and Iran air incidents', *Journal of Communication*, 41(4), 51–8.

Entman, Robert M. (1993). 'Framing: toward clarification of a fractured paradigm', *Journal of Communication*, 43(4), 51–8.

Entman, Robert M. (2007). 'Framing bias: media in the distribution of power', *Journal of Communication*, 57, 163–73.

Fornaciari, Federica (2011). 'Framing the Egyptian revolution: a content analysis of Al-Jazeera English and the BBC', *Journal of Arab & Muslim Media Research*, 4(2–3), 223–35.

Gamson, William A. (1998). 'News as framing: comments on Graber', *American Behavioral Scientist*, 33, 157–61.

Gamson, William A. and Modigliani, A. (1987). 'The changing culture of affirmative action', *Research in Political Sociology*, 95, 1–37.

Gans, Herbert J. (1979). *Deciding What's News: A Study of CBS Evening News, NBC Nightly News, Newsweek, and Time*. New York: Pantheon Books.

Hamdy, Naila and Gomaa, E. H. (2012). 'Framing the Egyptian uprising in Arabic language newspapers and social media', *Journal of Communication*, 62(2), 195–211.

Human Rights Watch (2014). 'Egypt: Raba'a killings likely crimes against humanity', 12 August. Available at: www.hrw.org/news/2014/08/12/egypt-rab-killings-likely-crimes-against-humanity (accessed 7 January 2015).

Jackson, Jasper (2015). 'National daily newspapers sales fall by half a million in a year', *Guardian*, 10 April. Available at: www.theguardian.com/media/2015/apr/10/national-daily-newspapers-lose-more-than-half-a-million-readers-in-past-year (accessed 4 May 2015).

Kiousis, S. (2004). 'Explicating media salience: a Factor analysis of *New York Times* issue coverage during the 2000 U.S. presidential election', *Journal of Communication*, 54, 71–87.

Luke, Douglas, Caburney, Charlene A. and Cohen, Elisia L. (2011). 'How much is enough? New recommendations for using constructed week sampling in newspaper content analysis of health stories', *Communication Methods and Measures*, 5(1), 76–91.

McQuail, Denis (2000). *Mass Communication Theory: An Introduction*. London: Sage.

Ozdemir, Cagri and Haddad, Mohammed (2013). 'Timeline: Morsi's rule over Egypt', *Al-Jazeera*, 4 November. Available at: www.aljazeera.com/indepth/interactive/2013/07/20137493141105596.html (accessed 7 May 2015).

Pierce, Anne R. (2014). 'US "partnership" with the Egyptian Muslim Brotherhood and its effect on civil society and human rights', *Society*, 51, 68–86.

Scheufele, Dietram A. (1999). 'Framing as a theory of media effects', *Journal of Communication*, 49(1), 103–22.

Scheufele, Dietram A. (2000). 'Agenda-setting, priming, and framing revisited: another look at cognitive effects of political communication', *Mass Communication & Society*, 3, 297–316.

Semetko, Holli A. and Valkenburg, Patti M. (2000). 'Framing European politics: a content analysis of press and television news', *Journal of Communication*, 50(2), 93–109.

Severin, Werner J. and Tankard, James W. (2001). *Communication Theories: Origins, Methods, and Uses in the Mass Media*. New York: Longman.

Shaalan, Khaled (2013).'Why the Western media are getting Egypt wrong', *Mada Masr*, 2 July. Available at: www.madamasr.com/opinion/why-Western-media-are-getting-egypt-wrong (accessed 2 January 2014).

Tadros, Mariz (2013). 'Egypt: growing anger with Western opinion', *Open Democracy*, 22 July. Available at: www.opendemocracy.net/5050/mariz-tadros/egypt-growing-anger-with-Western-opinion (accessed 2 January 2014).

4

Reporting Lebanon

Orientalism as News Practice

Zahera Harb

Lebanon has long taken centre stage in Middle East coverage as a country torn apart by conflict. Fifteen years of civil war, three major Israeli wars launched on its soil and various numbers of Israeli military assaults have made it synonymous with conflict. The war in Syria and its implications on Lebanon's security (including several suicide bombing attacks that ISIS committed against innocent civilians) has kept the country within the realm of conflict coverage that is usually seen in the context of a war zone. However, within that narrative of a 'war zone country', UK readers have been presented with many articles exploring the daily lives of the Lebanese people, and mainly the lives of the people of its capital Beirut, including issues related to gender roles and the position of women in society. As this chapter will show, many of these articles reflect simplistic and stereotypical views of the country and its people. This chapter will examine three stories that grabbed British newspapers' attention and are not related directly to war stories. These stories are selected due to the negative reaction they received from many Lebanese readers, in both Lebanon and the diaspora, with some people seeing the coverage as redundant, inaccurate, biased and deeply 'Orientalist'. The first of the stories is an article published by the *Daily Telegraph* in July 2015, entitled 'War is a million miles away when the Lebanese begin to party' by Ruth Sherlock. Lebanese bloggers' and social media activists' critical and sarcastic reaction to the article highlighted the problematic coverage of similar stories in Beirut and Lebanon. The second is the British press coverage of the story of Lebanese TV talk-show host Rima Karaki cutting off an Islamist preacher live on air, for being impolite to her as his host. The third story is that of Joumana Haddad, the Lebanese poet, journalist and writer, who because of her controversial position on sexual freedom has been hailed as the Germaine Greer of the Arab world, according to the *Independent* (Yaqoob, 2012).

The Roundtable Discussion as Research Tool

As part of the research for this chapter, the three stories mentioned above and the selected coverage related to them were presented to three high-profile Lebanese female journalists in a roundtable discussion organised by the author. One of the journalists lives in London and is a senior journalist/presenter at the BBC Arabic Service; the other two are print journalists. The first is an editor at the *Assafir* daily in Lebanon and the second is a former *Assafir* journalist and currently freelance journalist and researcher. All three selected for the roundtable have a lot of experience covering Lebanon.[1] The three female journalists, Najlaa Abumerhi, Sahar Mandour and Carole Kerbage,[2] were emailed links to five articles related to the stories mentioned earlier, in addition to links to two blogs written in response to the *Daily Telegraph* article mentioned above.[3]

The participants debated and deconstructed the five articles, dedicating time to each of the three stories and their coverage. Some of the in-depth analysis drifted at points towards assessing the professionalism of such coverage, particularly when inaccurate information about Lebanon and Beirut was embedded in the articles as facts. It is recognised that the research methods used depend on what sort of information one wants, as well as the nature of the available resources (Hansen et al., 1998). Each technique has a value, and different research questions and goals make one or the other more appropriate in a given application (Wimmer and Dominick, 1997). Since critical thinking is 'the engine that drives the moral reasoning machinery, and thus leads us away from the knee-jerk reactions towards a more rational approach to decision making' (Day, 2000: 63), an attempt to prompt such critical thinking seemed appropriate here.

Introducing case studies (selected articles in this case) to journalists for discussion and evaluation in a roundtable format is an appropriate method for accessing expert opinion on how Lebanon is reported in the British press. The format of the roundtable followed a prepared semi-structured format. The roundtable initiated for this chapter did not deliberately follow any of the recommended systems for case study analysis. The aim was instead to allow as 'natural' a discussion as possible to evolve, and then to see how this might be used to draw a view of what is right or wrong with the coverage of Lebanon in the British press. Some of the roundtable discussions were brought forward to Lebanese TV host Rima Karaki in a separate interview I conducted with her in Beirut. Karaki commented on the coverage her show has generated in the Anglo-American press and worldwide.

Orientalism as News Practice

Edward Said's thesis on Orientalism (1978) was spontaneously used as a reference point by the three participants several times during the discussion, to explain why the coverage in the five articles studied appeared as 'simplistic, stereotypical and superficial' as it did, mirroring what Said called 'the dogmatic views of "the Oriental" as a kind of ideal and unchanging abstraction' (Said, 1998: 8).

Orientalism, as Said advocates, is not simply a European fantasy about the Orient. It is a created body of theory and practice in which, for many generations, there has been a considerable material investment:

> Continued investment made Orientalism, as a system of knowledge about the Orient, an accepted grid for filtering through the Orient into Western consciousness, just as that same investment multiplied – indeed, made truly productive – the statements proliferating out from Orientalism into the general culture. (Said, 1978: 6)

The three participants in the roundtable – in which the author took the role of the moderator – agreed that there was a tendency towards generalisation and applying preconceived conceptions and prejudices in the selected coverage, especially when it comes to gender reporting.

Orientalism, as 'a system of knowledge about the Orient', and in the case of this chapter Lebanon, has been loosely incorporated (as the round-table discussion of the selected coverage will demonstrate) into a form of news practice that tends to reproduce the same discourses and narratives about Lebanon over generations. In these instances, accuracy as a journalistic norm becomes the first casualty.

'Oh Look, it is Another One of those Articles'

The first article, by Ruth Sherlock, was published on 18 July 2015 by the *Daily Telegraph*, titled 'War is a million miles away when the Lebanese begin to party'. Sherlock claims that she will be showing readers 'a side to Lebanon they don't often hear about'. The article shows an image of a young woman drinking champagne from the bottle with the caption saying it is an image of 'a Lebanese Christian woman partying after recent elections' (Sherlock, 2015). Bloggers and social media activists were quick to pick up on the fact that the last election Lebanon witnessed was in 2009, which makes the 'recent' not so 'recent'. They also noticed the stereotypical inclinations of the article's opening image in assuming the sect of the woman in the picture is Christian. She clearly ignored the fact that in the Lebanese context this woman could easily be a Lebanese secularist of Muslim background, or even an atheist. One of the first circulated blogs in response to the article was that posted on the *A Separate State of Mind*[4] blog and carried the headline: 'Foreign journalists, can you stop the cliché & poorly researched articles about Lebanon?' The blogger questions how the journalist concluded the woman is Christian:

> How is that woman Christian? I guess it is because she is unveiled? Because as we all know, there is not a single Muslim woman in the country who is not veiled. I should get the memo out to my friends. Is it because she is drinking alcohol? As if there is not a single Muslim who happens to be female who likes to drink alcohol in this country? I should also get the memo to my party-loving friends; but please do not get any ideas about writing articles about alcohol-loving Lebanese-Muslim women, I beseech you. (Fares, 2015)

A second prominent blog called *Blog Baladi* picked up on the fact that one Beirut neighbourhood the journalist refers to as mostly Shiʻa is a Sunni neighbourhood. Another factual error the article depicts is an image of one busy dining quarter in downtown Beirut. This quarter is almost deserted now and has not been buzzing with diners since 2005:

> I do not remember the last time I saw people dining in that area of Beirut. I think it goes back to 2003 or 2004. Whomever wrote this article obviously has not visited Beirut in a long time. (Najib, 2015)

The blog titled 'Ten things the *Telegraph* should know about Lebanon' listed ten factual errors in the *Telegraph* article, among them the statement 'Muslim and Christian communities rarely interact' (Sherlock, 2015):

> That is true. Christians rarely talk to Muslims and we rarely hang out at the same places. Yesterday I went to Verdun and I was a bit worried that Muslims on camels might attack me there, but then I spotted Christians wearing gold chain necklaces with a cross on it and I felt safe again. (Najib, 2015)

Across the different blogs that have been written by Lebanese bloggers in response to *the Telegraph* article, there was a unified call to avoid cliché and stereotypes about Lebanon and the Lebanese in the British press. For example:

> When you want to write an article about Lebanon, please do not interview a party planner for the 1 per cent, a businessperson who is among the 1 per cent and an old man who was probably taken aback by the presence of a foreigner, and was more than willing to blurt out anything, pile up the bunch together and call it an 'article'. (Fares, 2015)

Lebanese blogger and writer Rabih Salloum ran a spoof article on his blog under the title 'Occidentalist stories I: tea is a million miles away when the British begin to party'. He replicated the opening subheading note using the phrase 'London notes' instead of 'Lebanon notes', which appeared in the original *Telegraph* article. He wrote, 'London notes: vomit, bare feet and cosmetic dentistry – there's a side to England you do not often hear about' (Salloum, 2015). *Blog Baladi* questioned the distorted exaggerated unreliable information the journalist offered about what she calls 'the country's big spenders' and how they cannot sustain their lifestyles except through bank loans:

> Bank loans for $200,000 to hold a birthday party and get a nose job? Lebanese families who organize such parties do not need bank loans. They probably own banks themselves. Moreover, the phenomenon is not a consequence of the civil war, as most people tend to overspend on their credit cards. This is a universal problem for all credit card holders. (Najib, 2015)

The *Separate State of Mind* blog was clear in identifying the journalist's approach to covering Lebanon as being generalising and ostensible and not reflecting the reality of the country:

> I understand that Lebanon is not your target audience in such pieces; but we will be reading them anyway. Similarly, I assume you would also be appalled if I wrote an article about the United Kingdom and mixed up Scotland with England, or if I wrote an article about New York City and I assumed the entire city is nothing more than Manhattan's Financial District. (Fares, 2015)

As part of the roundtable discussion, the three participants said that they picked up the story on social media, two of them through the blogs mentioned above and one by reading the article after it was posted on Facebook. As Mandour said:

> I came to the *Telegraph* article through the reactions on social media and through the blogs that were criticising it. One of them wrote a parallel response to what it would be writing about Britain in the same manner.

While Abumerhi commented:

> A friend of mine who had lived for long time in Britain had posted it with a critical sarcastic comment. Most of the people that reposted it commented on it with disagreement. It is not factual and does not represent the reality or right image of Lebanon. (Abumerhi, 2015)

Based on analysis of the article and the response by the three journalists, it was clear that the coverage of Lebanon emphasised the timeless aspect of the place, echoing Edward Said's concept of the 'Orient' as the unchangeable other; it is 'the other' that is fixed in character and behaviour and is not capable of change (Said, 1978). It is as if nothing changes in Lebanon, all stays the same. The three roundtable journalists noticed the Orientalist tendencies that sneak into some of the British journalists' coverage of Lebanon. Sahar Mandour went further to relate some British journalists' attitudes to Lerner's (1958) Modernisation theory. The coverage tends at that point to be simplistic and fact checking becomes irrelevant. They apply the 'knowledge on the Middle East' thesis rather than the 'knowledge from'. They adopt Lerner's thesis (1958) that what the modern West is, the Middle East should seek to become. In his book, Lerner explains how societies move from backwardness into modernity following the West as their example. For Lerner, to be modern meant to be Western (Shah, 2011). The *Telegraph* article is describing a very 'savage place' rather than the reality of it:

> His book [Daniel Lerner] starts with a meeting with an old man giving him a rock and that is where he started the idea of how to bring the east into modernisation. That is what this journalist did: That old man told me not to go there. Muslims are there [...] Fear constructed around anecdotes. (Mandour, 2015)

The roundtable participants agreed that like most Lebanese who read the article, their reaction to it was merely sarcastic. As Mandour said:

> Many Lebanese became numb, the reaction was like 'seriously again' another such article on Lebanon and till when? [...] It is a collage of cliché on Lebanon that incorporate local myths and stories you hear at the local grocery shop. Sectarianism exists, but what she talked about is phobia. (Mandour, 2015)

Kerbage, however, believed that the reaction was also defensive, aiming to set the facts straight. She pointed out that on the face of it there is some truth to what was written, but it lacks depth and context:

> It lacks any deep nuances [...] It lacks any in-depth analysis as why all of those behaviours exist [...] You need to read about the country to understand its complexities, live in it to be able

to produce something that is not stereotypical and superficial. (Kerbage, 2015)

For Abumerhi the content of the article was out of context. She believes that the Lebanese public are ready to accept reasonable criticism and objective analysis of their state of affairs, but not an article that is factually incorrect:

> I do not expect from an ordinary person to understand the complexity of the Lebanese culture and politics, but I would from a journalist writing a story about Lebanon. Nevertheless, journalists seem to come to Lebanon with a superior attitude of pretending knowledge, or a 'we know better' attitude. (Abumerhi, 2015)

The three journalists, who (as mentioned earlier) have been covering Lebanon for a long time, mentioned the poor professional standards the article reflected. As practicing journalists, they believed that this article was produced in a hurry, mirroring many articles that are stereotypical, simplistic, generalising and sensational. It contained many factual errors and lacked context, a problem Marda Dunsky (2007) highlighted in an article on Western media reporting the Arab world. The roundtable participants agreed that the *Daily Telegraph* article was 'culturally positioned' coverage. Kerbage, who worked as fixer with Western journalists at the beginning of her journalism career, refers to the fact that some of these journalists visit Lebanon for a few days with the aim of putting together an article within the designated timeframe. 'I worked with journalists who hadn't read or done any research and they asked questions that were sometimes offensive. In many cases I had to tone down the question in Arabic.' In other words, some of the attitudes expressed were tainted with ignorance of the place and its social and cultural sensitivities. The three participants offered their responses to the article as Lebanese women and journalists. Mandour summarised it by saying:

> As a journalist and editor, I would not publish such an article. Someone has written a monologue on a very private visit on a country that suffered from wars and conflicts and is still suffering. The very active civil society, the everyday clash between modernity and heritage. To produce such a superficial simplistic article [...] Why? (Mandour, 2015)

The three summarised the coverage presented here as Orientalist and culturally positioned; full of applied generalisation, stereotype, exceptionalism and sensationalism.

The Orientalist 'Other' and Oppressed Arab Women

Another incident that clearly indicated Orientalist tendencies in reporting on Lebanon was that of Rima Karaki, the Lebanese female anchor, cutting off a self-declared religious scholar live on air, the London-based Islamist extremist preacher Hani Siba'i.[5] Karaki's action was hailed in many British and American online and print media as heroic in a society that is 'dominated by patriarchal oppressions' and 'it is a country where women's rights are still ignored' (Kabas, 2015). Much of the media in Western democracies are obsessed with stories about submissive Arab and Muslim women (Abu-Lughod, 2013). Rima's action was cited as an exception, a breakthrough, one of a kind – as for many Orientalist journalists Arab women are seen 'as exotic creatures whose value is derived solely from their imprisonment in a gilded cage' (Malik, 2015).

The story went global. I remember I was due to give a talk at the second Middle Eastern Studies conference in Rio de Janeiro in April 2015 when a colleague sent me the YouTube clip of Rima's show subtitled into Portuguese, with many Brazilian media organisations reporting on the story. The Middle East Media Research Institute TV Monitor project (Memri TV), an organisation dedicated to monitoring Arab media, distributing translated clips of newspapers and broadcasting to circles of power and media institutions free of charge in the United States and Britain, was first to broadcast the clip. Memri is specialised in monitoring Arab media and detecting 'anti-Semitic' or 'anti-Western' rhetoric, translating the passages to English and sending them to media organisations and political institutions (Whitaker, 2002). Following Memri's work, it seems that their intention was to highlight the Islamist preacher's repetitive hate speech rather than the 'bravery' of the presenter.

The first to use the story was an American website, the *Daily Dot*. The platform tainted the incident as exceptional in a society where 'women['s] rights are still abused' (Kabas, 2015). The perception that it is exceptional or novel for an Arab woman to do her job and demand respect is false. As

Nesrine Malik put it in the *Guardian*, the preacher would have acted in the same hateful manner if a male anchor interrupted him and cut him down to size (Malik, 2015).

Rima Karaki dismissed the heroic sentiments some media attached to her television act. In an interview with the author, she said she did not feel like a hero and that she acted out of self-respect. She added that the background of the guest played a big role in attracting media attention, 'especially with the political and religious concepts he expresses'. Rima, however, does not dismiss the importance of such an opportunity that allowed her to tell 'the whole world that women in my country [Lebanon] are strong and brave and tough, and any of them in my place would have done even better, they are my idols. They are not as everybody thinks, either plastic or submissive' (interview with author, 2015).[6]

Rima's reaction to the media attention she got matched the roundtable participants' reaction. The three female journalists made the point that the scale of attention was surprising and that this kind of scenario happens almost every day on Lebanese TV and other pan-Arab channels, whether with a female or a male anchor. Abumerhi believes that this encounter would not have got attention if the anchor were not wearing a headscarf. As Abumerhi noted:

> This thing happens in Lebanon every day. How many talk shows are there how many times this type of conflict happens on air? That is where the shock came from [...] the program has a sensational angle to it [...] it is in its making [...] he is a figure of hate speech [...] the coverage didn't reflect that what happened on this show is a common scene on Lebanon's TV and other TV shows in the Arab world. (Abumerhi, 2015)

Sahar Mandour takes this a bit further by asserting that this is not innocent coverage, and sees it as a repeated constructed scenario of the West's desire to jump in and help free the women of the East. Mandour's assessment echoes what Chakravorty Spivak described as 'white men saving brown women from brown men' (Spivak cited in Abu-Lughod, 2002: 784):

> It is the war on terror that is coming to rescue the Arab women from patriarchal control, give them their freedom [...] they are not free now they are bounded to the control of evil men [...]

all of that comes with the coverage [...] it has a political frame
to it, it is not innocent. (Mandour, 2015)

Carole Kerbage took the discussion to a wider context and pointed to the
fact that it could happen anywhere in the world, not just in Lebanon or in
the Arab world:

Being a woman it is how you are treated all over the world as
a female journalist [...] it seems there was a tendency to sum-
marise women's oppression in one form, one person – the icon
that says it all [...] that's what was irritating. (Kerbage, 2015)

Rima Karaki agrees that women's rights in Lebanon and the Arab world
should not be portrayed in light of what happened with her. Karaki, along
with the three debaters, asserts that women's rights movements in Lebanon
have long been fighting for gender equality. Much has been achieved and
much is yet to come (Karaki, interview with author, 2015). Roundtable
participant Najlaa Abumerhi highlights the fact that women's struggle
in Lebanon and the Arab world does not centre on the veil. 'Veil or no
veil that is not the central issue'. The narrative that has been used suits the
Western stereotypical narrative, says Sahar Mandour:

No one covered the women campaigning to empower women
for the end of domestic abuse in Lebanon, a massive campaign
that has gained momentum on a national level. It didn't not get
attention in the Western media [...] it works well along with
their narrative to have a beautiful woman with a veil standing
up to a religious preacher, it works well with their line of narrative about good and evil. (Mandour, 2015)

The coverage has been superficial, lacks context and is Orientalist in its
approach. We can argue that it is good to report on Arab women when they
are not being abused or enslaved, but as Nesrine Malik put in an article
in the *Guardian* countering the media fiesta on the incident, 'when everything that is not that is treated as a novelty, one is effectively reinforc-
ing the stereotypes by saying, "Look! Here is a woman NOT being beaten,
enslaved, force married or honour killed. How about that?"' (Malik, 2015).

Perhaps the coverage was good in the sense, as Rima Karaki says, that it
helped her to speak of the many female journalists and anchors that work

in Lebanon and the Arab world, and who are being brave and professional on all fronts. To echo Abumerhi's question, 'would the clip had attracted so much attention if Rima Karaki was not wearing the veil?' Did those who reported on the act know that Karaki is not a veiled woman and that wearing the veil loosely was in response to a request put by the interviewee as a condition to conduct the interview?

Generalising Gender Inequality

Edward Said wrote that, generally speaking, seeing Arabs 'as by nature lacking the same desirable qualities as the occidentals' (Said, 1978: 306), and hence the urge to 'empower women of the East', comes across vividly when considering my third case study.

Joumana Haddad is a writer-journalist who describes herself as a female activist advocating women's rights in general, but women's sexual rights in Lebanon and the Arab world specifically. As in the case of Rima Karaki, Joumana became the story of a defiant Arab woman in the British press after publishing her book *I Killed Scheherazade: Confessions of an Angry Arab Woman* (2010). She has become the symbol of Arab women, contesting the 'simplistic stereotype associated with oppression, victim and veil', as one advertisement for a talk she was scheduled to give at the Frontline Club in 2010 stated (Frontline Club, 2010). So here again, as in Karaki's case, Haddad's call for women's sexual freedom was represented as a novelty in the Arab world, as a novel act to be celebrated. The two articles discussed in the roundtable appeared in the *Independent* and the *Guardian* in the form of interview features. The *Guardian* feature presented Haddad as the victim of a country that hates her (Edemariam, 2010). The *Independent*, two years later, interviewing Haddad about another controversial book she had written, brings the novelty to a different level by proclaiming her to be the Germaine Greer of the Arab world (Yaqoob, 2012). The roundtable participants agreed that both the *Guardian* and the *Independent* celebrated Haddad as unique. Kerbage expressed her concerns that all women's rights struggles in Lebanon are brought down to one woman:

> They did not question her narrative as if all women in the Arab world are oppressed and under patriarchal oppression [...] As

if all women in the Arab world are brainwashed and she is the only women that knows [...] they simplified all women's problems down to male chauvinism and macho masculinity, neglecting the economic, political factors in shaping women's role and position in society. This speaks to the narrative the West like that – there is clash of civilisation between Arabs and Muslims on one hand and the West on the other. (Kerbage, 2015)

Mandour suggested that the article took Joumana's words for granted and managed to generalise them:

She [Joumana] is talking from a personal point of view and from personal experiences, it is the journalists who are generalising what she is saying to all [...] they are reading the society from her experience and she is reproducing the same discourse. I think she is not stupid [...] she knows what draws international media attention and she belongs to this world of generalization. (Mandour, 2015)

The roundtable participants agreed that both interview features bought into Joumana Haddad's narrative of generalisation. Abumerhi strongly believes that she is selling stereotypes in her books and the journalists, who conducted the interviews, are falling into generalising those stereotypes:

She is not exceptional in Lebanon [...] not more than a city woman in Lebanon [...] The Lebanese female image is so complex and not that black and white [...] two years between the articles and she is still selling the same product and they are still propagating the same image [...] nothing changed [...] the same portrayal [...] Simplistic [...] cliché. (Abumerhi, 2015)

Both interview features (two years apart) seem to buy into the image Haddad is selling about herself and the wider society. Sahar Mandour, who knows Joumana Haddad personally, believes the problem is not in what Joumana is saying, but in how these articles are generalising what she is saying to all:

Joumana has a very clear persona [...] she confronted many feminists with her approach [...] she has position [...] She

> is giving her opinion [...] She built her public persona on
> this discourse [...] 'Me and the society' [...] She personally
> believes that all men hate her [...] it is not representative, but
> that is her life her beliefs [...] and they generalised that to all.
> (Mandour, 2015)

Laila Abu-Lughod wrote, in her *Do Muslim Women Need Saving?* (2013),
about her astonishment as to how easily people in the West presume that
Muslim women do not have rights. That assumption led to the creation
of the stereotype of helpless, imprisoned women in desperate need of
Western liberation (Eltantawy, 2013). To borrow Abu-Lughod's words,
Arab women have been subjected to 'cultural framing' (Abu-Lughod,
2002: 784) as 'women shuffle around silently in burqas'. Reading the two
articles featuring Joumana Haddad's views, position and work and the
widespread coverage of Rima Karaki's 'TV performance' reflects what
Leila Ahmed (1992, cited in Abu-Lughod, 2002) called 'colonial femi-
nism', where all the struggles and problems of women in the region and in
Lebanon had been simplified to male chauvinism and male oppression.
The narrative neglected, as Carole Kerbage put it in the roundtable, 'the
economic [and] political factors in shaping women's role and position in
society'. The narrative presented here speaks to the simplified binary of
'us versus them':

> At one point, the journalist says we are surprised to know of an
> Arab woman that has such progressive ideas. For me that was
> insulting to us all Arab women [...] the amount of stories we
> covered of women who are struggling for her rights in Lebanon
> and the Arab world is countless. (Kerbage, 2015)

Kerbage was referring to the opening statement in the *Independent* which
reads 'Joumana Haddad is a voice rarely heard in the Middle East – an
unapologetic feminist who wants to challenge the way both Arab men and
women think' (Yaqoob, 2012). In all forms a very superficial and patronising contextualisation of what really matters for Arab and Lebanese women.
Generalising Haddad's argument to all brings home Evelyn Alsultany's
(2012: 79) question in her book *Arabs and Muslims in the Media*: 'What are
the alternative versions of reality that stories about the oppressed Muslim
woman omit?'

Conclusion

Simplifications and preconceived ideas used in reporting Lebanon in general and Lebanese women specifically are evident in the cases presented in this chapter. Orientalist tendencies to copy and paste experiences published and shared previously was clear, mainly in the *Telegraph* article. Depending on archival material and claiming it to be current is misleading and inaccurate. It represents Lebanon as a static state that does not change, and its complex social, cultural, religious and political realities as simple matters of either conflict between two religious rivals or as the land of all parties in the region. Stories fail to look equally at leisure tendencies among both Muslim and Christian women. They lack knowledge of realities on the ground. They tend to situate Lebanese women within the context of being weak, oppressed and submissive and subject to male domination. The articles featured here clearly indicate that those journalists writing or commenting on the situation of women in Lebanon lack knowledge about (or ignore) the realities of women's rights and the struggle in Lebanon. A tendency to generalise is also evident. Generalising the so-called 'female ignorance' of their rights and applying that to all Arab women is an act of Western prejudice about the 'Other' who needs saving. The journalists featured here have clearly not done their homework (their essential research) adequately before writing their stories, or, in the case of the *Telegraph* writer, she might not have left the neighbourhood that accommodated her in Beirut and thought it was correct to generalise her experience to the whole country.

As many Lebanese bloggers made clear, their advice to Western journalists parachuting in to cover Lebanon or sitting in offices in London or North America making assumptions about Lebanon and Lebanese women is this: avoid cliché and stereotypes, read about the subject or country you are writing on and don't apply your preconceived conceptions and Orientalist constructed knowledge about Lebanon and its people to your writings. Avoid pre-prepared stories. Avoid prejudicial assumptions of the 'Other'. One woman's struggle does not relate to all. Readers are not confined to national borders anymore. It is an era of the global readership and social media is their tool. Stories on Lebanon will be fact-checked by Lebanese readers in Lebanon and the diaspora.

83

Notes

1. The journalists selected for the roundtable have been practising journalism in and outside Lebanon for at least fifteen years.
2. The three journalists gave consent to the author to use their full names and identity when writing this chapter.
3. Links to full access to the articles and blogs discussed here are listed in the references at the end of this chapter.
4. The *A Separate State of Mind* and *Blog Baladi* blogs have been listed among the ten most shared and influential blogs in Lebanon according to Lebanese Blogs yearly stats. *Blog Baladi* was listed as the most influential blog in Lebanon and *Separate State of Mind* as the most shared on Facebook (http://stats2015.lebaneseblogs.com/). Internet users in Lebanon amount to 80.4 per cent of the population (World Internet Stats, 2015: www.internetworldstats.com/me/lb.htm).
5. Lebanese broadcaster Rima Karaki shot to fame when she cut off the microphone after her guest, an Islamist preacher Hani Siba'i, told her live on air to 'be silent and stop talking'. Full access to that section of the show, with English subtitles, is available here: www.dailymail.co.uk/video/femail/video-1165681/Rima-Karaki-shuts-scholar-tells-shut-up.html (accessed 15 February 2017).
6. Karaki, Rima, interview with author, Beirut, 26 August 2015. The interview was followed by email correspondence on 26 November 2015.

References

Abu-Lughod, Lila (2002). 'Do Muslim women really need saving? Anthropological reflections on cultural relativism and its Others', *American Anthropologist*, 104(3), 783–90.

Abu-Lughod, Lila (2013). *Do Muslim Women Need Saving?* Harvard, MA: Harvard University Press.

Alsultany, Evelyn (2012). *Arabs and Muslims in the Media: Race and Representations after 9/11*. New York: New York University Press.

Day, Louis (2000). *Ethics in Media Communications: Cases and Controversies*. Belmont, CA: Wadsworth.

Dunsky, Marda (2007). 'Reporting the Arab and Muslim worlds', *Neiman Reports*, 612, 41.

Edemariam, Aida (2010). 'Joumana Haddad: "I live in a country that hates me"', *Guardian*, 21 August. Available at: www.theguardian.com/theguardian/2010/aug/21/joumana-haddad-interview (accessed 23 July 2015).

Eltantawy, Nahed (2013). 'From veiling to blogging: women and media in the Middle East', *Feminist Media Studies*, 13(5), 765–9.

Fares, Elie (2015). 'Foreign journalists, can you stop the cliché and poorly researched articles about Lebanon?', *A Separate State of Mind*, 20 July. Available at: http://stateofmind13.com/2015/07/20/foreign-journalists-can-you-stop-the-cliche-poorly-researched-articles-about-lebanon/ (accessed 20 July 2015).

Frontline Club (2010). 'Joumana Haddad in conversation with Jeremy Bowen: confessions of an angry Arab woman', 7 September. Available at: www.frontlineclub.com/insight_with_joumana_haddad_confessions_of_an_angry_arab_woman/ (accessed 1 August 2015).

Haddad, Joumana (2010). *I Killed Scheherazade: Confessions of an Angry Arab Woman*. London: Al-Saqi.

Hansen, Anders, Cottle, Simon, Negrine, Ralph and Newbold, Chris (1998). *Mass Communication Research Methods*. London: Palgrave.

Kabas, Marisa (2015). 'A female Lebanese news anchor was told to shut up – here's what she did instead', *Daily Dot*, 6 March. Available at: www.dailydot.com/politics/female-lebanese-host-cut-mic/ (accessed 10 March 2015).

Lebanese Blogs (2015). '2015 year in review', Available at: http://stats2015.lebaneseblogs.com/ (accessed 30 January 2016).

Lerner, Daniel (1958). *The Passing of Traditional Society: Modernising the Middle East*. New York: Macmillan.

Malik, Nesrine (2015). 'A female Arab TV presenter put a rude male guest in his place. So what?', *Guardian*, 10 March. Available at: www.theguardian.com/commentisfree/2015/mar/10/rima-karaki-arab-tv-puts-male-guest-in-his-place (accessed 10 March 2015).

Najib (2015). 'Ten things the *Telegraph* didn't know about lebanon', *Blog Baladi*, 20 July. Available at: http://blogbaladi.com/ten-things-the-telegraph-didnt-know-about-lebanon/ (accessed 20 July 2015).

Ramazzotti, Georgina (2015). 'In this studio I run the show', *Mail online*, 4 March. Available at: www.dailymail.co.uk/femail/article-2986066/Lebanese-TV-host-Rima-Karaki-stands-sexist-Islamist-scholar.html (accessed 24 July 2015).

Said, Edward (1978–1995). *Orientalism*. London: Penguin Books.

Salloum, Rabih (2015). 'Occidentalist stories I: tea is a million miles away when the British begin to party', *Rabih Salloum Blog*, 21 July. Available at: http://rabihsalloum.com/occidentalist-stories-i-tea-is-a-million-miles-away-when-the-british-begin-to-party/ (accessed 21 July 2015).

Shah, Hemant (2011). *The Production of Modernization: Daniel Lerner, Mass Media, and The Passing of Traditional Society*. Philadelphia: Temple University Press.

Sherlock, Ruth (2015). 'War is a million miles away when the Lebanese begin to party', *The Daily Telegraph*, 18 July. Available at: www.telegraph.co.uk/news/worldnews/middleeast/lebanon/11748872/War-is-a-million-miles-away-when-the-Lebanese-begin-to-party.html (accessed 20 July 2015).

Whitaker, Brian (2002). 'Selective Memri', *Guardian*, 12 August. Available at: www.theguardian.com/world/2002/aug/12/worlddispatch.brianwhitaker (accessed 24 July 2015).

Wimmer, Roger and Dominick, Joseph (1997). *Mass Media Research: An Introduction*. Belmont, CA: Wadsworth.

Yaqoob, Tahira (2012). 'Joumana Haddad: "Arab women have been brainwashed"', *Independent*, 1 June. Available at: www.independent.co.uk/news/world/middle-east/joumana-haddad-arab-women-have-been-brainwashed-7804762.html# (accessed 23 July 2015).

Roundtable Participants

Abumerhi, Najla, Lebanese journalist, Roundtable, City University London, 29 July 2015.

Kerbage, Carole, Lebanese journalist, Roundtable, City University London, 29 July 2015.

Mandour, Sahar, Lebanese journalist, Roundtable, City University London, 29 July 2015.

Interview with Author

Karaki, Rima, Lebanese broadcaster, face-to-face interview, Beirut, 26 August 2015.

Karaki, Rima, Lebanese broadcaster, email correspondence, 26 November 2015.

5

Reporting the Israel–Palestine Conflict

Mike Berry

The Israeli–Palestinian conflict is one of the world's most bitter and protracted wars. It is also a conflict which has attracted an enormous degree of scrutiny from the international media. When set against the coverage accorded to other wars with far higher body counts, such as the conflicts in Syria, Darfur or the Democratic Republic of the Congo, the sheer volume of reporting dedicated to the conflict appears disproportionate. The international media's preoccupation with the conflict can in part be explained in terms of news values (Galtung and Ruge, 1965; Harcup and O'Neill, 2001): the involvement of elite geopolitical actors, the periodic stream of dramatic images of violence and bloodshed, the long continuity of the story and the ease of reporting from an accessible and technologically developed nation all explain, to some degree, why the conflict generates so much international attention. However, to explain the appeal of the story purely in terms of news values is to miss important dimensions which make this conflict unique. These include the fact the region is home to the holy sites of three of the world's major religions and has historically, particularly during the Cold War era, been seen as a critical flashpoint between East and West. Populations across the Arab and Muslim world take an intense interest in the conflict, as do significant Jewish and Muslim minorities in Europe and America. Furthermore, the region is inextricably tied to the history of European colonialism and in the post-World War II era and American foreign policy in the region. For Europeans, in particular, the creation of Israel is also intimately connected with their own dark history in terms of the Holocaust.

Whatever the factors underlying the international media's focus on the region, it is undeniably a story which has also exerted a fascination and pull for many leading international journalists. For some the challenge of covering such a complex story with its deep historical, political and religious roots has made working the beat a testing-ground or rite of passage. Former Reuters bureau chief Crispian Balmer has argued that 'it's one of those places that any journalist worth their salt wanted to come and try their time in' (cited in Rodgers, 2015: 59). However, it is also a posting that comes with a singular set of pressures and constraints. From the hazards of presenting competing historical narratives, to the challenges of navigating intense propaganda and public relations campaigns, to the difficulties of resisting the pressures of powerful lobby groups, covering the conflict is uniquely challenging.

In this chapter I will concentrate primarily on research which examined the second intifada (2000–2). This research formed part of a series of studies that were undertaken by the Glasgow Media Group between 2000 and 2010, which also covered events such as the 2008/9 Gaza war and the attack on the Gaza flotilla in 2010 (Philo and Berry, 2004, 2011). These studies examined the whole of what we describe as the 'circuit of communication' which encompasses the production, content and reception of media messages. We chose this approach because we don't believe it is possible to understand fully the exercise of communicative power without simultaneously studying all three levels, and how they interact. The Israel–Palestine conflict is, in part, an information war where both sides attempt to justify their actions and win the battle for public legitimacy in the court of international public opinion. So to understand this process it is necessary to examine both the content of media messages and how the public relations strategies of the protagonists are filtered through the social, economic and political factors which structure the production of news. However, the responses of audiences cannot simply be read off from an analysis of media content. Instead it is necessary to conduct close qualitative audience research which can unpack both the source of public beliefs and attitudes and the factors underlying the acceptance or rejection of media accounts.

To achieve this we adopted a mixed method approach where we combined: (a) the study of media content using thematic content analysis, (b) interviews with journalists and (c) the use of focus groups and questionnaires involving audience groups made up of members of the public.

This chapter will now provide some of the context to the outbreak of the second intifada in September 2000 in order to highlight the range of opinion that was available for journalists to draw on. This will be followed by an account of the key findings of our content analysis. Then it will turn to the results of reception study which will show how coverage impacted on public beliefs and attitudes. The chapter will conclude by discussing the various pressures and constraints which structure the production of journalism and noting how our findings resonate with research conducted in the United States.

Background to the Outbreak of the Second Intifada

The context leading up to the second intifada is complex and contested. For Palestinians the roots of the conflict lie in the colonisation of the historic land of Palestine by successive waves of Jewish immigrants in the late nineteenth and early to mid-twentieth centuries. This culminated in the war of 1948 when the state of Israel was created. During the war the forces of the nascent Israeli state embarked upon a military strategy which involved the destruction of Arab villages and the forced removal of their civilians (Shlaim, 2000). The war ended with more than 700,000 Palestinian refugees displaced from their homes and forced to live in countries such as Lebanon, Syria, Jordan and on the West Bank (of the Jordan) and in the Gaza Strip. There then followed a series of further conflicts between Israel and its Arab neighbours, the most significant of which was the 1967 war when Israel took control of the West Bank (from Jordan) and the Gaza Strip (from Egypt). The Palestinians living in these regions were placed under military rule and Israel began a process of colonising these areas by building fortified settlements. The building of settlements involved the exertion of strategic and military control of land and water resources such as the 'surrounding the huge Greater Jerusalem area with two concentric circles of settlements with access roads and military positions' (Shlaim, 2000: 282). The Israeli occupation and settlement-building are widely seen as violations of international law. They also, as Amnesty International have noted, have led to systematic human rights abuses committed against the Palestinians in the Occupied Territories:

> Amnesty International has for many years documented and condemned violations of international human rights and humanitarian law by Israel directed against the Palestinian population of the Occupied Territories. They include unlawful killings; torture and ill treatment; arbitrary detention; unfair trials; collective punishments such as punitive closures of areas and destruction of homes; extensive and wanton destruction of property; deportations and discriminatory treatment as com- pared to Israeli settlements. Most of these violations are grave breaches of the Fourth Geneva Convention and are therefore war crimes. (Amnesty International, 2002)

Israel has argued that the key issue in the conflict is that the Palestinians and the neighbouring Arab states have never accepted the legitimacy of the Israeli state. At the root of the conflict, it was argued, is anti-Semitism, Islamic extremism and terrorism. Many in Israel also defended the military occupation and argued that Israel had religious claims to the West Bank, Gaza and Jerusalem dating back to biblical times. Israel has also stated that the occupation is justified on security grounds because the borders of Israel are too narrow to be defensible.

The occupation produced two intifadas, or uprisings, in 1997 and 2000. In-between these periods there were a series of American-led peace ini- tiatives known collectively as the Oslo peace process. These granted the Palestinians some limited self-rule under the aegis of the newly created Palestinian Authority, led by Yasser Arafat. However, Israel still controlled access and roads, allowing it to close Palestinian areas. It also maintained a large military and undercover police presence. Palestinians had expected that the Oslo Process would lead to eventual statehood, but the period was marked by a huge increase in settlements and the construction of a network of Israeli-only roads to link them. This led many Palestinians to believe they would never be granted statehood. Eventually, in 2000, the peace process came to a head at final status negotiations conducted at

Camp David in America. However, no agreement was reached, with both sides blaming the other. Frustration with the peace process and the failure to end the occupation finally spilled over in September 2000 when Ariel Sharon, a figure notorious to Palestinians for his role in the massacre of refugees in Lebanon in 1982, walked through the Muslim holy places in Jerusalem. This was widely seen as a statement of Israeli sovereignty and led to riots which grew into the second intifada.

Media Content

In order to evaluate the coverage, we examined four separate samples of broadcast news coverage between September 2000 and April 2002. We focused on the mass audience (10.00 pm) bulletins on BBC1 and ITV because research has demonstrated that 80 per cent of the public rely on television news as their key information source on foreign news (ITC, 2003). We transcribed all news accounts and then subjected them to a thematic analysis. This method is based on the assumption that in any controversial area there will be competing ways of describing and explaining events and their history. These competing explanations are tied to particular interests which seek to justify their own position. So in this context there are competing perspectives on the origins of the conflict and who is seen as responsible for its persistence. There are also different accounts of the motives of the protagonists and who is seen as instigating the violence. Such accounts carry assumptions about causes, responsibility, legitimacy and consequences. Part of our job as researchers is to map the presence and absence of different accounts and examine the consequences of such patterns for public knowledge and understanding.

One of the key findings of our research is that coverage of the conflict is saturated with images of decontextualised violence. In one of our early samples, 28 per cent of news text was given over to accounts of stone-throwing, shootings, bombings, stabbings, military attacks and other forms of violence. In our audience groups these were the kinds of images which dominated people's recollections of the conflict. A BBC journalist who had reported on the conflict told us that his editor had told him that they did not want 'explainers', and instead the focus should be on 'bang, bang stuff'. The purpose of such coverage is to grab and hold the attention of viewers in what is a highly competitive media environment. However, as we will see, such coverage tends to leave audiences feeling confused, powerless and, ironically, more likely to turn away from news accounts.

Another key feature of news accounts was the almost complete absence of explanations for the conflict. As already indicated, to understand the conflict requires some knowledge of the events of 1948 and 1967. This provides the context which explains the rationale for the actions of the protagonists. However, in our first sample we found that out of more than 3,500 lines of news text only seventeen referred to the history of the conflict. When key issues in the conflict were discussed, journalists tended to speak in a form of shorthand which assumed that audiences possessed a level of background knowledge that was absent in most people. For instance, during a discussion of peace talks a journalist remarked:

> The basic raw disagreements remain – the future, for example of this city Jerusalem, the future of Jewish settlements, and the returning refugees. For all that, together with the anger and bitterness felt out there in the West Bank then I think it's clear this crisis is not about to abate. (ITV early evening news, 16 October 2001)

In order to understand the significance of these key political issues, viewers would need to have some knowledge of the fact that the Palestinians were driven out of their homes when Israel was created, that Arab East Jerusalem has been under an illegal Israeli occupation since 1967 and that the settlements play a key strategic role in the occupation.

In the absence of context, background or history most reporting tended to concentrate on the day-to-day fighting between the two sides. Such coverage tended to explain the continuation of the conflict in two ways. The first was in terms of a self-perpetuating cycle of violence. Here the conflict is presented, in the words of the BBC journalist Paul Wood, as a 'very large blood feud'. Violence is seen to begat more violence in a 'self-perpetuating tragedy':

> It has become a self-perpetuating tragedy. Each day starts with the funerals, but afterwards many Palestinian men make their way to the usual flashpoint to confront their enemy. Then there is the familiar exchange. Stones for rubber-coated bullets,

stun grenades and tear canisters. (ITV early evening news, 9 October 2000)

However, it is not possible to explain the genesis and persistence of conflicts using this kind of analysis. Underlying the conflict is a series of issues rooted in a historical process. Only by unpacking them can the conflict be explained. The second way the conflict tended to be explained was in terms of a framework in which Palestinians were presented as initiating violence to which the Israelis were described as 'retaliating' or 'responding'. In one sample we found that Israelis were described as 'retaliating' or responding to what had to been done to them six times as often as the Palestinians. Such a framework puts the onus for the continuation of the conflict on the Palestinians, whose actions are presented as perpetuating the violence. It also sidelines two alternative perspectives. First, that much Palestinian violence is driven by a desire to throw off occupation rather than just to respond to specific attacks, and second, that Israeli actions were driven not just by a wish for revenge but also by a desire to prevent the emergence of a Palestinian state.

Such patterns in coverage were part of a broader framework in which the Palestinian perspective on the conflict was substantially downgraded in relation to that of the Israelis. This can be seen for instance in the lack of reporting on the consequences of Israeli control of Palestinian land and water resources. The ongoing military occupation and the attendant human rights abuses are very rarely explored in news accounts. The head of a news agency in Jerusalem commented to us that television news covers 'the day to day action, but not the human inequities, the essential imbalances of the occupation, the day to day humiliation of the Palestinians' (interview cited in Philo and Berry, 2011: 196). We found that occasionally news accounts would use the word 'occupation', but its military nature and consequences were not explored, which left many viewers confused as to what it actually meant, with some believing that it just indicated that someone was on the land (as in a bathroom being 'occupied'). Therefore the lack of explanation of the military nature of the occupation and its consequences for the Palestinians had two important effects. First, it made it difficult for viewers to understand why the conflict was so bitter and intractable, and second, it severely disadvantaged the Palestinian position by removing their rationale for action.

The tendency to downgrade the Palestinian perspective in relation to that of the Israelis could also be seen in how broadcast news reported on the settlements. Israel regards these as Jewish communities under threat from Palestinian 'mobs' or 'terrorists', as in the following report: 'Israeli soldiers are accused of using excessive force in response to the violence but insist they are only defending their communities from the stone-throwing mobs' (ITV lunchtime news, 4 October 2000). However, for Palestinians, the settlements fulfil a key strategic role in allowing Israel to control the land and water resources of the occupied territories. Settlers have also been accused by human rights groups of committing widespread human rights abuses against Palestinians:

> Among the settlers' actions against the Palestinians are set-
> ting up roadblocks to disrupt normal Palestinian life, shoot-
> ing at rooftop water heaters, burning cars, smashing windows,
> destroying crops and uprooting trees, and harassing merchants
> and owners of stalls. (B'Tselem, 2003)

In BBC coverage we found that the view that settlements were vulnerable communities under attack from Palestinians predominated. Journalists spent time following the lives and concerns of settlers and were able to articulate these very clearly. However, journalists didn't question settlers about their role in the military occupation or whether they thought it was acceptable that they now controlled much of the land and water in the occupied territories. The fact that the settlements are widely seen as illegal was rarely mentioned and their strategic role was left unaddressed.

The imbalance in coverage can also be seen in the amount of time given to the two sides in interviews. Israelis received twice as much air-time as Palestinians. They were also far more likely to be interviewed in calm and relaxed settings. In contrast Palestinians were more likely to be interviewed in noisy street settings such as during a protest march. The Israelis were also able to restrict the movement of Palestinian spokes-persons and foreign journalists so that face-to-face interviews were frequently impossible, and instead interviews had to be conducted via telephone. This has important consequences both in terms of implied status and the ability to air perspectives. The broadcasters' decision to

accept this state of affairs effectively meant that they legitimised a structural imbalance in coverage.

Another crucial difference in reporting was the way that casualties were
reported. Israeli casualties were consistently given more attention, in comparison to their number, than Palestinian casualties. This does not mean
that Palestinian deaths, and particularly the deaths of children, were not
covered sympathetically. However, even here there was a significant difference in that journalists were more likely to provide a rationale when a
Palestinian was killed than an Israeli.

The language used to describe deaths and injuries were also markedly
different. Words such as 'murder', 'atrocity', 'lynching', 'savage cold-blooded
killing' and 'slaughter' were used to describe the deaths of Israelis but not
Palestinians. This was part of a broader pattern in which different language was used to describe the two sides. Israeli forces were described as
'soldiers', 'troops' and, on one occasion, 'brothers in arms', but most commonly as 'the Israelis'. In contrast Palestinians were described as 'guerrillas',
'militants', 'extremists', 'assailants', 'gunmen', 'bombers', 'terrorists', 'killers',
'assassins', 'fundamentalist groups', 'attackers' and 'fanatics'. For Palestinians,
the use of such labels obscures for them the fact that they see themselves as
engaged in a war of national liberation designed to throw off a brutal military
occupation. This is far removed from the view that the key issue is to 'catch
the terrorists'.

In summary then, broadcast news coverage of the conflict exhibited
clear and consistent features. There was an almost complete lack of historical background and a strong focus on decontextualised violence. The conflict tended to be explained as either part of a 'cycle' of attacks or a situation
where Palestinians initiated the trouble to which the Israelis responded. The
key element of the Palestinian case – that they were fighting against a brutal
military occupation – was largely absent from coverage, as was information
about the consequences of living under prolonged military rule. In contrast Israeli perspectives on the conflict were given far more space and were
sometimes directly endorsed by journalists. Israeli casualties were given
more airtime and described using markedly different language. As we shall
now see, such coverage had a dramatic impact on public understanding and
who was seen as responsible for the continuation of the conflict.

Audience Perceptions

Our audience studies involved two elements. We distributed question-naires to 743 students in the UK, Germany and America. These asked respondents about their knowledge of various aspects of the conflict, such as which nationality the settlers were and who was 'occupying' the occu-pied territories. The second element involved more in-depth qualitative research conducted with fourteen focus groups in London and Glasgow. In these groups we spent extended periods talking with respondents in order to unpack the structure and origins of audience beliefs about the conflict. We also used what we call the 'news game', where we supplied participants with photos from the conflict and asked them to pretend they were jour-nalists and produce their own news reports. These allowed us to examine what audience members retained from news accounts and whether they reproduced the patterns of explanation which we had identified in the content studies. We also brought leading journalists into our focus groups in order to generate a debate on how their coverage impacted on public understanding and how it could be improved.

Our research indicated that in our UK samples between 82 and 85 per cent of respondents depended on TV news as their main source of infor-mation on the conflict. Our US and German samples were less depend-ent on TV news and more likely to cite the influence of newspapers. In our focus groups, middle class and professional groups tended to be better informed about the conflict. This was primarily because they accessed a wider range of information sources and so were less reliant on TV news.

Most participants had little knowledge of the history or origins of the conflict. The proportion of students who knew that the Palestinian refu-gees had been created during the formation of Israel was between 4 and 8 per cent in the UK, 19 per cent in the USA and 24 per cent in Germany. The majority had no knowledge of the links between the wars of 1948 and 1967, in that many of the refugees of 1948 who had fled to the West Bank and Gaza were then placed under military rule. In the focus groups the mod-erator was sometimes asked about the historical context and in response the participants were provided with a brief account of the 1948 war from the Israeli historian, Avi Shlaim. As this exchange shows, this could have a dramatic impact on understanding:

Moderator:	Would it help when you are watching the news, if you knew that history?
First speaker:	Yes
Second speaker:	A lot more.
Third speaker:	Absolutely.
Second speaker:	If they did refer more to the history, the whole thing would mean a hell of a lot more for a lot of people.
First speaker:	That's right. We need to know more.
Third speaker:	It's so fragmented and vague, I mean I try and explain it to my children, I found it difficult – I'm not the sharpest tool in the box anyway, but having said that, on what I was given by the media, a great deal of it was blank, and you just filled in the blanks that I didn't have a clue about – 1948? Was there a war in 1948? Well now I know there was. (Low-income male group, cited in Philo and Berry, 2011: 289)

The lack of historical context made it difficult for participants to understand key aspects of the conflict. For instance, a number of participants mentioned the issue of land but were confused about what this meant, with many seeing the conflict as a border dispute between two countries or peoples. Few were aware that the land had been taken by one group from the other. In a similar vein there was a great deal of confusion over who was 'occupying the occupied territories' and the nationality of the settlers. In our sample of British students, 9 per cent in 2001 and 11 per cent in 2002 knew the correct answers to these questions, while in our focus groups the figure was 39 per cent. Bearing in mind how few understood that the Palestinians were subject to a military occupation, it is unsurprising that its consequences were not widely recognised. Even in our comparatively well-informed middle-class focus groups, few were aware of key issues such as control of land and water. Across our focus groups only 9 per cent mentioned water as an issue and in only two focus groups out of fourteen was the subject of human rights mentioned. Even in groups sympathetic to the Palestinians there was surprise to learn that there were pass laws and identity cards which restricted movement. We also found little knowledge of the large number of UN resolutions critical of the legality of the occupation and its impact on human rights. What is particularly striking is how these absences in public knowledge closely mirror the absences in news accounts.

When we discussed the settlements in our focus groups we also found that participants' views again closely paralleled their representations in television news. Generally the occupied territories were not seen to be subject to military control and the settlements were not seen to be part of this:

Moderator: Do you get the impression watching the news that it is a military occupation by Israel?

Male speaker: A military occupation? No, it's to give the Israelis land to work on, to live on and the army backs them up and keeps back the Palestinians. (Middle-class male group, Glasgow)

In another group a participant describes his impression of TV news coverage:

> I think you sometimes get the impression from the news these are people who happen to want to live there […] and the military backup is in pursuit of their peaceful wish to just go and live there, and I think that's the impression that I get from the news, rather than that it is a military occupation. (Teacher group, Paisley)

As noted earlier, TV news bulletins were far more likely to describe the Israelis, in comparison to the Palestinians, as responding or retaliating to what had been done to them. In our focus groups we found participants consistently seeing the conflict within this framework, which had clear effects on how they apportioned blame for the continuation of the conflict:

Female speaker: You always think of the Palestinians as being aggressive because of the stories you hear on the news. I always put the blame on them in my own head.

Moderator: Is it presented as if the Palestinians somehow start it and then the Israelis follow on?

Female speaker: Exactly, I always think the Israelis are fighting back against the bombings that have been done to them. (Student group, Glasgow)

We also found this initiation–retaliation framework reproduced repeatedly in the news-writing exercise:

> A new, more hard-line leader has come to power in Israel who has *retaliated* with force on attacks by the Palestinians on Israel. (Student, Glasgow, our italics)

> Palestinian snipers and suicide-bombers attacked Israeli targets and the Israeli army *retaliated* with tanks. (Teacher, Paisley, emphasis added)

The disproportionate emphasis on Israeli deaths and injuries in news reports also appeared to influence how our participants saw the relative scale of casualties. In our focus groups 42 per cent of participants saw the Israelis as having more casualties or the numbers being equal. This was primarily because of the strong emphasis on Israeli casualties in news reports. Other factors, such as the perception that the Palestinians were 'hostile' and the view that the conflict involved 'tit-for-tat' violence, were also significant. However, it is also true that some viewers used logic to discount the picture that was presented on the news. For instance, some assumed Palestinian casualties must be higher because Israel had more access to advanced weaponry and better care facilities for its wounded.

We also found in our focus groups that there was a very clear relationship between knowledge, understanding and audience interest. When participants didn't understand the context, the conflict appeared unintelligible and this engendered a sense of powerlessness. Although greater understanding does not necessarily translate into the power to influence change, the ability to see events as having causes can be the first step in seeing the possibilities for change, engaging with what is shown and having opinions. As one respondent put it:

> There is definitely an absence of explanation that causes an absence of feeling because I can quite easily sit and say I feel no way about it whatsoever. Because I haven't been there it's got nothing to do with me whatsoever, so I have a lack of feeling about it. But I also have a lack of understanding about it – maybe if I knew a lot more about it, I'd have more opinion and more feeling about it. (Low-income male group, London)

In another audience group the Channel 4 journalist Lindsey Hilsum explored the relationship between understanding and interest in following the story:

Moderator: Is there a link between you turning off and not being interested and that you actually don't quite understand what is going on?

First speaker: Sometimes if you are not up to speed ...

Second speaker: Sometimes things are more human and more real if you do understand the things that are behind it.

Moderator: I see you nodding [to third woman who has previously said she does not watch the news]

Lindsay Hilsum: [To the same person] Is there anything that would make you more interested in the news?

Third speaker: I can understand what you are saying and I think that it is probably one of the things if I was to turn on the news, if I was forced to for whatever reason, it would help if I knew what I was actually listening to, if I understood where they were coming from. So take this war, I don't know how it started, I don't know the background behind it, so I'm actually in effect listening to gibberish, so that would make a difference. (Middle-class female group, London)

Overall we found strong endorsement for the view that television news should feature clear, concise accounts for why the two sides were fighting. When these were provided, audience interest in the story increased substantially.

Our audience studies thus demonstrated how news coverage impacted public knowledge and understanding in important ways. Crucially, the lack of historical context left many bewildered about the key political issues in the conflict which made it so intractable. This absence, in particular, disadvantaged the Palestinians as their rationale is grounded in historical grievance. Furthermore, the consistent application of an initiation–response framework in reporting had important consequences for who was held responsible for the continuation of the conflict.

Why Does it Happen?

In our conversations with journalists we sought to understand the various constraints and pressures that structured the production of news in this area. We identified six key factors which were crucial. First, the time constraints of the medium were crucial in influencing how news was produced. The pressures of having to produce a constant flow of news items which would fit into a compressed time slot left little time to ponder issues of audience comprehension. Journalists also pointed out that the need to service the proliferation of new digital services, including 24-hour news, had cut down the amount of time that could be devoted to researching stories. The issue of time constraints was accentuated by the fact that most of the complex history of the conflict was highly contested, which meant that journalists would need to balance the opposing narratives. Second, the fact that most of the media were based in West Jerusalem meant that journalists were closer to the Israeli public relations machine and found it much easier to report on events in Israel. In contrast, reaching destinations in the West Bank could be time consuming and difficult due to roadblocks and closures. During the second intifada it also became dangerous, with groups such as Reporters Sans Frontières accusing Israel of targeting journalists with gunfire (Beaumont and Whitaker, 2001). Third, there is a substantial imbalance in public relations resources available to the two sides. The Israelis were widely seen to run a far more professional operation. Their press officers spoke good English, were efficient in providing documentation and took a highly proactive approach in bombarding journalists with emails and press releases putting across the Israeli case. In contrast Palestinian public relations were seen as reactive, incoherent and amateurish. The journalist Robert Fisk has described how public relations and the regular supply of information can structure the agenda of news organisations:

> The journalists' narrative of events is built around the last thing that someone has said and the last thing, given the constraints of time and the rolling news machine that they have heard on the agency wire. So what you would find on television in the last few weeks is that every time an Israeli statement was made, it was pushed across at the Palestinians. So the Israelis would say 'Can Arafat control the violence?' and instead of the television

reporters saying 'Well that's interesting, but can the Israelis control their own people?' the question was simply taken up as an Israeli question and became part of the news agenda. There seemed to be no real understanding that the job of the reporter is to analyze what's really happening, not simply to pick up on the rolling news machine, the last statement by one of the sides. And given the fact that the Israelis have a very smooth machine operating for the media, invariably what happened is, it was Israel's voice that came across through the mouths of the reporters, rather than [having] people who were really making enquiries into both sides and what they were doing (*The Message*, BBC Radio 4, 20 October 2000, cited in Philo and Berry, 2011: 322)

The fourth factor that structures the production of news is the existence of well-organised lobbying. The Israeli embassy has been extremely active in attempting to influence the news agenda in broadcasting and the press. This involves both projecting the Israeli line to news organisations and attacking organisations or journalists perceived to be critical of Israel. The main three political parties also have substantial internal pro-Israeli lobby groups. The CFI (Conservative Friends of Israel group), which is estimated to include around 80 per cent of Conservative MPs, lobbies vigorously for Israel. Part of this involves regular attacks on the media for perceived biased against Israel. It also involves organising regular lunches for senior journalists in the House of Commons. The CFI commented that 'for those working for organisations perceived as being biased against Israel these can be uncomfortable affairs' (cited in Philo and Berry, 2011: 325). There also exists internet-based sites, such as Honest Reporting and CAMERA, who coordinate letter-writing campaigns targeted at news organisations and individual journalists. Often these attacks make the very serious claim that journalists or organisations are anti-Semitic, which can have a chilling effect on reporting. The fifth factor which influences broadcasting is the strong support that Israel receives in much of the British press. The *Daily Telegraph*, particularly during the period when Conrad Black was proprietor, and Rupert's Murdoch's titles, have been strongly pro-Israel. Finally there is the closeness of Britain's relationship with the United States, the world's sole superpower and key player in the region. The power of the USA means that its representatives are guaranteed substantial media access which tends to tilt the balance of coverage even further in Israel's direction.

The media is not a completely closed system and there exist spaces where it is possible to balance reporting. However, the pressures of public relations, lobbying and criticism, as well as the climate created by the privileging of the Israeli perspective by politicians and other important public figures, does explain why broadcast journalists find it much easier to articulate Israeli, as opposed to the Palestinian, perspectives.

Conclusion

Although the research discussed in this chapter focused on British broadcast news reporting of the second intifada, its findings have been corroborated in studies of other media systems. For instance, research carried out on the US media has revealed that many of the key trends we identified in British reporting were visible in even greater prominence. For instance, the Palestinian initiation–Israeli retaliation framework was found in a study which examined reporting by the three main US networks (FAIR, 2002). American research also supported the findings that Israeli casualties were far more likely to be reported than Palestinian casualties (Ackerman, 2001; Friel and Falk, 2007; Viser, 2003); that Israeli representatives received much more airtime (Friel and Falk, 2007; Viser, 2003); and that little historical context or information about the occupation was provided in coverage (Dunsky, 2001; Friel and Falk, 2007).

The robustness of our findings were reinforced in our later study which examined UK broadcast news coverage of the 2008/9 Gaza war. Again we found an almost complete lack of historical context, a preponderance of Israeli perspectives and a tendency (routinely) to insert a rationale for Israeli but not Palestinian violence. The fact that these findings are discovered again and again is testament to the way in which the factors in production highlighted in the previous section structure coverage in a deep and consistent manner. Public relations, lobbying – in the USA there is an even more powerful pro-Israel lobby – and political pressure shape reporting in a way few journalists and news organisations find easy to resist.

However, the consequences of this kind of reporting are serious. Viewers are left confused and demoralised, with the consequence that they are likely to disengage from the story. This places a strong onus on journalists and news organisations to be more reflexive about their reporting and to consider how to modify it in order to provide the necessary context and explanation so that there can be a full and frank public debate on how the conflict can be brought to an end.

References

Ackerman, Seth (2001). 'The illusion of balance: NPR's coverage of Mideast deaths doesn't match reality', FAIR, 1 November. Available at: http://fair.org/extra-online-articles/the-illusion-of-balance/ (accessed 23 August 2015).

Amnesty International (2002). *Without Distinction: Attacks on Civilians by Palestinian Armed Groups.* AI Index: MDDE 02/003/2002.

Beaumont, Peter and Whitaker, Brian (2001) 'Focus: Reporting conflict: The first casualty of war: The Palestinians and Israel are resorting to propaganda as the main weapon in their fight for world opinion', *Observer*, 17 June, 17.

B'Tselem (2003). *Violence of Settlers Against Palestinians.* Available at: www.btselem.org/English/Settler_Violence/Index.asp/ (accessed 26 March 2004).

Dunsky, M. (2001) 'Missing: The Bias Implicit in the Absent', *Arab Studies Quarterly* 23(3): 1–21.

FAIR (Fairness and Accuracy in Reporting) (2002). 'In U.S. media, Palestinians attack, Israel retaliates', 2 April. Available at: http://fair.org/take-action/action-alerts/in-u-s-media-palestinians-attack-israel-retaliates/ (accessed 23 August 2015).

Friel, Howard and Falk, Richard (2007). *Israel-Palestine on Record: How the New York Times Misreports Conflict in the Middle East.* London: Verso.

Galtung, Johan and Ruge, Mari Holmboe (1965). 'The structure of foreign news: the presentation of the Congo, Cuba and Cyprus crises in four Norwegian newspapers', *Journal of International Peace Research*, 1, 64–91.

Harcup, Tony and O'Neill, Deirdre (2001). 'What is news? Galtung and Ruge revisited', *Journalism Studies*, 2(2), 261–80.

ITC (Independent Television Commission) (2003). *The Public's View.* London: ITC.

Philo, Greg and Berry, Mike (2004). *Bad News from Israel.* London: Pluto Press.

Philo, Greg and Berry, Mike (2011). *More Bad News from Israel.* London: Pluto Press.

Rodgers, James (2015). *Headlines from the Holy Land Reporting the Israeli-Palestinian Conflict.* London: Palgrave Macmillan.

Shlaim, Avi (2000). *The Iron Wall: Israel and the Arab World.* London: Penguin Press.

Viser, Matt (2003). 'Attempted objectivity: an analysis of the *New York Times* and *Ha'aretz* and their portrayals of the Palestinian-Israeli Conflict', *The International Journal of Press/Politics*, 8(4), 114–20.

6

Reporting Pre-1948 Palestine in Brazil

The Journalistic Narrative and the British Empire

Fernando Resende

This article analyses narratives on the Israeli–Palestinian conflict in the newspaper *Folha da Manhã* (Brazil, 1936–46). This historical perspective derives from long-running research that intends to discuss relations of power inscribed in the conflict and comprehend the ways in which journalistic narratives shed light on disputes for hegemony; this is a way to understand the process of producing meaning about the conflict in the Palestinian territories. The context in question allows us to understand how the British Empire, along with international news agencies, influences the narration, becoming an important agent in the process of meaning production on what relates to the conflict. And as the term terrorism diverts and attaches itself to distinct agents according to the interests of those who are in power, what one notices is how journalism effectively takes part in political, cultural and discursive practices of including and excluding individuals. Thus, by seeing journalism as a cultural discursive practice, this chapter provides a reflection on how this specific conflict becomes a journalistic event.

This chapter is part of wider research about how the Brazilian media reports the Israel–Palestine conflict. The long-run study discusses the idea that the power relations inscribed in the conflict become more evident as newspaper narratives put into play the leading characters and struggles for hegemony.[1] At this point, the conflict is no longer merely the content of the narrative; it is also constituted by the ways it is narrated.[2] Particularly in the case of Israel–Palestine, the analysis reveals how competition for the most truthful narrative about the conflict entails competing voices and meanings. The discussions presented in this chapter have a historical bias, since it presents analyses of narratives published in the first half of the twentieth century in the Brazilian newspaper *Folha da Manhã*[3]

The geopolitical materiality of the journalistic events discussed here – the Palestinian territory – is a key aspect, to the extent that it is the venue for battles over cultural geographies divided by political regimes, beliefs and lifestyles that are considered distinct *a priori*. The contradictory ways of apprehending and producing meanings for terms such as terrorism, the often inconsistent interpretations of the Arab–Israeli conflict produced by newspaper narratives in Brazil, confirm the status of Brazilian journalism, at least since the nineteenth century, as an important agent that contributes to the reaffirmation of so-called 'Western-ethnocentric' thinking. By playing this role, it sets identities, cultural differences and pathways through which Brazil has been producing meanings about the struggle in the Palestinian territories.

By extending the geographical location to where the Palestinian territories lie – the Middle East – we often witness an intrinsic relationship between narration and conflict. Matar and Harb (2013: 4), by discussing conflict and narration, call attention to the fact that 'nowhere is the competition over the imagination, construction and narration of conflict, as well as its meanings and its centrality to people's everyday lives more compelling', since in the Middle East, these competitions, above all, bring into play concepts of 'space, identity, discourse, image and narrative'. One relevant aspect therefore is the narrative approach taken by this chapter. In a geographical location where individuals face the dilemma of having been what they can no longer be, or of having lived where they cannot live anymore, stories assume a critical role: they become something between the struggle to retrieve/maintain the memory and the very construction of the meaning of the land. In this sense, the Palestinian territories are increasingly what the narratives say about them.

To the same extent, by addressing the problem this way, one seems to give rise to a more precise questioning of what it means to narrate such geography. In the narratives about this conflict, a considerable dispute surrounding the most truthful accounts becomes the war itself: who can better narrate (or who can narrate in the most legitimate way) the violence being inflicted on the Palestinian territories, or the 'retrieval of the Promised Land', as it was first termed by the Zionists? The research shows that the pursuit of the truth might also lie in the process of uncovering the forces hidden behind the powers that generate and narrate the conflict. Such an aspect becomes even more forceful in long-term conflicts, to the extent that they are fraught with layers of narrative, and give rise to a number of stories and multiple meanings.[4]

This chapter also brings to light the blatant pact between leading Brazilian communication groups and British rulers when it comes to narrating the events in that region. To understand the power games found in the narratives, we will focus on the use of the term 'terrorist' contained in the *corpus* of the research. The mobility of this word, sometimes referring to the Arabs, sometimes to the Jews, will reveal the extent to which the journalism of international news agencies showed their partiality in the conflict. For this purpose, we will focus on news published from 1936 to 1946. Up to 1936, there were very few articles in Brazil addressing issues in Palestine, and most of these used to adopt a Manichean approach, drawing attention, in general, to religious intolerance as the main (if not only) reason underlying the conflict.

When the Palestinians called a general strike (1936–9), the style of narration adopted by the newspaper changed. The newspaper *Folha da Manhã* set out to narrate the dissatisfaction of Palestinians both over the increasing number of Jewish immigrants and over British rule. There was an increase in the number of news articles published, other historical individuals were cited and the acts of violence in Palestine were then narrated from a terrorist perspective. Expressions like 'terrorist attack', 'terrorism' and 'terrorist' featured regularly in the journalistic narratives of that time.

First, we intend to show how the word 'terrorist' appears for the first time in reports of violent events in Palestine. It is by looking at what is 'unsaid' that we perceive the correlation between the Arabs and the word 'terrorist' in the newspaper. Along with that, the chapter focuses on the discourse adopted by *Folha da Manhã* to describe the Palestinians' resistance. And it is then, in the 1940s, that the usage of the word 'terrorist' shifts to refer to the Jews. By doing so, this chapter discusses how Great Britain, as a hegemonic power, used international news agencies to impose certain interpretations of facts relating to Palestine.

Thus, this chapter also intends to offer thoughts on the participation of journalism in processes that end up underpinning identities and creating stereotypes; processes in which the political, cultural and discourse-based practices and actions that include and exclude individuals are intertwined. One of the goals of this discussion is then to emphasise the pact among major communication groups and the logics of established powers, which allows us to discuss how the Israel–Palestine conflict is constructed as a journalistic event. In this vein, journalism is considered, above all, as a cultural discourse-based practice driven by a 'set of problems, orientations, intentions and sayings that inseparably produces meaning on and about the world we live' (Resende, 2011: 128).

The 'Hand-Washing' between Great Britain and the Zionist Movement

Some studies report that the conflict between Palestinians and Jews was sparked off in Palestine in 1890 after the Zionist movement was established. According to Finkelstein (2005), there was an 'ideological consensus' that brought about most of the doctrinal thoughts of this group. This consensus included the Zionist belief that Palestine should be eventually home to the majority of Jews. Such a condition would then confirm the Jews' constitutional right to have a state. This thought results in some of the root causes of the conflict with the Arabs, who have been the majority population in Palestine for many centuries. At the end of the nineteenth century, the Zionist movement attempted to establish in Palestine an allegedly homogeneous Jewish state, or at least one mostly made up of Jews.

Faced with the Palestinian resistance, the Zionists realised that, in order to settle in that area, they would need some sort of powerful protection. After all, the intention was to establish a Jewish state in an important region at the dawn of a new era of European imperialism in the late nineteenth century. For the Zionist leader Ze'ev Jabotinsky, that would require an 'iron wall that could not be knocked down [by the natives]' (Jabotinsky, cited in Finkelstein, 2005: 72). Underpinned by this political strategy, the Zionist movement sought an alliance with a major power in Palestine – England.

To get support from this leading power, the Zionists had to give up their own strategic interests. Therefore, it is the response to the British interest that Zionism had helped cover up the conflict between the Ottoman Turks and the Arabs in the early twentieth century, serving as an imperial bridgehead in a strategically important yet politically volatile region. Zionism also served as a lightning rod for local popular dissatisfaction and diverted attention away from the imperial power (Finkelstein, 2005). Therefore, in the 'hand-washing' established between Great Britain and the Zionist movement we also see the power relations forged in journalism.

In 1933, Great Britain was featured in the news on Palestine more often. This is due to the emergence of Arab nationalism, whose main concept was that the people from the Arab world, from the Atlantic Ocean to the Arabian Sea, should establish a single united nation with shared linguistic, cultural and historical heritage. As Vicenzi (2007) explains, the establishment of the British and French powers in the East, after the collapse of the Ottoman Empire, the Jewish immigration and the sale of land to Jews in Palestine, were factors that moved many Arab people in a unique and disconnected manner to pursue political unity. As Vicenzi puts it:

> The Palestine issue [...] strengthened the view that the whole Arabian world was a target of a stronger European colonial penetration – mainly motivated by the control of the main source of energy of our times: oil – and freedom depended on a wider perspective and on a specific organisation that would replace the local and regional frontiers. (Vicenzi, 2007: 101–2)

It is within this context that we understand how the international news agencies – critical for the development of international news reporting in the Brazilian media – served as spokespersons by helping spark off power disputes in the Palestinian territory. All agencies that provided news to the newspaper *Folha da Manhã* about the Arab–Israeli conflict in the first half of the twentieth century were based in the United States and Europe.[5] As it was expensive to send correspondents abroad, Brazilian newspapers grew dependent on the journalistic material published by foreign news agencies, through which it was possible to get more accounts from other continents. Those pieces of news very much presented perspectives of the economic power of that time. And it is for this reason, certainly, that for Natali 'the history of international journalism [in Brazil] is somehow the history of the winners' (Natali, 2004: 32).

Narrating the Conflict through the Unsaid

As the Jewish population increased and the British failed to interfere in local immigration policies, the Arab population engaged in public acts of resistance. A news article from 1936 reports a Palestinian strike that caused the shutdown of all commercial establishments. Such a position of resistance displeases established powers, and the news article says that the Palestinians would continue with their acts:

> The situation among Arabs and Israelis in the holy city is still very tense. The curfew was imposed to the Upper city. The Arabs dismissed the suggestion of sending an Arabian delegation to London and appointing a British Imperial Commission in charge of conducting investigations about the issue of the Israeli immigration. The Arabs refuse to negotiate while the said immigration is maintained. The campaign of civil contempt and the general strike is still in force. ('Considerados de extraordinária gravidade os últimos acontecimentos na Palestina' ['Recent incidents in Palestine are considered extremely serious'], *Folha da Manhã*, 19 May 1936)

Interestingly, the whole conflict takes place in Palestine and is sparked off by civilians – in this case, generally referred to as 'Arabs'. The narrative strategy presented here is subtle; *Palestinian* civilians are assigned a homogenising designation: being an Arab is the element that brings them together. This is important in the narratives analysed in the research, since very early in the conflict what is noticeable is the simplification of a relevant identity component, in the process of understanding what territory was about to be occupied and who owned it.[6]

At the time, a clear ideological and political confrontation between the Palestinians and the British emerged. The former were claiming independence from British rule in Palestine and requested that Jewish immigration be stopped. A news article from 1936 reported the dissatisfaction of the Palestinians towards the British government:

> The Arab hostility is no longer solely towards the Jews. It is also against the British administration and its racial and religious campaign may become a sort of war for independence. ('Continua grave a situação na Palestina' ['Situation in Palestine is still critical'], *Folha da Manhã*, 13 June 1936)

The Palestinians reacted with strategies of trade embargo, protests in public locations, civil contempt and, later, violent attacks on British troops and Jewish militia. After about a month, the newspaper's discourse referred to the Palestinians as terrorists (Arab terrorists).

The word 'terrorist' was introduced in the first half of the twentieth century in the news article 'Continuam as violências na Palestina' ['Violent events in Palestine continue'] (*Folha da Manhã*, 3 July 1936). In this news article, the use of the word 'terrorist' is evident and it was the Palestinians the article was pointing to:

> The last trials had some influence on the *Arab masses*. Despite that, violence continues. The police arrested many *terrorists* who were sent to the concentration camp of Serranand, where 150 of them were staying, some of which have gone on a hunger strike. The Arab rulers deny that the strike should end this weekend. (Emphasis added)

The context of the news revolves around the British law enforcement repression against the Palestinians' protests. The violent riots in Palestine were not clearly narrated. Apparently, although there was not a clear connection between them, 'terrorists' and 'Arab masses' were used to refer to the Palestinians. Another news article from 28 May 1936 exemplifies what Orlandi (2007) calls the 'said and the unsaid'. The article states: 'last morning, there were bombs and shooting in Jaffa but no one was injured'. Then, the narrative builds on another issue: the British guard protecting the Austrian Jews against attacks from the Arabs.

By then, it was assumed that the Arabs were attacking Austrian Jews in Palestine. And soon after this information was reported, accounts about

terrorist attacks on the previous day continued, with descriptions of out-
breaks of violence. The article refers to 'attacks on a police vehicle, discov-
ery of an explosive cargo, some bombs in Tulkarem, Nazareth' ('Perdura a
animosidade entre árabes e judeus na Palestina' ['Hostility among Arabs
and Jews in Palestine continues'], *Folha da Manhã*, 28 May 1936).

Nowhere in the account is it revealed who undertook the narrated acts
of violence. Who would have thrown bombs and fired shots in Jaffa? Who
would have attacked a police automobile? And whose were the explosive
cargo and the bombs thrown in Tulkarem, Nazareth? Silence. However,
it is said that the British guard was called upon to protect the Austrian
Jews against the Arabs' attacks. In the end, the article describes the apology
made by Arab authorities from the cities near the Jewish colony for attacks
against the Jews in that area.

After two years, we still find newspaper articles using the term 'terrorists' and not explicitly saying to whom the term should be imputed. In the
newspaper article 'Volta a agravar-se a situação na Palestina' ['Situation in
Palestine is exacerbated'] (*Folha da Manhã*, 8 July 1938), which reports acts
of violence, it says: 'Yesterday, a group of police officers put up a fight with
a gang of terrorists. Nine rebels died.' Once again, the 'gang of terrorists'
and 'rebels' are not identified, but the direct connection with those who
have been called 'Arabs' is inevitable. According to Orlandi (2007: 82), in
narrative constructions 'it is widely known that, within anything that is
said, there is a whole web of unsaid statements that also have a meaning'.
Therefore, whatever is said brings an assumption that is not materialised in
the narrative, but fills it up with its very presence.

The news narratives associate Palestinians with attacks against Jews.
Amid the huge amount of information about various attacks, it is implied
that the Palestinians are those who caused the scenes of violence described.
The newspaper does not directly assign to them any responsibility, but by
not saying anything, it gives hints to readers about who would have carried
out the attacks.

Added to this, it is noticeable that the violent acts undertaken by the
resistance movements were reported with some sort of disregard. Those
who read the news would feel that the actions were taken in a random way,
with no specific purpose, as if the Palestinians had no reasons to promote
acts of resistance. As we can see, the newspaper article 'Recrudesceram os

distúrbios na Palestina' ['Riots in Palestine have grown bigger'] (*Folha da Manhã*, 7 July 1936), presents the headline 'Attentado terrorista' ['Terrorist attack'], reporting that a bomb blast had hit three Jews. It mentions the involvement of civil Palestinians – referred to as Arabs – in setting off the bomb. In the end, the article says that British troops had to fire weapons against a 'gang of Arabs'.

In another article, the Arabs are called 'terrorist rioters'. ('Tropas britannicas enviadas para a Palestina' ['British troops sent to Palestine'] *Folha da Manhã*, 9 October 1936.) In both articles, the combination of the term 'terrorist' with the words 'rioter' or 'gang' asserts a fundamental view about the Arab struggle: those individuals are part of a group of rioters that unreasonably inflict horror (Figure 1).

The discourse, which is used to refer to the Palestinians, expressing some sort of disregard about the protests of civilians and their struggles, disturbed the Syrian Patriotic League in Brazil. A letter written by its then-Secretary-General Chafick Amad, expressed the dissatisfaction over the way the incidents in Palestine had been reported in the newspaper *Folha da Manhã*:

> On a daily basis, the newspapers publish telegrams mentioning 'terrorist attacks' undertaken by 'Arab bandits' against the Jews and English troops. [...] Just imagine, Editor-in-Chief, that such 'bandits' are precisely the *crème de la crème* of the Arab youth. Instead of going to schools and universities, these young kids go to the streets to fight for a cause, the first and foremost cause of Humankind: Freedom. Because of that, the news agencies call them 'criminals', 'bandits' and 'terrorists'. ('A Liga Patriotica Syria critica a maneira por que são apresentados os acontecimentos na Palestina' ['The Syrian Patriotic League criticises the way the incidents in Palestine are reported'], *Folha da Manhã*, 6 January 1938)

The fact that the Palestinians use violence when confronted with the British police and non-military Jewish organisations is the factor that criminalises the Arabs – representing them in an arbitrary way as if amid the forces that animate the conflict, the Palestinian resistance did nothing but inflict horror. Therefore, there is a direct connection between the terms 'Arabs' and 'terrorists'; an association, one should notice, that is widely recognised by the hegemonic media nowadays.

Fig. 1. Newspaper article 'Recrudescem os distúrbios na Palestina'. The photo shows an English police officer searching an Arab. The caption says: 'To avoid anti-Jewish and anti-British riots, the Arabs are searched by English soldiers in Jerusalem.'

A Redesigned Discourse in the Newspaper: The Terrorists are Now the Jews

Despite the pro-Jewish approach for setting up a State in Palestine, which filled the newspaper in the 1940s, the articles then set out to call the Jews terrorists. The newspapers were concerned, at the time, about laying the blame for any violent acts at the door of a specific group, dismissing those discourse strategies centred on an 'unsaid-based' approach used in the newspaper articles published in the 1930s. Now, the articles would just present brief descriptions about different groups, naming them according to their level of danger: 'the extremist Stern Gang'; 'extremist group Irgun Zvai Leumi'; 'para-military army Haganah':

> Today, Jewish terrorists have kidnapped five British officials
> [...] the five officials were held hostage while they demanded

the release of two members of the organisation 'Stern' – founded by Avraham Stern, a deceased Jewish terrorist [...] The terrorist organisation 'Haganah' officially claims responsibility for all acts of sabotage that have occurred [...] In turn, the organisation 'Irgun' distributed flyers calling the Jewish people to engage in the battle [...] ('Tropas inglesas em luta com os judeus.' ['English troops battling against the Jews'], *Folha da Manhã*, 19 June 1946)

The journalistic discourse of that time was inconsistent with how public opinion was voiced by *Folha da Manhã*. While newspaper articles since the 1920s recalled the promise of setting up a Jewish home in Palestine, the same newspaper published articles that blackened the activity of paramilitary Jewish groups.

The redesigned employment of the word terrorist, now referring to the Jews, was introduced by the publication of a secret English document called *The White Paper* in 1939. The document drafted by the British government addressed three issues: the political future of Palestine, the Jewish immigration and the sale of land to the Jews. The paper restrained the Jews by limiting the immigration and sale of land to them.

Once the British political strategies that were allegedly delaying the setup of a Jewish State in Palestine were announced, the Jewish organisations initiated activities against the British government. The explosion of the King David Hotel, which housed the British military and administrative headquarters, was the boldest attack carried out by the organisation 'Irgun'. After this attack, which killed ninety-one British individuals, the newspapers very narrowly assigned the Jews the title of terrorists.

In the article, 'Campanha de sabotagem à violência' ['Campaign of violent sabotage'] (*Folha da Manhã*, 25 July 1946), the journalist describes the morale of the city three days after the attack and specifies that the British police were closing in on those behind the terrorist attack, investigating the files of the one hundred most dangerous terrorists in Jerusalem. It is worth mentioning that all of those from that long list were Jews:

The Jewish neighbourhoods from Jerusalem were sustaining a growing feeling of apprehension while British soldiers patrolling the area indicate the alertness of the troops. While victims

115

from the explosion are searched in the debris of King David Hotel [...] British security agents review files of about one hundred of the most desperate terrorists of Palestine – *all of which are Irgun Zvi Leumi and Stern leaders*. (Emphasis added)

Although the newspaper articles from 1946 report 'agitations' among the Palestinians, there is no connection between the Palestinians and the term terrorist. Such treatment seems to demonstrate how the international news agencies were willing to meet British interests. Since that was a time when the non-military Jewish organisation Irgun was carrying out attacks of violence and horror against the British police, a degrading discourse is only targeted at the Jews. The article says:

> two Jewish terrorists from the organisation 'Irgun Zvai Leumi' who had been sentenced to death are now sentenced to life imprisonment [...] The secret broadcasting firm owned by the terrorist Semitic organisation 'Irgun Zvai Leumi' announced: 'Now that our men have been saved, the three British officials that we are still holding will be released. ('Comutada em prisão perpétua a pena de morte imposta pelos terroristas' ['Death penalty imposed by terrorist turned into life imprisonment'], *Folha da Manhã*, 4 July 1946)

The Ambiguity of the English

Still in 1946, besides the newspaper articles that addressed the attacks carried out by the Jews, we find articles that applied a different approach to reporting the conflict between Arabs and Jews. Those articles would produce interpretations of the Jews as representatives of democracy and Arabs as Soviet associates. This is quite clear in the article 'O povo árabe exortada à Guerra Santa contra a Grã-Bretanha e os EUA' ['Arabs encouraged to engage in Holy War against Great Britain and the USA'] (*Folha da Manhã*, 4 May 1946), in which an Arab leader says that the Arabs will fight against 'democratic despotism' and will do whatever it takes to make them safe, including 'seeking help from the Russians or even from the devil'. Note that such set of political and ideological stances presented by the newspapers are also a result of the context of that time, when the Cold War (1945–91) was going on.

According to Kellner (2001), these binary oppositions of ideology are rooted in a system of antagonisms between unequal forces and serve the purpose of legitimating the privileges and the domination of the most powerful ones. Journalism, therefore, was closely connected with power structures through Manichaeism and stereotyping, here serving the purpose of reaffirming the logic of the established power, i.e., Great Britain.

In this vein, the analysis reveals how Great Britain struggled to maintain an ambiguous position vis-à-vis the conflict. For instance, in 1933, Great Britain is portrayed by *Folha da Manhã* as the defender of the Jews while maintaining diplomatic relations with the Palestinians and other countries whose residents were mostly Arabs, as we can see in the article 'A situação na Palestina' ['The situation in Palestine'] (*Folha da Manhã*, 29 October 1933).

The article is made up of pieces of news sent by international news agencies reporting both the conflicts between Palestinians and Jews, and Palestinian attacks on official English offices. The last paragraph, however, narrates the ambiguous positioning of the English in the conflicts. The article says:

> Many members of the Arabian Executive branch have been received by the High Commissioner of England, who ensured that they should not fear the Jews taking over the supremacy of the country, even though they fulfilled some functions in an equitable way.

In the article 'Judeus e árabes na Palestina – Direitos iguais, mentalidades irreconciliáveis; aversão não confessada que vem de longe' ['Jews and Arabs in Palestine – Equal rights, irreconcilable mindsets; unconfessed aversion that comes from afar'] (*Folha da Manhã*, 25 August 1940), there is a full-page illustration of a Jew and an Arab arguing while an English soldier mediates between the two sides (Figure 2).

Once again, the readers are presented with an image in which the British imperialist forces appear to be neutral, mediating the conflict between Palestinians and Jews. Actually, by using these narratives, Great Britain is presented to the world as a power inclined towards solving a problem of worldwide relevance. As a result, the British Empire could stay

Fig. 2. 'Jews and Arabs in Palestine' published in the newspaper *Folha da Manhã*, 25 August 1940.

in Palestine longer and enjoy the benefits of such colonisation and enforce its hegemonic power in that region.

The concept of hegemony characterises the ideological and cultural leadership of a class over others (Gramsci, 1984). For Moraes, such a concept 'has to do with disputes of meaning and conflicting worldviews, as well as mediations of forces in a certain historic context' (Moraes, 2009: 35). Great Britain, as a hegemonic power, used international news agencies to impose interpretations of the events that took place in Palestine through fixed signs, attempting to protect anything that was held and presented as true from any sort of contradiction. This shows that any changes that may occur in how to narrate the conflict in Palestine are closely related to the interests at stake.

Conclusion

The shift in the usage of the term 'terrorist' reveals the extent to which the issue of impartiality in journalistic discourse was contingent upon the game of interests affecting the imperialist forces of Britain at the time. The use of this term to refer to the Arabs or to the Jews substantially helped the established hegemonic power prevent the contrast and the complexity that existed between the forces concerned from coming to light.

This is how Great Britain seemed to work as an 'iron wall' for the Jews and the Arabs by not allowing information to get through, while serving as its own iron wall whenever necessary, to protect itself from the eyes of public opinion. Regarding the representations of the Palestinian–Israeli conflict and the journalistic narratives analysed, Great Britain, as a hegemonic agent, influenced what could have and what should have been announced in the 'in-house setting' of global journalism.

From a wider perspective, this study leads us to consider that in long-term conflicts, the recognition of subjective aspects and intertwining of webs of power are critical to understanding how terms (terrorists, for instance) are made concrete, and the production of homogenisations disseminated by media narratives. In this scenario, where individuals and facts are described according to widely disseminated stereotypes, thought about their struggles and the ways that powers are established reveal the potential shifts in the usage of terms connected with them.

In journalism it is crucial to recognise that the events described are constructions made up of elements of discourse and culture inexorably involved in the production of meanings about the event itself. As Stuart Hall puts it:

> making an event intelligible is a social process – constituted by
> a number of specific journalistic practices, which embody [...]
> crucial assumptions about what society is and how it works.
> (Hall, 1999: 226)

These assumptions are part of a cultural scenario – styles of being and knowing – that is determinant in this process. Hall also says that:

> An event only 'makes sense' if it can be located within a range
> of known social and cultural identifications. If newsmen did
> not have available – in however routine a way – such cultural
> 'maps' of the social world, they could not 'make sense' of the
> events [...] which form the basic content of what is 'newswor-
> thy'. (Hall, 1999: 226)

The approach here is to consider that, while spinning the web of intrigue (Ricœur, 2010), recognising the marks of 'cultural maps' does not only mean revealing the process of producing meanings about the event. It also means understanding the ways of inscribing the dichotomies and stereo-types within the conflicts being described. Besides this, the approach also considers that the processes of 'producing meaning' (which according to Hall presupposes the reader) and 'assigning meaning' (a task undertaken by the writer) are interconnected in the very game of arranging the narra-tive. Ricœur reminds us that 'the full event is not only voicing something to an addressee; it is also aspiring to bring a new experience into language and share it with someone else' (Ricœur, 2010: 199).

The analyses reveal that narrating this conflict is not something thought to be objective, neutral or impartial. It is immensely more complex than that; it requires recognising the struggles taking place, in journalism nar-ratives influenced by the geographic space where these narrations are pro-duced. From the Palestinian perspective, the challenge is huge:

> One has to keep telling the [Palestinian] story in as many ways
> as possible, as insistently as possible, and in as a compelling way
> as possible, to keep attention to it, because there is always a fear
> that Palestine might just disappear. (Said, 1980: 187)

Having this in mind, how could/should journalism operate in that space where the act of narrating is understood as an action of resistance? This thought suggests that facing this challenge also means discussing, within the context of journalism, the idea that the power relations which are found in a certain event become more evident as one recognises how ways of speaking bring about disputes for hegemony. From this angle, the conflict – whatever it may be – is no longer the content of a narrative. According to Benetti (2010: 149):

A journalistic event is embodied in a highly complex hermeneutic order, or order of the senses – not only due to the procedures required for a phenomenon to be transformed into an event, but also due to the sets of references that help legitimise it.

This chapter's aim has been to help us understand that narrating the Israel–Palestine conflict is to narrate the struggles that lie in the conflict itself. These struggles and the ways to establish power unveil the potential meanings of the conflict, which are crucial aspects that make it become a journalistic event.

Notes

1. Hegemony as argued by Gramsci (1984), with ideology and culture as its main traces. It is used here as a perspective that connects disputes over meanings, worldviews and political power games in specific historical contexts.
2. The research study 'Poetics of the otherness: media narratives and the process of inventing the other' (CNPq) discusses the representation of conflicts in Brazilian, focusing on and comparing two specific conflicts: the riots of African-Muslim slaves in Bahia in the nineteenth century and the Israel–Palestine battle in the twentieth century. It is a long-running research programme being undertaken with the assistance of Letícia Rossignoli (a PhD student at the Graduate Program in Communication, at Federal Fluminense University, Rio de Janeiro, Brazil).
3. The newspaper *Folha da Manhã* was founded in July 1925. It is based in the city of São Paulo and is targeted at middle-class readers. *Folha da Manhã* had a significant influence in the south-east of Brazil. During the early decades of the twentieth century the conflict in Palestine was of relevance to Brazilian readers, due to the flux of migration from the Middle East to Brazil, and the arrival of European Jews fleeing the war in Europe.
4. Irit Rogoff (2000) considers long-term conflicts taking place in the Middle East. This author says that they require some deep thinking in order to recognise the depletion of epistemological apparatuses and the analytical resources that have been supporting all sorts of explanations about the conflicts. This is a key approach not only for this chapter but also for the research as a whole.
5. The agencies appearing in this research are the former Havas, based in France, Reuters in London and Associated Press in the United States.
6. Edward Said, specifically in *The Question of Palestine* (1980), but also in many of his other works, strongly reaffirms the diversities and identities that mark the differences in the space called 'the Arab world'. At the same time, the author is

very critical about the efforts to build a nationalist hegemony intended to produce homogeneous thinking concerning what it means to be Arabic.

References

Benetti, Márcia (2010). 'O jornalismo como acontecimento', in Márcia Benetti and Virginia Fonseca (eds), *Jornalismo e acontecimento: mapeamentos críticos*. Florianópolis: Insular.

Finkelstein, Norman (2005). *Imagem e realidade do conflito Israel-Palestina*. São Paulo: Record.

Gramsci, Antonio (1984). *Maquiavel, a Política e o Estado Moderno*. Rio de Janeiro: Civilização Brasileira.

Hall, Stuart (1999). 'A produção social das notícias: o mugging nos media', in Nelson Traquina (ed.), *Jornalismo: questões, teorias e 'estórias'*. Lisboa: Vega.

Kellner, Douglas (2001). *Cultura da mídia*. Bauru: EDUSC.

Matar, Dina and Harb, Zahera (2013). *Narrating Conflict in the Middle East: Discourse, Image and Communications Practices in Lebanon and Palestine*. London: I.B.Tauris.

Moraes, Dênis de (2009). *A batalha da mídia: governos progressistas e políticas de comunicação na América Latina e outros ensaios*. Rio de Janeiro: Pão e Rosas.

Natali, João Batista (2004). *Jornalismo Internacional*. São Paulo: Contexto.

Orlandi, Eni de Lourdes Puccinelli (2007). *Análise de discurso: princípios e procedimentos*. Campinas: Pontes.

Resende, Fernando (2011). 'Às desordens e aos sentidos: a narrativa como problema de pesquisa', in Gislane Silva, Dimas Künsch, Christa Berger and Afonso Albuquerque (eds), *Jornalismo contemporâneo: figurações, impasses e perspectivas*. Salvador: Edufba.

Ricœur, Paul (2010). *Tempo e narrativa*. São Paulo: Martins Fontes.

Rogoff, Irit (2000). *Terra Infirma: Geography's Visual Culture*. London: Routledge.

Said, Edward (1980). *The Question of Palestine*. London: Routledge and Kegan Paul.

Vicenzi, Roberta Aragoni Nogueira (2007). *Nacionalismo Árabe: apogeu e declínio*. São Paulo: tese doutorado USP.

7

Limited Perspectives

Reporting Gaza

James Rodgers

Even from the aged black-and-white photograph (Westmoreland, 1917),[1] the onlooker can begin to imagine some of the story. The caption offers few details: 'British troops with some of the inhabitants of a captured village. Third Battle of Gaza.' The year is 1917. The people in the picture are divided by what they wear. There are two British soldiers in pith helmets, one standing at either side of the frame. Their sleeves are rolled up. They have taken off their tunics. No weapons are visible. The 'inhabitants of a captured village' are all wearing traditional Arab clothing: loose-fitting garments to keep them cool; *keffiyehs* wound around their heads, or hanging down over shoulders, to keep off the sun. The clothing clearly identifies the two separate groups shown in the photograph. Look at the photograph a little longer, and it is the hands seen there which help us to imagine more of what is happening. The soldier at the left of frame has his arm hanging down by his side. He seems completely relaxed. The one on the other side of the frame is reaching out to something which has been offered to him. It could be a cup, or a piece of paper twisted into a cone. The way he holds his fingers suggests he is preparing to take something – perhaps a nut, or a sweet, which has been offered in greeting. Still more hands tell more of the story. A child stands near the soldier, its gaze fixed on the cup. The child's fingers are in its mouth: a gesture of alarm, excitement or expectation.

What is the stranger in strange clothes going to do? Another child's hand is visible near the soldier. Its owner's face and body are obscured, but the fingers reach out towards the soldier, seemingly about to touch his shirt, or his belt – perhaps to satisfy curiosity as to what these alien garments can be made of. It is the year of the Balfour Declaration. Soon, their victory over the Ottomans complete, the British will take on a Mandate for Palestine. It will last until the creation of the State of Israel in 1948.

In 1967, half a century on from the photograph, Israeli troops will take control of Gaza, as their British counterparts are seen doing in the picture. Almost half a century on again, they are still in charge. Much has changed, not least the clothes. Some things have remained the same. Even in George Westmoreland's faded black-and-white picture, you can still sense the 'blinding white sunlight' (Hass, 2000: 8) which shines on the land between the River Jordan and the Mediterranean. You can sense the air of suspicion, mistrust and the power relations, which still dominate the politics of the region. And you can sense the presence of the media. George Westmoreland, the photographer, was a serving British soldier 'instructed to take photographs for publicity purposes' by General Archibald Murray, who hoped it would assist 'his pleas for more troops' (Carmichael, 2003: 82). Even as the first outlines on the map of the twentieth-century Middle East were being drawn, the military were using the media to further their ambitions.

That is a pattern which continues today, when Israel, still the power which dominates the territory, takes arguably even more care over its media image than did its predecessors as masters of this corner of the Middle East. The Foreign Press spokesman for the IDF (Israel Defense Forces – the Israeli Army), Lieutenant Colonel Peter Lerner, describes himself on his Facebook page (Lerner, 2015) as 'commander of the IDF social media platforms'. The platforms themselves are virtually enlisted; lined up to serve on a front – the media war – where combat has become much more sophisticated since Westmoreland's day. This chapter will look at aspects of the Western news media's reporting of Gaza. It will do so from the perspective of recent history, as well as the events of the last few years. It will also include a degree of personal reflection based upon the time when, from 2002 to 2004, I was the BBC's correspondent in Gaza. Perhaps disappointingly from a journalist's point of view, the chapter will argue that, in the case of Gaza, international coverage has had limited influence on the political and diplomatic situation. However, it will also argue that Gaza's history, and the uncertainties in the wider Middle East, mean that good reporting from Gaza is more important than ever. International journalists have one great advantage over many others linked to the territory, or affected by the situation there: their access. Because of the restrictions placed upon them, Israelis, Palestinians and even foreign diplomats have limited perspectives on the situation in the regions. Journalists, while not exactly free to come and go as they please, are offered a rarer and broader view. That being the case, access will be one of the main aspects of Western reporting of Gaza which this chapter will consider. The second will be context. The third, political attempts to influence the journalism of the conflict; the fourth, the impact which the coverage has on policy making.

'These are the last pictures taken of members of the United Nations Emergency Peacekeeping Force in position on Egyptian Territory at the Gaza Strip frontier with Israel,' begins Alan Hart's report for Independent Television News (ITN), broadcast on 24 May 1967 (ITN, 1967). Almost fifty years later, they still have the exclusivity which Hart's script claimed then, for the peacekeeping force belongs now to history. The pictures show white cars with 'UN' on the side drawing up at a crossing point marked by a simple wooden barrier across the road, and an Israeli flag. Having given details of the date and time – 19 May, 2.00 pm – Hart concludes this section of his script: 'The Middle East was plunged into its most serious crisis since the Suez War in 1956' (ITN, 1967). His report can make a claim to be one of those placing journalism in the category of the first draft of history. What was coming a couple of weeks later, the June 1967 war, was indeed the 'most serious crisis' since Suez. It would also mean the end of the time when Gaza could be referred to, as in Hart's script, as 'Egyptian territory'. It would mean the beginning of the time when Israel, whether as a direct occupying military force, or as a superior military force surrounding Gaza on the land and on the sea, controlled the territory. That control has inevitably shaped the way that the Gaza Strip has been reported, as has Gaza's geographical location. One of the advantages for correspondents faced with the challenges of reporting the Israeli–Palestinian conflict is the relatively small geographical area involved.

In normal times, a return journey from Jerusalem, the main base of international correspondents, to almost anywhere in Israel, the West Bank, or Gaza, can easily be accomplished in a day – but 'normal times' is not a satisfactory way to describe the situation in the region. For correspondents are often the only people who are permitted to make the journey from Jerusalem to Gaza. Israelis, when they do at all, usually do so in armoured columns because they are serving in the army; Palestinians are rarely allowed to leave Gaza at all. Even so, international correspondents do not always make use of this access. Very few non-Palestinian journalists have ever been based in Gaza. The late, and highly respected, Graham Usher of the *Economist* was (*Economist*, 2013). The BBC's Alan Johnston lived in Gaza from 2004 until 2007, the last three months of his posting being spent in captivity after he had been kidnapped (BBC, 2007). This latter incident, although it happened in the last decade, may well still be one reason why no international journalists are based there. That perhaps matters less when there are excellent Palestinian journalists, such as Reuters' Nidal Al-Mughrabi, or the BBC's Rushdi Abualouf and Hamada Abuqammar (former colleagues of mine) working for many of the main international news organisations. Still, it is an oversight. An understandable one, perhaps, in a time when coverage budgets continue to spiral downwards, and when those limited budgets are stretched ever more thinly across a region which continues to demand massive editorial attention. That being the case, the Israeli–Palestinian conflict has in general slipped down the international news agenda.

Talking to international correspondents in Jerusalem in the summer of 2014, while researching my book *Headlines From the Holy Land: Reporting the Israeli–Palestinian Conflict* (2015), I got the impression that some of them wondered how much longer they would be there. There was less money, and too much to cover elsewhere in the region. The bigger organisations, such as the BBC and the *New York Times*, enjoy the benefit of having other correspondents elsewhere in the region. Those which do not, especially newspapers, seemed to be asking questions. The number of resident correspondents seemed to be falling every year. So there are many reasons – security, budgets, editorial priorities – why Gaza is likely to be covered in less detail than it has been at times in the past. Still, just a couple of weeks after those conversations, in late June 2014, Gaza was back at the top of the international news agenda as Israel launched Operation Protective Edge: seeking to limit the ability of armed Palestinian groups to fire rockets at Israel; killing hundreds of Palestinian civilians in the process.

Gaza was suddenly in the headlines again, even in a summer of instability where conflict in Ukraine, and the unprecedented military successes in Iraq of ISIS, provided strong competition for editorial attention. Because cause and context is such an important part of any discussion of the reporting of the Israeli–Palestinian conflict, and because Operation Protective Edge will be referred to throughout this chapter, it is worth here briefly recapitulating the events which preceded it. On Monday 15 June 2014, three Israeli students, Eyal Yifrach, Gil-ad Sha'er and Naftali Frankel, went missing while on their way back from a Jewish settlement on the West Bank (Heller, 2014). The students were believed to have been kidnapped. The Israeli authorities blamed members of the Palestinian group Hamas. Two weeks later, the three students were found dead (BBC, 2014a). Israel later identified those whom it held responsible for the students' deaths, and killed them (Sawafta, 2014) – but not before over a thousand more lives had been lost. Israeli forces first mounted a major operation on the West Bank, detaining Hamas suspects (even as rumours circulated that the students were already known to be dead (Horowitz, et al., 2014)), and then launched Operation Protective Edge against targets in Gaza. The assault lasted for several weeks. Journalists from across the world came to Gaza to cover it as it continued.

While, inevitably, there is not an undisputed figure for the numbers killed during Operation Protective Edge, the BBC, citing UN figures, gave the Palestinian death toll as 2,104, of whom 1,462 were civilians (BBC, 2014b). The same BBC news story said that, 'An Israeli government official told the BBC that the Israel Defense Forces (IDF) had killed 1,000 "terrorists" during the assault on Gaza' (BBC, 2014b). That means that some of those whom the United Nations identified as civilians were identified by the Israelis as 'terrorists'. This was an important part of Israel's media campaign. Israel was seeking to justify a military operation which caused large-scale civilian casualties, and which, it must have known, would draw widespread international criticism. In 2008–9, during Operation Cast Lead, which was also launched against Gaza, Israel went as far as to prevent international journalists from entering Gaza. The move prompted a protest from the Foreign Press Association in Israel (FPA), which described it as 'unprecedented denial of access to Gaza for the world's media'. Access, as always, was key. The FPA was eventually successful in overturning the ban, with Israel's Supreme Court 'endorsing the principle of unfettered access to the Gaza Strip for the International Media', a decision which the FPA welcomed as 'a noteworthy decision for freedom of access to journalists in situations of conflict' (Foreign Press Association, 2009). Despite the court deciding in the FPA's favour on that occasion, it would be wrong to get the impression that journalists enjoy 'unfettered access'. While it would also be wrong to single out Israel as a particularly egregious offender in a world where many countries place great restrictions on the press, especially in time of war, there are still obstacles placed in the way of journalists wanting to report from Gaza.

To begin with, Israel controls access to the territory. There is a crossing point from Egypt, where it borders the southern edge of the Gaza Strip, but at the time of writing, in May 2015, this crossing point is completely closed. In any case, any international journalist arriving in the region to work in Gaza would normally fly to the nearest airport, which is in Tel Aviv. That means that access to the territory is only possible with the knowledge and permission of the Israeli authorities. In order to enter Gaza from Israel as a journalist, you need to have a press card issued by the Israeli Government Press Office (GPO). According to the GPO's website, these are only issued to 'Those whose main profession is in the news media in the year preceding the application' (Israel Government Press Office, 2015a). This condition is presumably designed to prevent pro-Palestinian activists from entering the territory as journalists. Even in the early years of the previous decade, during the second Palestinian intifada, or uprising against Israel, it was relatively easy for any foreign passport holder to enter the territory. That changed as time went on. The suspicion that two suicide bombers carrying British passports had visited Gaza before carrying out their attack on a bar in Tel Aviv (McGreal et al., 2003), and the killings the same year by Israeli forces in Gaza of two foreign activists, Rachel Corrie and Tom Hurndall (Rodgers, 2013: 128), were followed by stricter conditions for entry. For a journalist, a GPO press card is now indispensable. In order to obtain such a card, the applicant has to accept working under the procedures set out in the 'Censorship Declaration'. Any applicant for a press card has to tick a box on the GPO's website indicating that they 'have read and agree to accept' (Israel Government Press Office, 2015b) the declaration. The Censorship Declaration itself seems fairly draconian, especially when point 1 begins: 'All written material, photographs and recordings dealing with security and defense matters intended for transmission abroad, must be presented to the Censor's Office' (Israel Government Press Office, 2015b). In practice, the cards are relatively easy to obtain – provided that the applicant can prove that he or she is a full-time journalist.

Hundreds of visiting correspondents were able to report from Gaza during Operation Protective Edge in the summer of 2014. In practice, the conditions placed on 'all' material 'dealing with security and defence matters' are not enforced. Were that the case, then presumably all the material relating to all of Israel's military activity in the occupied Palestinian territories would theoretically have to be submitted for censorship on the basis that Israel justifies its occupation on the grounds of its security. As will be discussed later, a country which so closely identifies itself with Western values of democracy and press freedom would not want to be seen as failing to live up to these values by curbing legitimate journalistic activity. It cares too much about its international image. Is there another language which has, as Hebrew does, a word, *hasbara*, which combines the ideas of public relations and public diplomacy? Nevertheless, these conditions remain, and can therefore technically be invoked at will. Agreeing to them is a condition of journalists' entrance to Gaza, and it is Israel, not the Palestinian Authority, or the Hamas government of the Gaza Strip, which has drawn them up, and imposes them or not as it sees fit. Even if access is, in principle and in law, 'unfettered', there is no guarantee that it will be so in practice. When it is possible, though, it offers a very rare perspective.

As noted above, Israelis and Palestinians have increasingly little to do with one another unless it is in circumstances of confrontation. The throngs of thousands of Palestinians who used once to cross into Israel from Gaza are no more. Even third-country diplomats, who might once have travelled regularly to Gaza from Tel Aviv or Jerusalem (depending upon how their country's foreign ministry divided up ambassadorial and consular duties) do so increasingly rarely. They are restricted by the security situation – the United States still recalls the roadside bomb which blew up its convoy more than a decade ago (BBC, 2003) – and, in the case of diplomats from the European Union and the United States, there are government bans on talking to Hamas officials, on the grounds that they consider them representatives of a terrorist organisation.

Journalists are not subject to the latter constraint. They are not immune to the former. Even where access is granted, there are other hazards. The 2007 kidnapping of the BBC's Alan Johnston is one; the dangers inherent in reporting armed conflict are others. In 2003, the British cameraman James Miller was killed by Israeli fire while filming a documentary in Rafah, at the southern edge of the Gaza Strip (Committee to Protect Journalists, 2003). In 2014, the Associated Press journalist, Simone Camilli, was killed during Operation Protective Edge, when unexploded ordnance blew up (Stern, 2014). These two cases are cited here because the focus of this chapter is Western reporting from Gaza. It is important to note that, as Shazdeh Omari of the Committee to Protect Journalists (CPJ) wrote of the Middle East in general, 'Despite increased risks to Western journalists working in conflict zones, the overwhelming majority of journalists under threat for their work continue to be local.' As Omari goes on to say, 'At least four journalists and three media workers were killed while covering the 50 days of conflict in July and August in Israel and the Occupied Palestinian Territories' (Omari, 2014). One of those was Ali Abu Afash, killed in the same explosion as Simon Camilli (Stern, 2014).

Even when the territory is open to Western journalists, to enter can be to take a risk. In July 2014, Sky News' Andrew Wilson, formerly his organisation's Middle East correspondent (he had returned to the region to cover the escalating conflict), broadcast a report which focused on the challenges involved just in getting into the territory to start reporting: the lengthy security checks; the long walk through the concrete tunnel which leads from the Israel crossing point into the rest of the Gaza Strip; then, at the height of Operation Protective Edge, the perilous bus ride from the northern side of Gaza City to the city centre and down to the seafront (Wilson, 2014). The first part of the ride followed, at high speed to lessen the chance of being fired on, on deserted roads, passing homes from which civilians had fled to seek safety. The report provided a valuable view for outsiders who had never been there, and almost certainly never would, of the reality of life in the war zone. It offered the audience an important additional perspective, in at least two ways. First, it gave an impression of the conditions and circumstances in which the material they were seeing was being gathered, explaining the time, trouble and danger involved in making what ends up being a few minutes of television news. It gave the viewer a picture of what they might see and experience were they to make the same journey themselves. Second, it gave a broader perspective, however brief in time, of what life was like in the territory. No Western journalist has to live under the restrictions imposed on the Palestinian population. They may experience, or witness, them from time to time, but that is all. Exposing them in this way can help to provide one of the most important requirements of news coverage from Gaza, and one which is often the most difficult to meet: context.

Four days after Andrew Wilson gave audiences an insight into what was involved in just getting to the area where he could start work, Channel 4 News' Paul Mason, then also reporting from Gaza, posted a blog entry, 'As a Brit in Gaza, "it's all your fault," is a line I've heard a lot'. 'Sit down with any Palestinian over the age of fifty on a street in Gaza and, if you're British, you'll soon be discussing Arthur Balfour', Mason began. He went on to reiterate, '"It's all your fault," is a line I've heard – delivered reasonably calmly' (Mason, 2014). Mason explained that his interlocutors were 'very capable of joining the dots', as they drew connections between the expulsion from what is now Israel of grandparents in 1948 – a fate which they in turn traced back to the Balfour Declaration, and its endorsement of 'the establishment in Palestine of a national home for the Jewish people' (BBC, 2001).

Mason is not the only British correspondent to face such an accusation. It was also levelled at me shortly after my arrival in Gaza in 2002 (Rodgers, 2013: 121). To the BBC's credit, the significance of the Balfour Declaration was one of the questions I was asked to discuss at my interview for the post of correspondent in the territory. No one who has reported from Israel and the Palestinian territories for more than a couple of days can fail to notice the great importance which both sides in the conflict place upon history. Increasingly, as I argue elsewhere (Rodgers, 2015) those national narratives are reinforced by religious ones. Such views challenge the two-state solution, that is, the idea that the land between the River Jordan and the Mediterranean Sea can eventually accommodate both Israel and a Palestinian State. This has been the focus, in one form or another, of all recent attempts at a negotiated peaceful solution to the conflict – the 2003 Roadmap being the most high-profile example. The Roadmap's stated aim was to 'resolve the Israel-Palestinian conflict, and end the occupation that began in 1967' (United Nations, 2003). As noted above, it was the 1967 war which established Israel's control of the West Bank and Gaza, a control which endures today. Yet in the historical narratives which exert such influence on the thinking on both sides of the conflict, 1948, not 1967, is not the year which looms largest. Writing in the *New York Review of Books* in 2013, Nathan Thrall of the International Crisis Group suggested that:

> Both Palestinian and Israeli hard-liners have gained support-
> ers by casting doubt on the notion that the conflict could be
> resolved in an exchange of land for peace. This central axiom
> of the two-decades-old peace process made sense for Israel's
> negotiations with Egypt, Jordan, and Syria, but never with the
> Palestinians, who believe that the core of the conflict is Zionist
> settlement in Palestine and the expulsion of Palestinians during
> the 1948 war that established the Israeli state. (Thrall, 2013)

Israel, for its part, generally remembers 1948 as a heroic military strug-gle which led to independence. 'Israel's Independence Day is an occasion for genuine celebration. Jews celebrate the rebirth of our national freedom in our restored homeland,' as the newly re-elected Israeli prime minis-ter, Benjamin Netanyahu, put it in his address marking the day in 2015 (Netanyahu, 2015). These contrasting views of the same event – 'rebirth of our national freedom', or *nakba* (catastrophe) in Arabic – might not matter too much if history in the Middle East were a matter largely confined to academic study. It is not. As the Brit in Gaza being told, 'It's all your fault' will discover, events which happened almost a century ago are seen as hav-ing direct and visible consequences in the present.

Much international reporting relies on knowledge of a region or a nation's history. Considered coverage of Yugoslavia in the 1990s, or of Ukraine in this decade, would be quite impossible without it. So a cor-respondent reporting on Gaza needs to have at least a passing knowledge of the main events going back to the time of the photograph mentioned at the beginning of this chapter, and the Balfour Declaration of the same year. They also need to know something of the territory's troubled, more recent history – especially its changing experiences of two intifadas – or uprisings against Israel. Since the first began in 1987 (for an account of the circumstances of its outbreak, see Shindler, 2013: 204–7), the territory has known times of hope, and an easing of restrictions, to renewed rebellion and conflict, to the state of almost complete isolation and siege which characterises the present. News reporting cannot constantly refer to these violent vicissitudes – its principal role is to tell audiences what is happening in the present – yet reporters must be aware of them. They are the forces which have shaped the people of Gaza's view of their neighbours and enemies; they are the events which, though in the past, dominate Gaza's present, and its population's often bleak view of its future.

That bleakness comes from experience of the last century. The reason why context is important is precisely because it is seen to shape the present in a much more immediate way than the newly arrived reporter can perhaps appreciate. At its heart, the Israeli–Palestinian conflict is about land, specifically 'homeland' as Mr Netanyahu referred to it in the extract cited above. This idea is expressed especially keenly among the Palestinians, too: in a national anthem which repeatedly refers to 'My country' (Palestinian American Council, 2015), and in countless other songs and stories of exile and loss. The *nakba* is remembered every year in the Palestinian territories. In Gaza in 2003, some members of the crowd gathered in Gaza City centre held up outsize cardboard keys to symbolise those to the properties they had lost (Rodgers, 2013: 63). Any visiting correspondent spending any time discussing family history with a Palestinian may well find that treasured documents are brought out to show to the visitor: the deeds to houses in what is now Israel, what was once Palestine, and home. This is where context is the greatest challenge for news reporting. The ideas expressed both by Mr Netanyahu and a Palestinian grandfather bringing out the carefully preserved papers are in the heads of the belligerents every day. That level of detail is quite impossible to reflect in the amount of space or airtime generally available for a news report, but it shapes the events which news reports are meant to chronicle. As, of course, does religion.

In a BBC documentary, 'Israel: facing the future', broadcast in 2013, the former Israeli intelligence chief, Ephraim Halevy, summarised well the importance of faith when he spoke of 'holy land'. In consequence, he suggested, 'no side can in any way forego its rights on every inch of territory' (Ware, 2013). How adequately to present these ideas to audiences? One reporter came up with a solution in a book on the conflict which he co-authored. Referring to 'tradition accepted both by the Arab and the Jews,' this correspondent's introductory chapter begins by taking its reader back to the time of the biblical Abraham (or Ibrahim). Its first paragraph concludes, 'They both claim Palestine as their home' (Churchill and Churchill, 1967: 1). The chapter continues with a succinct summary of Moses' leading the Jewish people out of Egypt to the promised land, and the era when Rome was the leading power in the region. Biblical text and more widely accepted historical fact are presented as equally reliable sources. Perhaps this is the only way adequately to prepare an audience for an account of the Israeli–Palestinian conflict. The Churchills (the authors were the son and grandson of Britain's wartime prime minister) though, were writing a book, and they were writing one in 1967. Even then, as the modern Middle East dramatically took shape, the requirements of context were perplexing those who had come to cover the conflict.

Paul Mason's reflection on the Balfour Declaration came during the bloody events of the summer of 2014. They are worth considering in detail not only because they are the most recent occasion when world media attention was focused on Gaza. They demand attention for at least two other important reasons. Covering conflict in any part of the world usually involves reporting not only on violence, but also on a political process, or the prospects for one. Especially since the failure earlier in 2014 of the US Secretary of State John Kerry's attempt to restart negotiations between Israel and the Palestinians, there has been no peace process. The Israeli general election of 2015 returned Benjamin Netanyahu to the post of prime minister. His victory followed a statement he had made during the final stages of the campaign that there would be no Palestinian state while he was in office (Ravid, 2015). Some weeks after Mr Netanyahu's electoral triumph, his deputy foreign minister, Tzipi Hotovely (who was then, given that Mr Netanyahu was himself acting foreign minister, Israel's most senior official working full time on foreign policy) was the subject of the following report from the Associated Press:

> 'We need to return to the basic truth of our rights to this country,' she said. 'This land is ours. All of it is ours. We did not come here to apologise for that.'

Hotovely, an Orthodox Jew, laced her speech with biblical com-
mentaries in which God promised the land of Israel to the Jews.
(Associated Press, 2015)

Ms Hotovely's remarks seemed the latest restatement of the phenomenon
– that of the role of religion as a justification, and motivation – identified by Mr Halevy in the extract from the BBC documentary cited above.
This came at a time in the Israeli–Palestinian conflict when there was no
political process. The reporting of Gaza in 2014 is therefore especially significant, which leads us to the second reason. It may be that what happened in the territory that summer marks the way that the conflict will be
fought in the foreseeable future. Operation Protective Edge, after all, was
unprecedented only in its scale, not in its nature. Two previous Israeli military campaigns aimed at Gaza, 'Cast Lead' (2008–9), and 'Pillar of Defence'
('Pillar of Cloud' in Hebrew) (2012), had attempted similar objectives: the
limitation of the military capacity of Gaza's armed groups. Somewhere
along the way, a ghastly euphemism emerged for these assaults: 'cutting'
or 'mowing' the grass (see, for example, 'Mowing the grass in Gaza', Inbar
and Shamir, 2014). Presumably, this phrase is supposed to mean reducing
military capacity which has increased. The use of the mowing metaphor
has hideous echoes of Death the Reaper with a scythe, and must surely, in
many minds, suggest killing rather than harvesting: the death of people –
many of them civilians – rather than simply the destruction of armaments.

In the absence of a political process, in the absence too of sufficient
political will to start one – renewed failure being the most easily foreseen
outcome – the media war seems almost to have become a substitute for
the political process which might normally have been expected to coex-
ist, if perhaps not to prosper, alongside a military conflict. In the absence
of news conferences and statements which might form part of the public diplomacy of a negotiation process, the belligerents are left to speak to
each other – and to third parties – through their statements to the media.
The media, distracted by events elsewhere in the region, and around the
world, and fatigued by the failure of countless rounds of talks and talks
about talks to produce anything approaching a permanent settlement, only
find their attention drawn to Gaza in times of extreme violence. Those
times of extreme violence in Gaza, therefore, are now the times when this

public diplomacy, aimed at world opinion, is likely to be conducted. Even as they face death and injury to report what is happening in Gaza, journalists' words and images are another battleground. Advocates, apologists and activists, not only in the region but around the world, are keen to join in. The last three times the Israeli–Palestinian conflict has featured prominently in international news coverage have all been during large-scale Israeli military operations in Gaza. Given that absence of a political process there may well be more 'cutting the grass'. The combined factors outlined here put the reporting of Gaza at the centre of international impressions and understanding of the Israeli–Palestinian conflict.

Hundreds of international correspondents crossed into Gaza during the summer of 2014, taking the same time-consuming and potentially dangerous route described by Sky News' Andrew Wilson in the report referred to above. Because crossing in and out of the territory every day was both a risk, and a potential waste of time, most of the reporters were out of contact with the Israelis – and least, out of personal contact with the Israelis. Israel, keen as ever to seek to get its point of view across, found its opportunities to do so limited. This was for a number of reasons: as already noted, Israeli officials were not in a position to hold news conferences for correspondents who were in Gaza; second, official spin was complemented and challenged by social media content posted both by Israeli troops, and Gazans. Kuntsman and Stein's description of the way this worked during Israel's 2012 Operation Pillar of Defence seems relevant for 2014, too:

> The mobile uploads from individual soldiers differed markedly from the official output of the Israeli military, with its emphasis on PR didacticism and the production of an institutional record. And they contrasted sharply with the viral content from Gaza's Palestinian residents that saturated global social networks. (Kuntsman and Stein, 2015)

Perhaps because of this – particularly because of that 'viral content from Gaza's Palestinian residents' – Israel faced a challenge to justify military action which was causing so many civilian casualties. This was especially difficult when many of the civilians who were directly affected were able to share on social media pictures of their suffering. Israel may control access to Gaza. It has little control over what the territory's residents can post on social media, or on the activities of international correspondents once they are there. That does not mean that the Israeli authorities are content to sit back and let their version of events go untold. The social media battle was joined along with the military one during Operation Protective Edge. The Israeli army's Twitter feed worked hard to counter suggestions that they were thoughtlessly causing civilian casualties, suggestions often illustrated by pictures of dead or mutilated children. Their approach was to try to blame Hamas for the deaths and hardship which were being visited upon the population of Gaza. One of their graphics claimed that the resources used to construct the network of tunnels amounted to millions of dollars which could otherwise have been spent on homes, mosques, schools and clinics (Israeli Army Twitter feed, 2014). These social media exchanges – Palestinians and their supporters were quick to mock the Israeli army's graphics – seemed, as the conflict went on, to take the place of political dialogue. The Twitter abuse was both unilateral and multi-directional: taking the place of diplomatic exchanges between the two sides, and also carried out for the benefit of an international audience – including the international news media.

The main phase of Operation Protective Edge was completed in early August, when Mr Netanyahu gave a news conference. It was an exercise in patronising and belittling the journalists who had covered the conflict, and their work. This is an extract from his opening remarks:

> I expect, now that the members of the press are leaving Gaza, or some of them are leaving Gaza, and are no longer subjected to Hamas restrictions and intimidations, I expect we'll see even more documentation of Hamas terrorists hiding behind the civilian population, exploiting civilian targets. I think it's very important for the truth to come out. (Netanyahu, 2014)

Officials' placing pressure on journalists has become so routine in contemporary political communication that words such as these barely strike the reader as out of the ordinary. What is remarkable is that here they are made publicly by a prime minister, rather than snarled out by a sharp-suited spin doctor lurking in a corner or corridor. It shows the importance that Israel places upon the way the story in Gaza is reported internationally. It shows the kind of high-level political pressure to which reporters covering the

Israeli–Palestinian conflict, and especially the Gaza Strip, can be subjected. In the case of Gaza, Israel finds itself in a very difficult situation. Many Israelis may well share the desire, expressed by their then prime minister, Yitzhak Rabin, more than two decades ago, for the territory to sink into the sea (Peters, 2013: 198). While that will not happen, Israel faces domestic political pressure to 'mow the grass' every so often, a response which brings international condemnation (although Israel has become used to this, and is ready to withstand it as long as it remains limited to words, rather than actions). Still, as long as Israel's self-image relies upon its being an outpost of democracy, with all that entails regarding respect for human rights and freedom of the press, in a region where such values are said to be lacking, if not absent, it must try as hard as it can to polish its international reputation. Mr Netanyahu's words, cited above, seem to say: 'The international reporting of the recent conflict in Gaza was flawed because Hamas restricted and intimidated journalists.' They are patronising precisely because such an assessment suggests that reporters would be incapable of seeing this for what it was, or coping with it. Such remarks are also misleading. While there may have been isolated cases of Hamas fighters seeking to put pressure on people, no evidence has emerged of any kind of systematic attempts to intimidate international correspondents. Anyone who has reported from the territory knows that in times of heightened tension, members of the Palestinian armed groups are either fighting, or in hiding to avoid being killed. To its credit, the Israeli newspaper *Ha'aretz* challenged Mr Netanyahu's assertion a couple of days later in a piece headlined 'Foreign press: Hamas didn't censor us in Gaza, they were nowhere to be found' (Pfeffer, 2014).

Why then, does international reporting from Gaza matter? Why did Mr Netanyahu bother to suggest that correspondents' accounts were incomplete, for whatever reason? Israel has been able to weather outrage at previous instances of mass civilian casualties. If stories of civilian deaths from Gaza really had any effect, then Israel might have been subject by now to much more severe sanctions than the kind of diplomatic censure to which it has become accustomed. It matters because even in the connected world in which we live, perspectives on Gaza – today the most violent front in the Israeli–Palestinian conflict – are limited. Israelis and Palestinians know increasingly little of each other's lives. Diplomats often rely on secondary information. International reporting from the territory, whatever its flaws and failures might be, whatever obstacles are placed in its way, offers a rare and valuable viewpoint.

Note

1   See image at http://www.iwm.org.uk_www.iwm.org.uk/collections/item/object/ 205067197 (accessed 16 February 2017).

References

Associated Press (2015). 'Israel's new deputy foreign minister: "This land is ours. All of it is ours"', *Guardian*, 22 May. Available at: www.theguardian.com/world/ 2015/may/22/israels-new-deputy-foreign-minister-this-land-is-ours-all-of-it- is-ours (accessed 27 May 2015).

BBC (2001). 'The Balfour Declaration', 29 November. Available at: http://news. bbc.co.uk/1/hi/in_depth/middle_east/israel_and_the_palestinians/key_docu- ments/1682961.stm (accessed 20 May 2015).

BBC (2003). 'Gaza bomb hits US convoy', 15 October. Available at: http://news.bbc. co.uk/1/hi/world/middle_east/3194432.stm (accessed 22 May 2015).

BBC (2007). 'Timeline: Alan Johnston abduction', 4 July. Available at: http://news. bbc.co.uk/1/hi/world/middle_east/6518873.stm (accessed 21 April 2015).

BBC (2014a). 'Missing Israeli teens found dead near Halhul', 30 June. Available at: www.bbc.co.uk/news/world-middle-east-28095831 (accessed 12 May 2015).

BBC (2014b). 'Gaza crisis: toll of operations in Gaza', 1 September. Available at: www.bbc.co.uk/news/world-middle-east-28439404 (accessed 22 April 2015).

Carmichael, Jane (2003). *First World War Photographers*. London: Routledge.

Churchill, Randolph S. and Churchill, Winston S. (1967). *The Six Day War*. London: Heinemann.

Committee to Protect Journalists (2003). 'Journalists killed: Israel and the Occupied Palestinian Territory'. Available at: https://cpj.org/killed/2003/james-miller. php (accessed 13 May 2015).

Economist (2013). 'Graham Usher: a correspondent of integrity and courage', 15 August. Available at: http://www.economist.com/blogs/pomegranate/2013/ 08/graham-usher (accessed 6 December 2016).

Foreign Press Association (2009). 'The Foreign Press Association'. Available at: www.fpa.org.il/?categoryId=74290 (accessed 12 May 2015).

Hass, Amira (2000). *Drinking the Sea at Gaza*. New York: Owl Books.

Heller, Jeffery (2014). 'Israel says Hamas militants behind abduction of three teens', Reuters, 16 June. Available at: http://uk.reuters.com/article/2014/06/16/uk- palestinian-israel-idUKKBN0EQ0A620140616 (accessed 12 May 2015).

Horowitz, Adam, Roth, Scott and Weiss, Phillip (2014). 'Israel maintains gag order in missing teen case, leading to charge of media "manipulation"', *Mondoweiss*, 23 June. Available at: http://mondoweiss.net/2014/06/maintains-missing-manipulation (accessed 12 May 2015).

Inbar, Ephraim and Shamir, Eitan (2014). 'Mowing the grass in Gaza', *Jerusalem Post*, 22 July. Available at: www.jpost.com/Opinion/Columnists/Mowing-the-grass-in-Gaza-368516 (accessed 21 April 2015).

Israel Government Press Office (2015a). 'GPO press cards'. Available at: http://gpo.gov.il/English/presscards/Pages/GPOPressCards.aspx (accessed 13 May 2015).

Israel Government Press Office (2015b). 'Application for a GPO card'. Available at: https://forms.gov.il/globaldata/getsequence/getHtmlForm.aspx?formType=gpocardeng@pmo.gov.il (accessed 13 May 2015).

Israeli Army Twitter feed (2014). @idfspokesperson. Twitter. Available at: https://twitter.com/IDFSpokesperson/status/493371173669855232?lang=en-gb (accessed 27 May 2015).

ITN (1967). 'Middle East crisis: Israel report', Available at: http://jiscmediahub.ac.uk/record/display/042-00053220;jsessionid=E538E2D962B1353657DF226F5E7F77BE#citation (accessed 21 April 2015).

Kuntsman, Adi and Stein, Rebecca L. (2015). *Digital Militarism: Israel's Occupation in the Social Media Age*. Stanford, CA: Stanford University Press.

Lerner, Peter (2015). Facebook. Available at: www.facebook.com/Lt.Col.PeterLerner (accessed 21 April 2015).

Mason, Paul (2014). 'As a Brit in Gaza, "it's all your fault", is a line I've heard a lot', Channel 4, 4 August. Available at: http://blogs.channel4.com/paul-mason-blog/brit-gaza-fault-line-heard-lot/2094 (accessed 20 May 2015).

McGreal, Chris, Urquhart, Conal and Norton-Taylor, Richard (2003). 'The British suicide bombers', *Guardian*, 1 May. Available at: www.theguardian.com/world/2003/may/01/israel5 (accessed 13 May 2015).

Netanyahu, Benjamin (2014). 'Israeli Ministry of Foreign Affairs: PM Netanyahu holds press conference'. Available at: http://mfa.gov.il/MFA/PressRoom/2014/Pages/PM-Netanyahu-holds-press-conference-6-Aug-2014.aspx (accessed 27 May 2015).

Netanyahu, Benjamin (2015). 'PM Netanyahu's greeting for Independence Day 2015'. Available at: www.youtube.com/watch?v=umjgzMftZV0 (accessed 20 May 2015).

Omari, Shazdeh (2014). 'International journalists killed at high rate in 2014: Middle East deadliest region', Committee To Protect Journalists. Available at: https://cpj.org/reports/2014/12/international-journalists-killed-at-high-rate-in-2014-middle-east-deadliest-region-for-press.php (accessed 13 May 2015).

Palestinian American Council (2015). 'The Palestinian anthem in English'. Available at: www.pac-usa.org/anthem1.htm (accessed 20 May 2015).

Peters, Joel (2013). 'Gaza', in Joel Peters and David Newman (eds), *The Routledge Handbook on the Israeli–Palestinian Conflict*. Abingdon: Routledge.

Pfeffer, Anshel (2014). 'Foreign press: Hamas didn't censor us in Gaza, they were nowhere to be found', *Ha'aretz*, 8 August. Available at: www.haaretz.com/news/features/.premium-1.609589 (accessed 27 May 2015).

Ravid, Barak (2015). 'Netanyahu: if I'm elected, there will be no Palestinian state', *Ha'aretz*, 16 March. Available at: www.haaretz.com/news/israel-election-2015/1.647212 (accessed 15 April 2015).

Rodgers, James (2013). *No Road Home: Fighting for Land and Faith in Gaza*. Bury St Edmunds: Abramis.

Rodgers, James (2015). *Headlines from the Holy Land: Reporting the Israeli-Palestinian Conflict*. Basingstoke: Palgrave Macmillan.

Sawafta, Ali (2014). 'Israel says its troops kill Hamas men accused of slaying teens', Reuters, 23 September. Available at: http://uk.reuters.com/article/2014/09/23/us-palestinians-israel-idUKKCN0HI09H20140923 (accessed 12 May 2015).

Shindler, Colin (2013). *A History of Modern Israel*, 2nd edition. Cambridge: Cambridge University Press.

Stern, Jason (2014). 'After journalist killings, potential violations in Gaza must be investigated', Committee to Protect Journalists, 28 August. Available at: https://cpj.org/blog/2014/08/after-journalist-killings-potential-violations-in-.php#more (accessed 13 May 2015).

Thrall, Nathan (2013). 'What future for Israel?', *New York Review of Books*, 15 August. Available at: www.nybooks.com/articles/archives/2013/aug/15/what-future-israel/ (accessed 20 May 2015).

United Nations (2003). 'A performance based roadmap to a permanent two-state solution to the Israeli-Palestinian conflict'. Available at: www.un.org/News/dh/mideast/roadmap122002.pdf (accessed 20 May 2015).

Ware, John (2013). 'Israel: facing the future', BBC2, 17 April.

Westmoreland, G. (1917). 'Third battle of Gaza'. Available at: http://jiscmediahub.ac.uk/record/display/061-oaiwwwculturegridorgukIWM5132649 (accessed 20 April 2015).

Wilson, Andrew (2014). 'Getting to Gaza', Sky News, 31 July.

8

Stoning Iran

*Strategic Narratives, Moral Authority and the
Reporting of a Stoning Sentence*

Esmaeil Esfandiary and Shahab Esfandiary

On 7 July 2010, just over a year after the contested 2009 presidential elections in Iran that resulted in the mass circulation in Western media of
disturbing and graphic images of violence on Tehran's streets, another
'shocking story' provided invaluable 'material' for another year of the
Western media's fixation on Iran. This time, they told us, a woman named
Sakineh Mohammadi Ashtiani had been convicted of adultery and was
about to be punished to 'death by stoning' (Fletcher, 2010a). The Murdoch-
owned British newspaper *The Times* became the surprising front-runner in
covering the story in the subsequent months. In fact, the paper launched
an 'international campaign' to spare the life of Ms Ashtiani, inviting human
rights luminaries, including Nicholas Sarkozy, Tony Blair, John Bolton and
Condoleezza Rice, to condemn this 'barbaric' and 'inhumane' sentence. In
one of its early reports, *The Times* carefully detailed a very graphic and
daunting account of what was about to happen to 'the convict':

> Ms. Ashtiani, 43, will be taken from the prison in the northern
> city of Tabriz in which she has spent the past five years and be
> wrapped head to toe in a white shroud. She will then be buried
> up to her chest and stoned. The stones will be large enough to
> cause severe injury but not so big that she will be killed outright

[...] It can be more than 30 minutes before she is dead or unconscious. (Fletcher, 2010a)

This marked the beginning of an unprecedented international media campaign intended, apparently, to put pressure on the Iranian government into sparing the life of Ms Ashtiani. In a couple of weeks, this campaign for a woman in a provincial town of Tabriz in Northwest Iran grew into a massive and extensive human rights campaign. Between July 2010, when the initial news of stoning broke out, and December 2010 when Ms Ashtiani was spared from death, *The Times* published more than 200 articles and reports, including many front-page headlines and editorials on her case. In the present chapter, we aim to examine this campaign through an analysis of the discourse and narratives of the published stories in *The Times*. We also seek to find out why this case, among many other cases of stoning in the region, as well as other gross violations of human rights that happened over the same period, gained such a global momentum.

Strategic Narratives and the Battle for Moral Ground

In their book *Strategic Narratives: Communication Power and the New World Order*, Alister Miskimmon et al. (2013), provide valuable insights into understanding 'strategic narratives' and their role in constructing national identity and exercising power in international relations. 'Strategic narratives are a means for political actors to construct a shared meaning of the past, present, and future of international politics to shape the behavior of domestic and international actors' (Miskimmon et al., 2013: 2). But this is not merely true about narratives regarding one's own identity: 'actors work to frame their own character *and that of others*, by selecting and highlighting some facets of their history or actions in order to promote a particular interpretation and evaluation of their character' (Miskimmon et al., 2013: 5, emphasis added).

The authors refer to 'history, analogies, metaphors, symbols, and images' as potential resources for constructing these narratives (Miskimmon et al., 2013: 7). From a similar perspective, Monroe Price, in his comprehensive volume titled *Free Expression, Globalism and the New Strategic*

Communication (2015) argues that 'a state is, in part, a collection of stories connected to power. Remembered traditions, obligations and laws – all stories in themselves – shape internal and external perceptions of a state and the range of its efficacy' (Price 2015: 41).

According to Miskimmon et al. (2013: 17), strategic narratives have a twofold power effect: they are 'an instrument of power in the traditional Weberian or *behavioural* sense of A getting B to do what B otherwise would not' (emphasis in original); but they also constitute 'the experience of international affairs and thus the identity of its actors and the meaning of the system'. For example, a carefully designed and promoted narrative may imply that military intervention is the only way to save indigenous populations from dictatorship and tyranny, and thus persuade allied states to participate in military coalitions serving such purposes. But at the same time such narratives also define the 'real world' for pertinent actors and ascribe identities to them. It is true that hard facts exist on the ground, but strategic narratives connect facts with ideologies and histories in order to make them meaningful – to construct a coherent new 'reality'. In other words, a combination of both external facts and discursive practices enable narratives to show us 'the real' world, as they want us to see it.

Also relevant here is the concept of soft power famously formulated by Joseph S. Nye (1990). Basically, Nye defined soft power as the attractive and exemplar status of a state in a way that others would naturally want what it wants. This has a direct connection to the functions of strategic narratives: 'Central to Nye's initial formulation was a concern to forge a new US narrative of international affairs to give meaning to the post-Cold War era' (Miskimmon et al., 2013: 3). In other words, Nye's concern was to determine how the world should make sense of the new unipolar, post-Cold War international order in a way that best serves US interests around the globe.

Iran and the US have had their own rival strategic narratives in the Middle East for the past thirty-seven years. More recent ones include their narratives on crises in Iraq, Syria and Yemen. 'Whether it is the clash of civilizations, the loss of "values," or the need to protect jobs or economies', argues Price (2015: 60), 'competition for national narratives of legitimacy – for good and for ill – will persist'. As Price indicates, 'legitimacy' is at the core of all efforts to win the hearts and minds of people within a nation or across the world. In order to persuade people about the legitimacy of its foreign policy initiatives, a state has to project them in a moral light; to imply that they are, in essence, *virtuous*. Even in the most violent military interventions, certain narratives are employed to indicate that intervention is moral and *humane*; to protect vulnerable people (like women), and to uphold values such as democracy, human rights and economic development.

An example of employing – or appropriating – such narratives for military interventions can be found in Cynthia Weber's (2005) analysis of the film *Kandahar*. The 'US moral grammar of war' is, according to Weber, made up of a tripartite axis: foreign policy, popular (often filmic) imaginaries, and narratives of the family (2005: 359). She argues that in US national narratives at times of war the feminine functions in a stereotypical way: 'as a figure in need of physical and moral security'. As Weber notes, this theme informed both the US and the UK's official justifications of the 'war on terror' (Weber 2005: 360).

Thus, it may be argued that the wars of narratives are inherently wars of moralities, i.e., how different systems of morality are used to justify and promote national interests and foreign policy initiatives. In the context of the US–Iran war of narratives, America emphasises the themes of democracy, freedom and human rights, while Iran capitalises on Islamic traditions and culture to project itself as the protector of Islamic values and morality in the face of the West's 'corrupting influence'. 'The revolutionary rhetoric,' Price (2015: 137) writes, 'still salient and sustained thirty-five years later, is situated as a bulwark against those seen to be meddling in Iran's domestic affairs, with the regime imagined as the righteous defender of Islam and caretaker of a moral society.' In other words, the geopolitical battle between the US and Iran is fought more on soft fronts, on values and moralities, than on military fronts.

Finally, it should be noted that new communication technology, obviously, has a major impact on the way these wars of narratives are fought in the digital age. In his seminal book *Communication Power* (2013), Manuel Castells explains how new communication technology has changed the practice of national and international politics. He demonstrates how digital networks of communications have forced political actors to adapt themselves to the new environment and to construct and project their policies, institutions and constituencies accordingly.

Miskimmon et al. (2013: 10), likewise, recognise these changes: 'Projection of strategic narratives in a new media ecology presents significant opportunities and challenges for actors [...] including increased reach of communication technologies, increased transparency, increased interactivity, and accelerated and distorted time horizons.' As shall be argued below, the 'Free Sakineh' campaign took full advantage of the new possibilities in this media ecology.

The 'Free Sakineh' Campaign

In the days after news of Ms Ashtiani's stoning sentence broke, major national and international media outlets dedicated immense time and space to the coverage of the case. A website (FreeSakineh.org) was set up with a petition requesting her amnesty. Tens of street protests and sit-ins were organised in major European and North American cities. An effort to invite intellectuals, celebrities, artists and playwrights to join was staged, and of course Western politicians jumped on the bandwagon too, using the harshest language possible to condemn the Iranian government for this case. All in all, an extensive, multi-platform international campaign was in place in a matter of days (McArthur, 2010).

Famous artists, intellectuals and philosophers also participated in this campaign:

> Bernard-Henri Levy, the French philosopher, [launched an initiative] to step up the pressure on the Iranian regime to spare Ms. Ashtiani [...] Each day Mr Levy's website *La Regle du Jeu*, the French newspaper *Liberation*, the US women's magazine *Elle* and the news website *Huffington Post* intend to publish a letter by an artist, intellectual or politician to show solidarity with Ms. Ashtiani. (Fletcher, 2010b)

Recovering from the internal and external scars and bruises of the 2009 post-election turmoil, the Iranian government was caught totally off-guard by this media campaign. Initially, the government reaction was low profile. Two days after the story broke, the Iranian embassy in London issued a statement that clearly denied the stoning punishment:

> this mission denies the false news aired in this respect [...] according to information from the relevant judicial authorities

in Iran, [Ms Ashtiani] will not be executed by stoning punishment. (CNN, 2010)

Since the ambiguous statement left the impression that Ms Ashtiani may be executed by a means other than stoning, the international campaign continued. A few weeks later, witnessing the intensification of the campaign's activities, the Iranian government went on the defensive, trying to explain to the world what 'the real story' of Ms Ashtiani was. This task was mainly carried out through a televised interview with Ms Ashtiani on the Iranian 24-hour English News channel, PressTV, in which she apparently confessed to her crimes. As the international media campaign drew more celebrities and politicians in to support Ms Ashtiani, some government-owned media in Iran grew more and more angry and tried to stage their own offence against the West.

The story increased in dramatic temperature when Iran's leading conservative newspaper *Kayhan* called the French First Lady Carla Bruni a 'prostitute', following a letter she had issued portraying Ms Ashtiani as 'a symbol of true love and liberty' (Fraser, 2010). *Kayhan* wrote:

> Studying Carla Bruni's personal record [i.e., her previous high-profile relationships] clearly shows the reason why this immoral woman is backing an Iranian woman who has been condemned to death […] In fact, she herself, deserves to die. (Purcell, 2010)

These provocative words clearly show the anger and rage within certain Iranian circles two months after the campaign was first triggered.

The Hidden Side of the Story

One important aspect of the campaign about Ms Ashtiani's case in the Western media is that it initially excluded a significant piece of information about her case. The dominant 'narrative' in Western media was that she was an 'innocent' woman about to be stoned by 'savage barbarians' merely and simply for having 'an affair' with her lover. This is perhaps why Carla Bruni called her a symbol of love and liberty. However, Ms Ashtiani's lawyer who broke the story of her stoning sentence to the world, acknowledged in his official blog on 14 July 2010 – that is, just a week later – that there was also a dark aspect to her case. According to

Mohammad Mostafaei, his client had been 'seduced' by a man in 2006 and was an accomplice to the murder of her husband (Mostafaei, 2010). According to the head of the city of Tabriz's judiciary, Sakineh Ashtiani had collaborated with her lover by sending her two children away from home and injecting her husband with an anaesthetic shot, enabling her lover to kill her husband by electrocution in the bathtub (Yong and Worth, 2010). Ms Ashtiani's lawyer did not refute this claim in his public response; in fact he confirmed that she had been sentenced to ten years in prison for this charge (Mostafaei, 2010).

Due to an appeal by her husband's relatives and/or scrutiny by judiciary authorities, her case was reopened and examined by another court, and this time she was also convicted of having an extramarital relationship while being married; an offence that if proven – on condition that four people give testimony that they have witnessed it – could lead to the death penalty by stoning in Iran's previous Islamic Penal Code. When the second case was coming to a conclusion in juristic proceedings, her lawyer published some details of her case on his blog and the story was quickly picked up by Western media. Yet the murder case was omitted when her story was initially reported to Western media by her lawyer and family. Clearly it would have been difficult to launch an international campaign for a woman who had colluded in electrifying her husband in a bathtub. It would be much easier to do so for an 'innocent' woman who was being harshly punished for 'a forbidden love affair'. Clearly, this is not to say that because Ms Ashtiani was complicit in murder, she deserved the stoning verdict, or that she should not have been supported when facing such as verdict. The issue, here, is the way Ms Ashtiani's case was appropriated to launch a moral and political 'media war' that had objectives far beyond condemning stoning or saving a person's life.

It should be acknowledged that, despite a directive by the head of Iran's judiciary in 2002 that barred judges from issuing stoning verdicts, and although the amendment of the Islamic Penal Code in 2013 removed reference to stoning as a punishment in the laws regarding 'adultery while married', there have been a number of cases where judges have issued such verdicts based on *fatwas* of certain senior clerics outside the government. So in accusing the Iranian government for Ms Ashtiani's sentence, the media were also in a sense misleading their readers, since the head of

Iran's judiciary, who banned the practice of stoning in 2002, was appointed by the religious leader of the Islamic Republic, and those few judges who have issued this sentence after 2002 have done so by reference to *fatwas* of senior clerics other than the leader of Iran. According to some reports by Iranian opposition activists, since 2002 five men and three women have been stoned to death (Afshin-Jam, 2010). Yet apparently in some of these cases the verdict had been issued years before the 2002 directive (BBC News, 2007). In the case of Ms Ashtiani, the stoning verdict was reversed in September 2010 (*New York Times*, 9 September 2010: A8). On 19 March 2014, after spending eight years of her ten-year sentence in prison for complicity in murder, Ms Ashtiani was pardoned and freed (Tomlinson, 2014). Yet as at this time the international fervour and attention on her case had dried up, few even noticed her release.

Unveiling the 'Human Rights Activists'

'The whole truth' about Ms Ashtiani was concealed by the many expatriate pundits and 'human rights activists' who fed Western media with daily input from their 'sources' in Iran. Mina Ahadi, for example, the secretary of a little-known group named Iran Committee Against Stoning, was actively involved in propagating Ms Ashtiani's case in the West. Letters in eloquent prose by Ms Ashtiani were supposedly smuggled out of prison and very articulate interviews with her were published in Western media by these intermediaries, regardless of the fact that she was a poor, illiterate woman from a remote province who could not even speak Farsi and only spoke in the local Azeri language (Kamali Dehghan, 2010). Of course 'the human rights activist' is generally perceived as having the moral authority to speak the truth. Yet Western media failed to inform their readers that self-proclaimed 'human rights activists' like Mina Ahadi were in fact politburo members of Iranian opposition groups such as the Worker-Communist Party of Iran. A simple search in Google or Wikipedia would have clarified for media editors not only her political affiliation, but also her staunch anti-Islam agenda that positions her far from anything close to an impartial and balanced human rights observer. Of course this is not to say that all human rights activists in Iran or outside who have campaigned over the years to improve human rights in Iran are politically motivated or have Islamophobic tendencies. In fact, one may argue that many of them, particularly those inside Iran who have included negotiation with the authorities as part of their campaign strategy, have been more successful in reforming the laws – including those regarding stoning as mentioned above – rather than activists whose main ambition has been launching high-profile 'anti-Iran' campaigns in the Western media.

The Selective Reporting of Human Rights Violations

As mentioned above, the authors of this chapter do not seek to under-mine or question the intentions or objectives of all the varied person-alities and activists who participated in the campaigns in order to save Ms Ashtiani's life. In fact, having both lived in the West, we were our-selves deeply disturbed and outraged by Ms Ashtiani's verdict, and were also delighted that her stoning sentence was withdrawn and that she was eventually freed.

What matters to our study is the accuracy and reliability of Western media's reports on this case and the discourse they applied to represent it, as well as the functions or uses of such reports for Western governments' political and strategic projects. We believe that coverage of human rights violations in Western media, and the responses of Western politicians to them, are highly selective and in accordance with political and strategic alliances and calculations. For example, at the height of the international campaign for Ms Ashtiani, actual stoning cases happened in Pakistan and Afghanistan with no Western coverage or condemnation (Worth, 2010; *The Times*, 13 July 2010: 25). The case in Pakistan received only one line in the last paragraph of a report on Ms Ashtiani in *The Times*, while the case in Afghanistan received only one line in a *New York Times* op-ed. Violent punishments in Saudi Arabia – a key ally of the West in the region – usually take place without much international attention. Even systematic and gov-ernment-sponsored human rights violations on a much larger scale such as US drone killings or Israel's war crimes in Gaza did not trigger such a wide-scale global media campaign as the one for Ms Ashtiani. The selec-tive, purposive and strategic representation of her case, thus, has functions beyond saving an individual's life.

To address this issue, we must first examine the themes that these strategic narratives in Western media incorporate. What are the major themes in the extensive coverage of this case? How is the Iranian nation, as a whole, portrayed by Western officials in this extensive campaign? To this end, we first analysed all the accounts published by *The Times* in the five-month period between 7 July 2010, when the news first broke out, and 7 December 2010. *The Times* was chosen because it was the leading media outlet active in this extensive international campaign. All its stories were retrieved and analysed through Proquest Databases.

Analysis of *The Times* Coverage

In this section, the recurring themes in news reports and articles published by *The Times* on this subject over the aforementioned five-month period will be examined. Two types of stories are examined here based on our research aims. First are the reports that include statements by Western governments and officials who have commented on the case; and second, the editorials published in *The Times* regarding Ms Ashtiani's case.

Examining Western officials' statements regarding the case of Ms Ashtiani, we noticed the large scale and level of attention paid to this single issue. The avalanche of condemnations that continued for months at all official levels shows that this campaign was seen as an important opportunity and valuable asset for Western governments. Second, a lexicon of salient terms and phrases such as 'medieval', 'barbaric', 'torture', 'cruel', 'disgusting', 'inhumane', 'despicable', 'Middle Ages' and 'barbarity' were used by those officials in this regard. As already discussed, these terms imply a position of moral authority and civilisational superiority for the persons that use them. Finally, the forceful tone of such statements that include examples such as 'Iran should ...', 'Iran must ...' and 'we urge Iran ...', clearly places Iran in a subordinate discursive position in relation to the West. In other words, both the morality-based lexicon and the power dynamics of the language seeks to place Western officials in the position of moral authority and the Iranian government in a position of moral bankruptcy.

John Kerry, then-chairman of the US Senate Foreign Relations Committee, declared: 'Stoning is an appalling and barbaric punishment. The Government of Iran should abolish this act as a legitimate form of punishment' (Fletcher, 2010c). The US State Department also issued a statement declaring that it was 'deeply troubled by reports of the proposed stoning execution, which it called "a form of legalised death by torture". The governments of Canada and Norway have summoned their Iranian ambassadors to protest' (Fletcher, 2010d).

A similar positions was taken by the British government. Alistair Burt, a British Foreign Office minister, called stoning 'a medieval punishment that has no place in the modern world' (Fletcher, 2010c). David Miliband, the foreign secretary at the time, referred to stoning as a 'barbaric punishment', adding that 'people will not tolerate grossly inhumane acts of cruelty and barbarism' (Fletcher, 2010d). Tony Blair also jumped on the bandwagon, stating that 'the world is rightly outraged that such a cruel and disgusting punishment could even be contemplated in today's world' (Fletcher and Bannerman, 2010). And finally, David Cameron joined the campaign for Ms Ashtiani, calling her sentence 'completely inhuman and despicable' (Fletcher and Watson, 2010).

The French Foreign Minister, Bernard Kouchner, said at the time that 'Everything about [Ms Ashtiani's] case offends the universal conscience' (Fletcher and Bannerman, 2010), adding that Iran's treatment of her was 'the height of barbarity and a return to the Middle Ages' (*The Times*, 8 September 2010: 2). President Sarkozy's intervention, however, was more clearly self-congratulatory, as one would expect. The man best known for his 'zero tolerance' policy during the French riots in 2005, told a meeting of French ambassadors that France considers itself responsible 'for the woman', adding that 'the regime [of Iran] exercises control by repression and resorts massively to capital punishment, including its most medieval form, stoning' (Fletcher, 2010e).

Moreover, *The Times*' editorials clearly illustrate how the campaign for Ms Ashtiani was all about declaring moral authority and constructing a narrative that projected Iran as a morally corrupt system of government. For example, in its very first editorial on the subject, titled 'An act of barbarism' that also became the front-page headline, the author writes that 'stoning is a brutal medieval punishment', adding that 'Iran must repeal this law, and spare Sakineh Ashtiani' (*The Times*, 8 July 2010: 2). The editorial continues: 'This degraded practice is more than a judicial punishment. It is a political instrument of repression [...] Not all sentences of stoning are actually carried out, but the threat of such a terrifying torture is a way to deter opposition'. Considering the stoning punishment to be a 'political instrument' used to 'deter opposition' is a completely baseless claim, as such a punishment, even in the previous laws, could only be applied for certain convicts of extramarital relations.

The Times' next editorial, titled 'Stone cold shame', clearly recognises that there is a battle between Iran and the West – with the definition of morality at its heart:

> When the Iranian mullahs consider their domain, they do not see their country as we would necessarily recognise it. They see a proud nation that dates back to biblical times, cultured since its foes dwelt in holes, and beleaguered these past decades by Satanic enemies who refuse to acknowledge the beacon of Islamic sophistication [...] Iran is not the only country to practise stoning, but it is the only one to marry this backward village morality with the presumption of a right to global significance [...] In the global scheme of things, the planned murder of one woman may seem a minor matter. But the Iranian regime must recognise that this case has represented a microcosm of all that the rest of the world recognises is so terribly and glaringly wrong with Iran. (*The Times*, 9 July 2010: 2)

In other words, this whole campaign is not merely about the 'minor matter' of sparing a woman's life, but a strategic project that aims to demonstrate to the world that Iran is neither 'a proud nation' nor a 'beacon of Islamic sophistication', and does not have a 'right to global significance' because it is 'terribly and glaringly wrong'; unlike 'us' in the West who are incredibly and brilliantly right. This campaign, the editorial implicitly admits, is part of a strategic battle over moral authority in the field of international relations.

Other editorials also include a plethora of emotionally loaded, even hateful terms about 'the Iranian rulers', without mentioning that the stoning verdict issued by a judge in one of the provinces of Iran was not condoned by any of the Iranian senior authorities. 'Ms Ashtiani has come to symbolise the barbarity of Iran's rulers', reads one editorial, adding that 'She represents all victims of a singularly vile regime' (Fletcher, 2010f).

Another editorial, titled 'Defiance and delusion', falsely speaks of 'Tehran's stance' on the stoning verdict, emphasising that it 'harks back to the Middle Ages not only in the grotesque barbarity of the chosen punishment, but in insisting that Iran can make its own laws without reference to others. It ignores the interconnectedness of the modern world' (*The Times*, 8 September 2010: 2). So, Iran belongs to the Middle Ages because it insists on making its own laws without reference to 'us' in the modern world. The author of an editorial titled 'The meaning of freedom' considers the campaign to release Ms Ashtiani as 'a challenge to state-sponsored brutality', adding that this campaign is 'a stand against barbarism and a test of Tehran's humanity' (*The Times*, 10 December 2010: 2).

It is also interesting to note that many of the reports and articles published in *The Times* on this case, have titles that attribute terms such as barbarism, cruelty, medieval, and inhumane to Iran as a whole, and not to a particular verdict or even to 'the regime' or 'the rulers of Iran'. This attitude can be observed in titles such as: 'Cameron attacks "inhuman" Iran over stoning case' (16 September 2010); 'Hague appalled at "medieval" Iran over stoning plans' (8 July 2010); 'Outrage over Iran's plan to stone woman to death' (8 July 2010); 'Iran's cruel calculation' (2 November 2010); 'Iran's abuse of justice' (13 August 2010) and even 'Iran calls [Carla] Bruni a "prostitute" in stoning row' (29 August 2010).

Conclusion

Stories of human rights violations have had a strategic value and function for Western governments in their decades-old battle of narratives with the Islamic Republic of Iran. As the responses to, and reporting of, the case of Ms Ashtiani's stoning sentence has demonstrated, moral themes are at the centre of these narratives. In responding to such cases in the media, Western officials are portrayed as being in a position of moral authority where they are instructing a morally corrupt system what it *must* or *must not* do in order to become less barbaric and medieval. In its own narratives about the West, Iran has also applied moral ideals when blaming the West for oppression, exploitation, neocolonialism and corruption. Thus, the human rights campaigns play a secondary role in constructing counter-narratives that would neutralise Iran's claims to moral authority and discredit it on the international stage.

The Free Sakineh Campaign – with street protests and sit-ins, government condemnations, multimedia reports and commentary, billboards and street banners, performances and endorsements by artists and celebrities – was, in our view, not merely targeting the Iranian leaders. More significantly, it was targeting Western public opinion, capitalising on the legacy of the Enlightenment and the deep-rooted ideology of liberalism, as well as the fear of the horrors of the Middle Ages in Europe and the contempt for certain medieval traditions. The recurring cliché of 'death by stoning for adulteress', with all the horrific imagery that it signified, had a function of leaving a long-term impact on the mindset of Western citizens about the 'immoral nature' of the Iranian government. Thus, as Edward Said tells us in his seminal work *Orientalism*, Westerners use the imagery of their own wicked past to define an immoral, thus inferior, 'Other' (Said, 1978). This is not merely about Iran; it is about a Western projection of immorality based on the collective memory of its own immoral past.

The scale of this campaign took the Iranian government by surprise and pushed it into a corner, not knowing exactly what to do or how to react. This was an win-win narrative for the West and a lose-lose for the Islamic Republic in their decades-old war of narratives over hearts and minds. One key factor in the success of the campaign was the skilful recourse to literary and filmic narratives such as 'the female in need of rescue' and 'the forbidden love affair' that are very familiar to Western popular imaginary. The campaign took full advantage of all possible networks of influence as well as new communication technology to spread its message. From the very first days, a highly effective network of activists was shaped (McArthur, 2010). They used social media and online outlets to promote their agenda. More importantly, they used their influential connections to bring in large media corporations, public intellectuals and artists, and politicians and governments. At one point they even managed to persuade Brazilian president Lula da Silva to discuss offering asylum to Ms Ashtiani in a meeting with his friend Mahmoud Ahmadinejad (Barrionuevo, 2010). Traditional media outlets such as television and newspapers joined forces with new media technologies such as social networks to get the message of this campaign across to as wide a public as possible.

Finally, it should be noted that the effectiveness of this campaign does not mean that Iran does not continue to produce its own moral-based narratives against the West, specifically against the USA. In fact, Iran has aggressively increased its media activity, both in the cyber space and in broadcasting, by launching many international and multilingual media outlets and websites. During the nuclear negotiations between Iran and the E3+3 (or P5+1) nations, the Iranian negotiators actively used social media to post photos, messages and videos in English that targeted Western audiences and sought to put pressure on Western diplomats through public opinion. In a similar fashion, the religious leader of the Islamic Republic issued a personal letter addressed to 'the youth in Europe and America', following the terrorist killing of twelve journalists at the offices of the *Charlie Hebdo* magazine in Paris (Khamenei, 2015). Ayatollah Khamenei's letter aimed to encourage the youth of the West to study Islam through its original sources rather than paying attention to Islamophobic content in Western media that is prejudiced by acts of terrorists. The message was translated into several languages and posted on different social media through accounts in the leader's name and also via the robust social network of his followers. All in all, the strategic narrative wars continue to be fought on moral grounds at a time when military interventions have become less likely due to the increasing risks and costs of wars and progress in the field of diplomacy.

References

Afshin-Jam, N. (2010). 'This is only a reprieve: Sakineh's life is still in danger', *The Times*, 17 July. Available at: Proquest Databases (accessed 15 May 2015).

Barrionuevo, Alexei (2010). 'Brazil's president offers asylum to woman facing stoning in Iran', *New York Times*, 1 August. Available at: www.nytimes.com/2010/08/02/world/americas/02brazil.html (accessed 29 June 2015).

BBC News (2007). 'Iran "adulterer" stoned to death', 10 July. Available at: http://news.bbc.co.uk/2/hi/middle_east/6288156.stm. (accessed 30 August, 2015).

Burke, Kenneth (1969). *A Grammar of Motives*. Berkeley: University of California Press.

Castells, Manuel (2013). *Communication Power*. Oxford: Oxford University Press.

CNN (2010). 'Iran denying woman will be executed by stoning', 9 July. Available at: http://edition.cnn.com/2010/WORLD/meast/07/08/iran.stoning/ (accessed 10 July 2015).

Fletcher, M. (2010a). 'Death by stoning ordered for woman given ninety-nine lashes for alleged adultery: Iran', *The Times*, 7 July. Available at: Proquest Databases (accessed 15 May 2015).

Fletcher, M. (2010b). 'Bruni call to spare woman from stoning', *The Times*, 25 August. Available at: Proquest Databases (accessed 15 May 2015).

Fletcher, M. (2010c). 'Stop the stoning', *The Times*, 8 July. Available at: Proquest Databases (accessed 15 May 2015).

Fletcher, M. (2010d). 'Iranians back down', *The Times*, 9 July. Available at: Proquest Databases (accessed 15 May 2015).

Fletcher, M. (2010e). 'If Iran can stone her to death, it can get away with anything', *The Times*, 28 August. Available at: Proquest Databases (accessed 15 May 2015).

Fletcher, M. (2010f). 'One among hundreds, she now represents all victims', *The Times*, 28 August. Available at: Proquest Databases (accessed 15 May 2015).

Fletcher, M. and Bannerman, L. (2010). 'Iran is silent on fate of woman sentenced to death by stoning', *The Times*, 10 July. Available at: Proquest Databases (accessed 15 May 2015).

Fletcher, M. and Watson, R. (2010). 'Cameron attacks "inhuman" Iran over stoning', *The Times*, 16 September. Available at: Proquest Databases (accessed 15 May 2015).

Fraser, Christian (2010). ' "Carla Bruni is a prostitute", says Iranian newspaper', BBC News, 30 August. Available at: www.bbc.com/news/world-europe-11133178 (accessed 1 July 2015).

Kamali Dehghan, Saeed (2010). 'Sakineh Mohammadi Ashtiani "confesses" to involvement in murder on Iran state TV', *Guardian*, 11 August. Available at: www.theguardian.com/world/2010/aug/12/sakineh-mohammadi-ashtiani-confesses-murder-iran (accessed 10 July 2015).

Khamenei, Seyyed Ali (2015). 'To the youth in Europe and North America', khamenei.ir, 21 January. Available at: http://farsi.khamenei.ir/ndata/news/28731/index.html#en (accessed 13 July 2015).

McArthur, G. (2010). 'Women unite worldwide to save Iranian from execution', *Globe and Mail*, 9 July. Available at: LexisNexis Academic (accessed 1 July 2015).

Miskimmon, Alister, O'Loughlin, Ben and Roselle, Laura (2013). *Strategic Narratives: Communication Power and the New World Order*. New York: Routledge.

Mostafaei, Mohammad (2010). 'Responding to all the ambiguities and statements regarding the case of Sakine Mohammadi', modafe.com, 14 July. Available at: https://web.archive.org/web/20110621080250/http://modafe.com/NewsDetail.aspx?Id=421 (accessed 10 July 2015).

Nye, Joseph S. (1990). *Bound to Lead: The Changing Nature of American Power*. New York: Basic Books.

Price, Monroe E. (2015). *Free Expression, Globalism and the New Strategic Communication*. New York: Cambridge University Press.

Purcell, I. M. (2010). 'Iranian daily brands Bruni prostitute for opposing stoning', *The Times*, 30 August. Available at: Proquest Databases (accessed 15 May 2015).

Said, Edward (1978). *Orientalism*. New York: Vintage.

The Times (2010a). 'An act of barbarism', 8 July.

The Times (2010b). 'Stone cold shame', 9 July.

The Times (2010c). 'Defiance and delusion', 8 September.

The Times (2010d). 'The meaning of freedom', 10 December.

Tomlinson, Hugh (2014). 'Ashtiani freed after 9 years on death row', *The Times*, 19 March. Available at: www.thetimes.co.uk/tto/news/world/middleeast/article4037975.ece (accessed 10 July 2015).

Weber, Cynthia (2005). 'Not without my sister(s): imagining a moral America in Kandahar', *International Feminist Journal of Politics*, 7(3), 358–76.

Worth, Robert F. (2010). 'Crime (sex) and punishment (stoning)', *New York Times*, 21 August. Available at: www.nytimes.com/2010/08/22/weekinreview/22worth.html (accessed 29 June 2015).

Yong, William and Worth, Robert F. (2010). 'Iran shows what it says is murder confession', *New York Times*, 12 August. Available at: www.nytimes.com/2010/08/13/world/middleeast/13iran.html (accessed 29 June 2015).

9

Reporting Turkey

*Somewhere between the European Self and
the Oriental Other*

Birce Bora

East is East, and West is West
And never the twain shall meet.

(Rudyard Kipling)

Light cannot be defined without dark and good cannot be
defined without the existence of evil. Similarly, identities need
an opposite to define themselves.

(Paksoy, 2012: 67)

The idea of 'self's need for the other to exist' was first introduced by
Claude Lévi-Strauss in his book *Structural Anthropology* (1976) and
was developed by many others, including Hegel, Fichte, Sartre, Levinas
and Beauvoir. The concept has been studied in disciplines such as cultural studies, international relations, sociology, philosophy and history
(Criss, 2008).

But it was Edward Said who made the process of 'othering' a major
topic of discussion in European identity formation and representation of
Oriental cultures in the West, by claiming that the traditional idea of a
European identity, a European Self, that emerges from the idea of a common history, culture and morality was in need of an opposite against which

to define itself (Kösebalaban, 2007) and it used (and is still using) the Orient as this opposite, or 'Other' (Bryce, 2009a; Hall, 1995; Kösebalaban, 2007; Neumann, 1996; Neumann and Welsh, 1991; Robins, 1996; Said, 2003; Strasser, 2008; Tekin, 2008)

European nations defined the similarities that make them 'one' by defining their differences with nations of the East (and their most obvious commonality, 'Islam'). Europe differentiated itself from the Other, and that Other, in turn, consolidated the European identity (Neumann and Welsh, 1991). So, the civilised, moral and superior 'European Self' came into existence by defining the underdeveloped, passive and immature Orient (Aissaoui, 2007; Amin, 1989; Bhabha, 1990; Hall, 1997; Harasym, 1990; Hobson, 2004; Landry, 2011; Said, 2003, 1997; Spivak, 1988; Young, 1990).

Said formulated this idea by redefining the word Orientalism as the acceptance in the West of 'the basic distinction between East and West as the starting point for elaborate theories, epics, novels, social descriptions and political accounts concerning the Orient, its people, customs, "mind," destiny and so on' (Said, 2003: 4).

According to Said (2003) there are three separate designs of 'Orientalism', or in other words 'ways of dealing with the Orient': academic, imaginative and historic. While academic Orientalism is to Said what 'anyone who teaches, writes about, or researches the Orient either in its specific or its general aspects' does, he defines imaginative Orientalism as the works of novelists, philosophers, poets, theorists, painters and musicians (Said, 2003: 3).

The third meaning is defined as historical material. This is Orientalism as 'something more historically and materially defined than either of the other two'. Taking the late eighteenth century as a roughly defined starting point, he discusses and analyses Orientalism as 'the corporate institution for dealing with the Orient – dealing with it by making statements about it, authorizing views of it, describing it, by teaching it, settling it, ruling over it' (Said, 2003: 3).

These three different designs of Orientalism are all interdependent, and European or Western journalism is under the influence of all the types of Orientalist thinking since it is a product created by Europeans, for Europeans, that frequently deals with the Orient.

Today, Western media are labelling Muslims as 'intolerant, misogynistic, violent or cruel, and finally, strange or different' on a regular basis (Whitaker, 2002: 55; see also Amel et al., 2007)

So Orientalism has a 'central importance for an investigation of representations of the Islamic other as the cultural contestant against which "the West" first had to define itself' (Bryce, 2009b: 67, see also Kösebalaban, 2007: 97; Paksoy, 2012: 67).

Said's Orientalism is also a tool commonly used for analysing European media's representation of the Turk and Turkey (Akca and Yılmaztürk, 2006; Bryce, 2007; Devran, 2007; Kejanlıoğlu and Taş, 2009; Oktem, 2005). Yet there are also some doubts about Turkey's appropriateness as Europe's Oriental Other.

It is unanimously accepted that the Turk was one of the most dominant Others in the history of European identity creation (Delanty, 1995; Kylstad, 2010; Neumann, 1999), since there were several reasons for Europe to see the Turk, or the Ottoman, as an important Other:

> The Ottoman had the military might, physical proximity, and a strong religious tradition that made it a particularly relevant other in the evolution of the fledgling international society that evolved from the ashes of Western Christendom and that took up a pivotal position in the forging of European identities. From the fourteenth century to nineteenth century, Ottoman Empire occupied and controlled a quarter of the European continent, comprising some of the Europe's most coveted territory. (Neumann, 1999: 40)

Yet it is not possible to say that Turkey was ever a straightforward Other to the West (Çirakman, 2005; Findlay, 2005; İnalcık, 1994):

> The West's historical relationship with Turkey has been characterized by an inability to appropriate it materially or indeed discursively with any degree of assurance. Western travellers in the Ottoman Empire over several centuries referred to its Islamic and Oriental 'otherness' while also admiring aspects of its political and social organization and were obliged to deal with it, functionally, as one of the great states of Europe. (Bryce, 2007: 181).

This two-sidedness to the Turk's identity in the eyes of Europeans became even more apparent in the nineteenth century (Neumann, 1999). For the first time, in 1856 with the treaty of Paris, the Ottoman Empire was recognised as a permanent part of the European power balance. And the treaty, which gave the Ottoman Empire a right to benefit from international law and the Concert of Europe,[1] somehow included the Other into the Self (Neumann, 1999). During the same period the Ottoman effort to become European also escalated. And with the creation of the secular, Western-minded Turkish republic in 1923 and the Turkish application to join the European Union, this complex relationship between identities made the Turk's status as the European Other somewhat questionable.

This caused several pertinent criticisms against the use of Said's *Orientalism* as a theoretical base for analysing Turkish representation in the European media.

Critics of applying Said's theories to the case of Turkish media representation in the West argue that discussions in Said's work about Turkey or the Ottoman Empire are limited, and it is even possible to say that he purposefully ignored Turkey's case because it may have weakened his claims about Western othering towards the Orient (Bryce, 2009b: 112).

With its Westernisation efforts, secular constitution, European aspirations, NATO membership and geographical proximity, Turkey does not fit into the static description of the Oriental Other presented by Said, and as a result is not treated as such by the West. But this does not mean representations of Turkey in the West are immune to Orientalism and, in a more general sense, othering.[2]

It is true that Turkey, a predominantly Muslim country and the successor of the main European Other, the 'Ottoman Empire', is often presented as 'an ally, a NATO member, an EU candidate' or the 'good', 'model' or even the 'tame' Muslim country.[3] Looking at these 'positive' representations of Turkey, it is easy to reach to the conclusion that the country is a strong example for the inadequacy of Orientalist theory in explaining the representation of Islam and the Orient in the Western media.

But, as Milica Bakić-Hayden explained in her 1995 article titled 'Nesting Orientalisms: the case of former Yugoslavia', Self and other relationships and Orientalism are in fact not static but gradual:

> Asia is more 'East' or 'other' than Eastern Europe; within Eastern Europe itself this gradation is reproduced with the Balkans perceived as most 'eastern'; within the Balkans there are similarly constructed hierarchies. (Bakić-Hayden, 1995: 918)

And if we extend this gradation to Europe's external Others in the Middle East and beyond, we can see that modern Turkey, as a result of its Westernisation efforts, secular nature and geographical proximity, is also a 'lesser' Other to Europe than its Middle Eastern neighbours.

Turkey is not a straightforward member of either European or Oriental civilisation and thus it is not a straightforward Other to Europe. Turkey is a 'torn' country, as Huntington puts it (1993), between Orient and Occident, and the way it is perceived and represented in the Western media is also affected by this fact. While being presented as the 'good' or even 'model' Muslim country, Turkey is also being Orientalised in many ways in Western media texts.

This chapter will analyse Turkish representation in the Western media using the concepts of othering and Orientalism, and will try to determine whether Westernised, secular and allegedly European Turkey is being included in to the European Self,[4] or whether it is still being othered and, as Said puts it, Orientalised as a result of its religion, cultural heritage and history.

While arguing that Turkey is situated somewhere between 'the European Self' and the 'Oriental Other', this chapter will seek to understand how this unique position is affecting the way Turkey is being covered by the Western media.

The analysis will be conducted on articles about Turkey published in four British broadsheets (*The Times, Daily Telegraph, Independent, Guardian*) and their sister Sunday papers (*Sunday Times, Sunday Telegraph, Independent on Sunday,* and *Observer*) between 2007 and 2013.[5]

Othering Turkey by Excluding it from the 'Self' in Media Narratives

As Coleman and Ross pointed out in their book *The Media and the Public: 'Them' and 'Us' in Media Discourse*, media narratives are based on an 'us vs. them' dichotomy that reflects the concepts of Self and Other (Coleman and Ross, 2010: 135).

In media narratives, the first-person plural pronoun is used to refer to the 'Self', but this 'Self' can represent different identities in different contexts.

While reporting on domestic affairs, media outlets generally only refer to a small section of the public (that they identify as their target audience) as 'us' and hence present it as the 'Self'. For British broadsheets that group is the educated, tax-paying, predominantly white and Christian middle class. For example, they rarely refer to British Muslims, immigrants or people living in municipal housing (public housing) as 'us' even though these groups constitute a large percentage of the British population (Coleman and Ross, 2010: 135–6).

Yet, in news items about Britain's foreign affairs, the British media stretches the first-person plural to embrace the whole of the British public, European community and in some cases the entire 'Western civilisation'.

In news items about Britain's relations with the European Union, media outlets use the first-person plural pronoun to refer to the British public' and 'Britain' in general, but in news items about the country's relations with, for example, Syria, 'us' can refer to a large range of allies and 'friends'.

As a result, in many narratives dealing with international affairs, 'us' becomes an entity that is based on a certain set of values and alliances. And since the use of the first-person plural is a clear indication of who and what is included in the 'Self' in that given context, one wonders if Turkey, an important ally and economic partner, ever gets to be included in it.

As seen in the editorials published about Turkey between 2007 and 2013, British broadsheets constantly claim Turkey should be seen as a European country.[6] They emphasise Turkey's importance for the region, underline the fact that Turkey and rest of the European Union are bound together by shared interests (*Daily Telegraph* – Miliband, 2007) and criticise France and Germany for alienating the Turks by blocking their EU membership bid (*The Times* – Straw, 2011; *Daily Telegraph* – Hannan, 2010). Also, the most common adjective they use in their coverage to define directly Turkey is 'ally'.

Yet, if we look at the general narrative closely, we see that Turkey is never included in the first-person plural, and as a result the European or the Western 'Self'. Just to give some examples: the *Daily Telegraph* once said 'Turkey's role in the flotilla affair should worry *us* all in the West' (Coughlin, 2010); while the *Guardian*, commenting on the Syrian civil war, stated that 'There is a moral case for intervention, but with *the West* reluctant, Turkey and other powers will be the ones to decide' (Ash, 2012).

These narratives, like many others, plainly draw a line between 'the West' which is the 'Self' (us) and Turkey, the 'Other' (them). They make it clear that even though Turkey is an ally, it is not a part of *them*. And even when Turkey's former president Abdullah Gül said 'There is no reason to have doubts about Turkey, we are European', *The Times* went with the subhead 'President Gül assures Martin Fletcher and Suna Erdem that the West can trust its *powerful Islamic ally*' (Fletcher and Suna, 2010, emphasis added).

This attitude shows that even when the highest-ranking representative of the Turkish republic openly declares the country to be European, or acts as an ally, it is never included in the European or Western 'Self' in British media narratives.

Western civilisation's reluctance to include Turkey in the Self was most obvious in 2007, when Turkey decided to launch a cross-border attack into Iraq under the banner of the so-called 'war on terror'.

The British media, who supported Turkey's EU membership bid and classified the country as an important strategic ally (alongside other Western media organisations), started to question the legitimacy of Turkey's involvement in the Self and its desire to wage its own 'war against terrorism'.

Slavoj Žižek, international director of the Birkbeck Institute for the Humanities, explained this in a commentary for the *Guardian*:

> With the likelihood of Turkey launching a cross-border attack under the banner of the war on terror growing by the minute, it is as if an intruder has gate-crashed the closed circle of 'we', the domain of those who hold the de facto monopoly on military humanitarianism. What makes the situation unpleasant is not Turkey's 'otherness', but its claim to sameness. What such a situation reveals is the set of unwritten rules and silent prohibitions that qualifies the 'we' of the enlightened humanity. (Žižek, 2007)

In other words, Turkey was an ally, a partner and even a possible future EU member, but at its core it was not a part of the European or Western Self that can participate in 'military humanitarianism'. That kind of action was reserved for the European/Western Self.

Differentiating Turkey from the European Self by excluding it from the first-person plural in the coverage is a powerful proof for Turkey's status as the 'Other' in the British media coverage. It shows that Turkey, while being a 'lesser' Other, which is in the periphery of the Self, is still not being seen as an acceptable member of the so-called civilised world or European/Western identity by the British media.

This attitude was also prominent in the coverage of Turkey's EU membership bid between 2007 and 2013. French and German media outlets oppose Turkey's membership bid, claiming that Turkey is not European (or in other words 'part of the European Self') and hence should not be in the European Union. On the other hand, British media, following British foreign policy, gave their full support to Turkey's membership bid between 2007 and 2013.

But the British media's support for Turkish accession during this period was not an indication of their belief that Turkey can ever be a part of the European identity or in other words, the European Self. Rather, it was just another indication of how they see Turkey as an Other.

Othering Turkey in the Coverage of EU Membership Negotiations

In 2010, within three months of becoming the British prime minister, David Cameron visited the Turkish capital, Ankara. When asked 'Why Turkey?' and, 'Why so soon?' he said: 'Because Turkey is vital for our economy, vital for our security and vital for our politics and our diplomacy' (Cabinet Office et al., 2010).

After acknowledging Turkey's importance for Britain with this grand gesture, the prime minister continued to show his support to the country by promising to 'fight' for its membership to the European Union. He even claimed that a European Union without Turkey at its heart was 'not stronger but weaker [...] not more secure but less [...] not richer but poorer' (Cabinet Office et al., 2010).

Cameron's support for Turkey's European aspirations was simply a continuation of longstanding British foreign policy. Britain has been a strong supporter of Turkey's European Union membership bid since it applied to accede to the European Economic Community, the predecessor of the European Union, on 14 April 1987.[7]

News items about Turkey's membership bid published in the British media between 2007 and 2013 show that British broadsheets, liberal and conservative alike, followed the prime minister's lead in showing support for Turkey's accession to the European Union.

For example, the *Guardian*, in a leader titled 'Turkey: a vital player', said 'Mr Cameron is fundamentally right to keep hammering away at what much of the Europe now considers a lost cause: Turkey's membership of the EU' (*Telegraph View*, 2010). Similarly *The Times* stated, 'The EU carrot doesn't look that tasty, but it's in everyone's interest for Ankara to take it' (Senior, 2010), and in an editorial titled 'Stabilising Turkey' the *Daily Telegraph*, rather directly, said 'This newspaper has long supported Turkey's European ambitions' (Telegraph View, 2010).

Yet, while their unanimous support for the membership bid shows that British broadsheets wanted to see Turkey in the European Union, it does not necessarily mean that they perceived Turkey as a 'European country' or a part of the 'European Self'.

Britain's support for the Turkish accession is based on the country's functionalist view of the European Union and does not necessarily mean that it perceives Turkey as an integral part of the European identity, and British broadsheets seem to be on the same page as their government on this issue.[8]

British media outlets used several arguments in their narratives to support Turkey's accession to the European Union, but none of these arguments actually portray Turkey as a part of the European Self. In their coverage, British broadsheets mainly argued that they are supporting Turkish accession because it may change the identity of the European Union itself, to the benefit of Britain.

British governments have long been opposed to the idea of a federal Europe (an attitude which goes hand in hand with the essentialist approach to European integration), in which Brussels will have more power than national governments. British broadsheets (especially the conservative ones, which are more Eurosceptic in nature) also supported this line of thought in their narratives, and their fierce opposition to a 'federal Europe' played a significant role in their undisputable support for Turkey's EU membership bid.

They claimed that Turkey's accession to the European Union would not validate its identity as a European nation but instead would make the European Union a weaker and looser free trade area. In an editorial published in 2008, the *Daily Telegraph* explained this by saying Turkey's accession to the EU 'would also help Europe move towards a broader and looser free trade area and away from the top down, over regulated super state dreamed of by the Brussels establishment' (Telegraph View, 2008).

Also, again in line with the functionalist approach to European integration, British broadsheets based most of their arguments on Turkey's value as a political, economic and military ally, and underlined the role of Turkey as a 'bridge' between Europe and the Middle East.

Yet, while making these points, none of the British broadsheets ever claimed that Turkey is a part of the shared history, culture or values that shape modern European identity, and they never openly declared Turkey to be 'a European country'. For example, while commenting on Turkey's possible EU membership the *Daily Telegraph* said:

> The country [Turkey] is demonstrating its usefulness to the West in myriad ways – providing a link to less sympathetic nations in the Middle East, such as Iran; remaining a faithful member of NATO and supplier of troops in Afghanistan and playing a crucial role in the development of secure energy routes [...] the West should do its utmost to ensure our friend and ally remains a stable, democratic and prosperous nation. The best way to do that is to push forward the accession talks. (*Daily Telegraph*, 2010)

In this editorial, the *Daily Telegraph* clearly showed that it strongly backed Turkey's EU membership bid, just like the British government. But, the argument to do so was based on Turkey's *usefulness for the EU* rather than its belongingness to it. In other words, the *Daily Telegraph* was welcoming a treasured ally into a political and economic union, but not into the European identity.[9]

In their coverage, British broadsheets were also pointing out that 'Muslim' Turkey's accession to the European Union would be highly beneficial in ensuring the peace and stability of the European community. Broadsheets used narratives indicating that they saw Turkey as a 'model' Muslim nation, which does not participate in 'Islamic extremism' and is eager to adjust itself to Western values. They argued that Turkey could be a useful 'bridge' between two conflicting civilisations.[10]

The Times columnist Antonia Senior explained this in a 2010 commentary titled 'Frenemy or enemy Turkey should be in Europe' (Senior, 2010):

> You can see it [Turkish accession] as a way for moderate, secular but nominally Christian states to extend a hand of friendship to a moderate, Islamic but nominally secular, state. Alternatively, you can take the view that Islam is an implacable enemy of Western values [...] But even if you take this line, Turkish membership of the EU is still the answer [...] It can only aid European relations with the rest of the Islamic world if we build a close fraternal bond with Turkey.

In her article, Senior strongly supported Turkey's accession to the EU, on the basis that Turkey is 'the model Muslim country' or the 'best in a bad bunch'. Yet, she did not even hint at Turkey's Europeanness. As the use of the words 'Frenemy or enemy' in the title indicates, she was still presenting Turkey as an Other.

In her conclusion she even stated that Turkey's accession to the European Union could be seen as '[either] binding the bastards closer, or embracing your Muslim brothers' (Senior, 2010), further illustrating the fact that Turkey is either a 'Muslim' ally or a straightforward enemy, but never a 'European brother' or a part of the European Self in the eyes of the British media.

All in all, British broadsheets' positive attitude towards Turkey's eventual accession to the EU cannot be interpreted as a sign of their acceptance of Turkey into the European Self.

The narratives used in the coverage regarding Turkey's European Union bid indicate that the British media perceive and present Turkey as a *useful* and *necessary* Other but not as a part of the European Self.

As explained above, arguments against Turkey's EU membership bid (as well as some arguments that are supportive of accession) focus on Turkey's Muslim identity, but this focus also affects the rest of the Turkish coverage.

Islam is still the quality that unifies the Oriental Other in the eyes of Western civilisation (Just like Judeo-Christian heritage is still a unifying factor for the European Self/European identity), and Turkey's Muslim identity affects the way it is represented and othered in British media texts.

Othering Turkey by Emphasising its Religious Identity

According to the 'Turkish Religious Life' report published by the Turkish Directorate of Religious Affairs in 2014, 99.2 per cent of the Turkish public defines themselves as 'Muslim' (Turkish Directorate of Religious Affairs, 2014). So it is a fact that Turkey has a predominantly Muslim population. Yet, since the annulment of the constitutional clause that states, 'The religion of the state is Islam' in 1928, and the addition of the adjective 'secular' to the definition of the Turkish state in the constitution in 1937, Turkey officially is a secular country (Tanör, 2014).

Since the British media almost never refers to Greece (98 per cent Christian according to the CIA Fact Book), Italy (80 per cent Christian) or Poland (89.3 per cent Christian) as 'Christian nations' when covering news events related to them, it is intriguing to see that a quarter of the adjectives directly towards defining the republic of Turkey were based on religion.[11]

In their coverage of Turkey, even when they were presenting the country as an important ally or a welcomed edition to the European Union, British journalists kept reminding their audiences that Turkey is an 'Islamic nation.'

Adjectives like 'overwhelmingly Muslim', 'predominantly Muslim' and 'Islamic' were scattered in the narrative, and labels and definitions like 'Muslim democracy' (*The Times* – Halpin, 2010), 'Muslim inspired democracy' (*The Times* – Bremner, 2010), 'tame Islamists' (*Guardian* – Tisdall, 2010), 'chief Muslim democracy' (*Daily Telegraph* – Telegraph View, 2010), 'moderate Islamic State' (*Independent* – Cockburn, 2012) and 'Nato's Muslim ally' (*The Times*, 2013) were commonly used throughout the coverage.

It can be argued that by stating Turkey is not simply a 'democracy' or an 'ally' but a 'Muslim or Islamic' one, British journalists implied that even though Turkey is on 'their' side, it is still fundamentally different to Europe and as a result they underlined Turkey's 'Otherness' against British and European selves (Devran, 2007: 13).

Of course, this chapter does not claim that the labels and definitions about Turkey's religious identity should have been completely omitted from the coverage, since the emphasis on Turkey's religion in certain stories, which are directly dealing with issues related to Islam, is understandable and even necessary. For example, it would be unreasonable to expect the British media (or any media), to cover news items about the secular–Islamist divide in Turkish politics or the developments on the headscarf ban in Turkish universities without pointing out the dominant religion in the country. Also, it cannot be denied that under the government of the AK Parti (Justice and Development Party, known for the Turkish abbreviation AKP), religion became a more substantial part of the daily political discussions in Turkey.

Yet, these religion-based adjectives, labels and definitions also pop up in the coverage of subjects that have no relevance to the dominant religion in the country. For example, in an article published in the *Daily Telegraph* about US President Barack Obama's planned visit to Turkey in 2009, the title 'Obama reaches out to Muslims with Turkey visit' was used. The introduction of the article said 'President Barack Obama will seek to extend America's key alliances beyond Europe by using a visit next month to Turkey, which is ruled by a moderate Islamic party, to court the Muslim world' (*Daily Telegraph*, 2009).

The rest of the article clearly states that Obama never talked about 'courting the Muslim world via Turkey' and the White House clearly denied any suggestion that he may give a speech to 'Muslim crowds' in İstanbul. Yet, instead of presenting the story as what it is: 'American president Barack Obama is going to make a planned visit to Turkey, a long term American ally', the *Daily Telegraph* chose to use the words 'Islam' and 'Muslim' five times in the first paragraphs of the article.

While the unnecessary emphasis on Turkey's religious identity in the article can be seen as a sign of Oriental Othering on its own, there are several other complementary examples of Orientalism in the 'religion-based' narrative of this news item.

First of all, the article claims that 'President Barack Obama will seek to extend America's key alliances beyond Europe', and places Turkey outside of the European region. This particular news item was published in the *Daily Telegraph*, a news outlet that clearly stated that it supports Turkey's European ambitions and wants to see the country in the EU (Telegraph View, 2010). But the narrative used in the article shows that even though the media outlet supports Turkey's EU bid and claims to see it as an essential part of Europe, it does not in any way perceive 'Muslim' Turkey as a part of the European Self/identity or as a country that is in fact 'in Europe'. In a way, the reporter uses Turkey's religious identity to differentiate it from the 'genuinely' European countries.

Furthermore, the article assumes that a speech directed to the Turkish public will be the equivalent of 'courting the Muslim world'. According to the numbers provided by the Pew Research Center, as of 2010 there are 1.6 billion Muslims in the world, constituting 23.4 per cent of the planet's total population (Pew Research Center, 2011). The Muslim world includes a variety of people from Indonesia to Iran, Saudi Arabia to Lebanon, who have significantly different cultures, worldviews, political interests and views about the United States and its president. Turkey is home to more than 80 million Muslims but it is not in any way the representative of the 'Muslim world' on its own. Claiming that the American president will be courting a quarter of the world's population by giving a speech in Turkey (a speech that most certainly would not be about Islam or the USA's relations with Islam, but about the USA's strategic partnership with a secular country) is a clear example of how the media ignores the particularities of different Muslim nations and perceives them as a singular homogenous entity.

In his book *Covering Islam*, Said also touched upon this particularity of the Western media by stating '[in the Western media] "Islam" seems to engulf all aspects of the diverse Muslim world, reducing them all to a special malevolent and unthinking essence. Instead of analysis and understanding, as a result, there can be for the most part only the crudest form of us-versus-them' (Said, 1997: 117).

In other words, labels like 'Muslim' or 'Islam' carry deeper meanings than just a religious identity for the Western media, and in fact they show a country, a nation or an individual's place in the Self–Other axis. By unnecessarily underlining Turkey's religious identity in news items that have no relevance to religion, the British media is including Turkey in an Orientalist discourse that uses labels about Islam to bind the highly diverse

Muslim nations and communities together and consequently present them as a singular Oriental Other.

This can be seen clearly in the coverage of negative news events regarding the 'Muslim world' in the Western media. As Said discussed in *Covering Islam*, atrocities committed in any country with a Muslim population or a government are reported in the Western media with an emphasis on religion, while similar acts in the Western world are never connected to Christianity:

> Of course no one has equated the Jonestown massacre or the destructive horror of the Oklahoma bombing or the devastation of Indochina with Christianity, or with Western cultures at large; that sort of equation has been reserved for Islam. (Said, 1997: 117)

This can also be observed in the British media's coverage of Turkey. For example, in an article about the Armenian genocide published by *The Times*, the atrocities committed by the Ottoman Empire at the beginning of the twentieth century were explained with the phrase 'Christian Armenians living in what was eastern Anatolia died in blood-letting by Muslim Ottoman troops' (*The Times*, 2010c).

By emphasising the fact that Armenians are 'Christian' while Ottomans are 'Muslim', this atrocity was presented as an example of 'Islamic' violence towards Christians. Since this massacre was not committed in the name of religion and was actually ordered by nationalist leaders from the Young Turk movement, the emphasis on the religious identity of the Ottoman Empire in the coverage of the Armenian genocide is unjustifiable. It is not common ground in the Western media (and rightfully so) to claim the Holocaust is a 'Christian' crime. They don't refer to Nazis as 'Christians' in media narratives, even though the Nazi party was endorsing 'positive Christianity' to combat the so-called 'Jewish materialist spirit' (Noakes and Pridham, 1974).

Thus, it can be argued that the emphasis on the Ottoman Empire or Turkey's religious identity in the coverage of the Armenian genocide is another sign of the Western media's tendency to present the Muslim world as a singular, interconnected and homogenous Oriental Other, especially when it comes to negative occurrences. Also, this type of coverage shows that Turkey, as a result of its Islamic identity, is seen and presented as a part of the Oriental Other and not the European Self in the British media.

But as explained above, Turkey is not a straightforward Islamic Other to Europe or the West. Turkey, as a result of its relatively well-functioning democracy, secular constitution and non-violent brand of political Islam, is frequently referred to as a 'Muslim model' in the British media. This label, while being positive on the surface, causes Turkey to be Orientalised by the West. The effect of this discourse has led to the othering of Turkey.

Othering Turkey by Presenting it as a Model 'Bonne pour l'Orient'

In the twenty-first century, Turkey under AKP rule has been frequently defined as a 'Muslim model for the Middle East' in Western narratives. For years, at least until the Gezi Park uprising in mid-2013, this narrative was commonplace in Western political discussions, academic articles and media texts.[12]

Discussions about the legitimacy of the Turkish model are ongoing in the West, Turkey and the Middle East.[13] But this narrative also has a prominent effect on the way Turkey is represented in the Western media.

Representations of Turkey as a 'model' Muslim democracy for the Middle Eastern region seem to be positive and even complimentary for the country on the surface; yet these narratives also carry an Orientalist mindset.

This narrative causes Turkey to be represented as a 'model Other' in media texts: an Other that is more friendly and even represents the Western perception of an 'ideal' Islamic society, but still perceived as inferior and less civilised compared to the (European) Self.

First of all, democracy is a secular concept at its core and describing Turkey, a secular country, as a model *Muslim* democracy instead of just a model democracy implies that it is not being viewed as a 'proper' democracy and differentiates it from Western democracies as a somewhat lesser variation. Also, it implies that Muslim nations are only capable of achieving a religion-based, 'modified' version of democracy and reduces the discussions about democratisation of the Middle Eastern region to religion (Gürsel, 2011; Mert, 2011; Musil, 2011; *Guardian*, 2007).

As Musil states, the narratives that present Turkey as a 'model' for the Middle East

> indirectly supports the opinion that Islam is a barrier that needs to be overcome in democratization efforts and that is what Turkey has managed to do. It simplifies the democracy problem of the Arab world by downgrading the causes of authoritarianism to Islam. (Musil, 2011: 15)

Kadri Gürsel also touches upon this subject in his article for the *Turkish Policy Quarterly* entitled 'Who wants a Muslim democracy?' and asks:

> Why would the inventors of the 'Turkish model' not suggest to the Muslim Middle-East a much more developed and complete model such as the ones that American, British, German or other consolidated democracies are based on? (Gürsel, 2011)

In his answer to this question he believes this attitude is the result of the West's Orientalist perception of the Middle East. He also argues that the West is presenting Turkish democracy as a model for the Middle East, because it perceives Turkish democracy (even though it is not from any point of view perfect or complete) as being 'Bon pour l'Orient' (good enough for the Orient).

'Bon pour l'Orient' is a French term referring to the stamps affixed to the diplomas of colonial students (and also some coming from the Ottoman territories) subjected to a less intensive level of education in Western educational institutions. These diplomas, which were useless in Europe, were good enough to get employment in colonial territories.

And this term perfectly describes the perception of Turkey, and also Turkish democracy, in the West as a 'model Other' since it is possible to say that, in Western eyes, Turkey is an Oriental model that is 'good enough for the Orient'.

Turkey's role as the 'Muslim model for the Middle East' directly influences the perception of Turkey in the British media. This narrative causes some British media outlets, as a result of their commitment to Turkey's role as a model Other against more Islamic, more threatening and more problematic Others to its east, to condone some developments in the country that would be seen as unacceptable in a proper, European, liberal democracy (Karli, 2007).

175

This attitude can be seen most clearly in the coverage of the criticisms directed at the AKP government in Turkey before the Gezi Park uprising in 2013. Until the Gezi Park uprising, the British media embraced a supportive narrative towards the AKP, even though they perceived the party as being the representative of political Islam, an ideology that they normally present as an Other. They chose to defend the AKP as a shining example of a 'tame' and 'benign', 'model' of political Islam and classify any criticism regarding their commitment to democracy, human rights and secularism as 'exaggerations'.

For example, in an article examining 'the model Muslim democracy' or 'Democracy alla Turca [*sic*]' created by the AKP in Turkey, the *Economist* said:

> Life has been made easier for pious Muslims in ways that secular Turks dislike; but so far, at least, Turkey is a long way from any Iranian-style enforcement of female dress, let alone a clerical class that has the final say in all big decisions. (*Economist*, 2011)

In other words, instead of discussing the situation of rights and freedoms in Turkey through the criteria to which they subject Britain or any other Western democracy, they preferred to dismiss criticisms and warnings about the AKP's conservative policies on the grounds that the situation in Turkey is 'not as bad as Iran' or 'good enough' compared to some other countries in the region. Mert (2011) responded to the *Economist* article and similar narratives used by other Western media outlets in late 2000s by saying:

> There is a disturbing connection between the idea of 'democracy à la Turca' and 'democracy bon pour l'Orient'. It sounds as if Westerners preach us to stop complaining and stop asking for more, but to confine ourselves to the limits of the Turkish model. Moreover it implies that, although it is no proper definition of democracy, this is more than enough for the Turks, Muslims or Orientals! In this respect, it is a new version of Orientalism that reinvented itself in multiculturalist lines.

This attitude was also apparent in the *Guardian*'s 2007 leader titled 'Islam and democracy' which was discussing Turkish army and secular concerns about Abdullah Gül, Recep Tayyip Erdoğan and the AKP's alleged 'Islamist agenda'. After listing these concerns and criticisms, the broadsheet said that 'From a European liberal perspective, some of this is worrying, but in parts of the Middle East – among reformers in Egypt, for example – it is often seen as a model', and they concluded the article by indicating that the illiberal actions of the AKP government should not be condemned (*Guardian*, 2007).

In other words, the news outlet openly argued that some allegedly illiberal actions of the AKP and its leaders, which were unacceptable for a Western liberal democracy, were 'good enough' for a 'Muslim democracy' like Turkey.

This entails a deep Orientalist mindset, which implies that a Muslim society cannot be (or should not aspire to be) as liberal as a European one. These narratives show that Turkey, even though it is a 'lesser' and 'more acceptable' other in the eyes of the British press compared to the rest of the Muslim world, is still not being treated as an equal.

Conclusion

Turkey is a country that is in the headlines all around the world nearly every day, not only because it has a strategic location between Europe and the Middle East, but also as a result of its unique condition as a predominantly Muslim country that has a relatively well-functioning, fundamentally secular democracy.

As explained above in detail, the British media's perception and representation of Turkey, due to its unique position between the European Self and the Oriental Other, is more positive compared to their perception and representation of Islam and predominantly Muslim countries in general. Yet, it is not completely free of othering and Orientalism.

Today, Orientalism is being seen (and is actively being used) by the Turkish government as a way to brush off any Western criticism towards Turkey. While arguing that any negative comment about Turkey coming from the West is a baseless Orientalist defamation is unacceptable, this does not mean Orientalism does not affect the coverage of Turkey in the Western media.

Orientalism is not a static, meaningless hatred or a baseless criticism, but rather a general, patronising Western attitude towards Oriental societies. And this patronising attitude is very much present in the British media's representation of Turkey.

Between 2007 and 2013, Turkey was presented as a 'lesser' or a 'model' Other in British media texts. It wasn't seen as being 'civilised' enough to be accepted into the first-person plural, but it was presented as a 'good enough' model for the rest of the Middle East.

This narrative, which was rooted in the idea that Muslim nations should be evaluated by lower standards than their Western counterparts, reduced the diverse Muslim world to a singular and homogenous mass that should be content with a lower grade of democracy, represented by Turkey. Also, it caused the British media to gloss over the illiberal and anti-democratic attitudes of the Turkish government and dismiss criticisms coming from Turkish seculars as exaggerations.

Today, in the post-Gezi Park era, it is commonly accepted that the idea of a 'Turkish model' is losing ground, as the Turkish government is becoming more and more authoritarian and less accommodating to Western interests and ideals.

This gives an opportunity to Western journalists to evaluate their perception of Turkey and to create a new, more accurate and more just representation of the country that won't Orientalise it by assuming it should be subjected to lower standards regarding its democracy.

Also, to be able to provide accurate coverage of the Middle East, journalists need to be willing to step out of the us vs them dichotomy when reporting on the region, and refrain from seeing and presenting Turkey as a model 'Bonne pour l'Orient'.

Notes

1. The Concert of Europe (the Vienna system of international relations), also known as the Congress System after the Congress of Vienna, represented the balance of power that existed in Europe from the end of the Napoleonic Wars (1815) to the outbreak of World War I (1914).
2. Othering is any action by which an individual or group becomes mentally classified in somebody's mind as 'not one of us' (that group or individual is classified as being in some way less human, and less worthy of respect than 'we' are). On the other hand, Orientalism is a specific term coined by Said to define the othering of the Orient (Asia, especially the Middle East) by the Occident.

3. Quantitative analysis of 731 news items published in four British broadsheets and their Sunday sister papers (*The Times*, *Guardian*, *Daily Telegraph* and *Independent*) between 2007 and 2013 showed that the most common adjective used to define Turkey was 'ally'. The country was frequently described as a 'regional ally of the West', a 'Nato ally' or 'Europe and US ally in the region'. The second set of adjectives that were frequently used to define the country were based on its religious identity, such as 'Muslim' and 'Islamic'. Turkey was also, very occasionally, defined as a 'secular' country. Yet, the ratio between the adjectives that emphasise Turkey's religion and its secular nature was approximately 2 to 1, indicating that Turkey was mostly categorised as a Muslim nation. The fact that Turkey was referred to as an ally above anything else shows that the country was represented as a positive actor in British media texts. Yet, the strong emphasis on Turkey's religion (and the relatively low interest in the country's secular nature) indicated that Turkey's status as an 'Islamic Other' was also prominent in the coverage. Quantitative analysis showed that the emphasis on religion was even higher in adjectives/labels that were used to define the AKP and Turkish Prime Minister Recep Tayyip Erdoğan. Overall, 67 per cent of the adjectives that were used to define the AKP and Erdoğan in British media texts were based on religion. This finding demonstrates that the Turkish government and the Prime Minister were presented as 'Muslims' above anything else, even though they were identifying themselves as conservative democrats. Over all, solely looking at the adjectives/labels that were used to define Turkey and its government in British media texts, it can be argued that the country was presented as an ally and a positive actor, but that it was not perceived as a part or even an extension of the European Self.

4. In this chapter, as explained previously, the term 'European Self' is used to describe the European identity, or the concept of Europeanness that started to materialise when nations in continental Europe and Britain formed their allegedly more civilised and superior collective identity against the 'Barbaric' Oriental Other. This identity differs from the EU and what it represents, since it was formed centuries prior to the formation of a politically or economically united Europe under the EU banner (Kösebalaban, 2007; Said, 2003).

5. The British media provides a particularly good research sample for understanding Turkish representation and Turkey's place in the European Self–Other axis, because unlike other European countries, Britain itself has an exceptionalist attitude towards the European identity. And this attitude is reflected in the British media's representation of Turkey. Unlike media outlets in the rest of Europe, they unanimously support Turkey's EU membership bid and frequently claim that 'Turkey should be a part of Europe', while simultaneously othering Islam in their narratives. But it needs to be noted that this chapter is focusing on the representation of Turkey in the British media from 2007 to 2013, a period prior to the start of EU membership discussions and

consequently a more aggressive representation of Turkey's EU membership ambitions.

6. This attitude, of course, changed significantly prior to the EU referendum debate in Britain in 2016. During this period, British politicians and the British media withdrew their support for Turkey's EU bid.

7. While Britain stood firmly with Turkey for nearly three decades, other member states like Germany, France and the Netherlands openly objected to the country's European aspirations. In June 2013, in the wake of Ankara's fierce crackdown on the Gezi Park uprising, Germany blocked the start of new EU accession talks with Turkey (Traynor and Letsch, 2013). However, in 2016, prior to Britain's EU referendum, British politicians and the British media changed their attitude towards Turkey's EU bid completely.

8. Britain fully embraces the Kantian understanding of the EU identity and differentiates it fully from the historico-cultural and religious European identity. On the other hand, Germany and many other member states embrace an essentialist understanding of the European Union and believe it should be founded on Europe's common history, culture and values. These attitudes affect their approach to European integration and Turkey's membership bid. This attitude became particularly apparent before Britain's EU membership referendum. The referendum and discussions surrounding the referendum campaigns further demonstrated Britain's Euroscepticsm and showed that the UK's decades-long support for Turkey's EU membership bid was simply pragmatic.

9. For other examples of this approach to Turkey's EU membership bid see: *Guardian*, 2010; *The Times*, 2010a.

10. For other examples of this narrative see: *The Times*, 2010a; *Independent*, 2007; Telegraph View, 2013; *The Times*, 2010b; Harris et al., 2010.

11. The quantitative analysis of 731 news items primarily about Turkey, published in four selected British broadsheets between 2007 and 2013, showed that 26.76 per cent of these news items included direct adjectives that define Turkey by its religious identity.

12. The West has described Turkey as a 'model' since the end of the Cold war for a variety of pragmatic reasons. As Benlioğlu explained, 'First, it was the Clinton administration right after the end of the collapse of the Soviet Union that talked about the "Turkish model" in the context of the Central Asian and Caucasus states. Then the issue for the US was to encourage these newly independent countries to choose the secular Turkish model as opposed to Iranian theocracy. After that, came the Bush administration. This time the context was post-9/11 era and the "war on terrorism". In that context, Turkey was made the model for reconciliation between Islam and democracy, an example of "moderate Islam," much to the dismay of seculars in Turkey' (Altunışık,2011).

13. See: Kaddorah, 2010; Göksel, 2012; Altunışık, 2005; Dede, 2011; Eligur, 2010.

References

Aissaoui, Rabah (2007). 'History, cultural identity and difference: the issue of Turkey's accession to the European Union in the French national press', *Journal of Southern Europe and the Balkans*, 9(1), 1–14.

Akca, Emel Baştürk and Yılmaztürk, Songül (2006). 'Turkish image in the EU media: Turkey's representation through the 3rd October process', 4th International Symposium Communication in the Millennium, 14–16 June 2006, Anadolu Üniversitesi Yayınları, Eskisehir, Turkey.

Altunışık, Meliha Benli (2005). 'The Turkish Model and democratization in the Middle East', *Arab Studies Quarterly*, 27(1/2), 45–63.

Altunışık, Meliha Benli (2011). 'What is missing in the "Turkish model" debate?', *Hürriyet Daily News*, 23 June. Available at: www.hurriyetdailynews.com/ default.aspx?pageid=438&n=what-is-missing-in-the-8216turkish-model8217-debate-2011-06-23 (accessed 2 June 2015).

Amel, Saied R., Marandi, Syed M., Ahmed, Sameera, Kara, Seyfeddin and Merali, Arzu (2007). *The British Media and Muslim Representation: Ideology of Demonization*. The Islamic Human Rights Commission. Available at: www. ihrc.org.uk/file/1903718317.pdf (accessed 1 July 2015).

Amin, Samir (1989). *Eurocentrism*. New York: Monthly Review Press.

Ash, Timothy G. (2012). 'Europe has left Syria to a distinctly Ottoman fate', *Guardian*, 12 April. Available at: www.theguardian.com/commentisfree/2012/ apr/11/europe-left-syria-to-ottoman-fate (accessed 5 October 2015).

Bakić-Hayden, Milica (1995). 'Nesting Orientalisms: the case of former Yugoslavia', *Slavic Review*, 54(4), 917–31.

Bhabha, Homi K. (1990). *Nation and Narration*. London: Routledge.

Bremner, Charles (2010). 'Ankara turns away as EU ambitions fade', *The Times*, 13 May. Available at: www.thetimes.co.uk/tto/news/world/europe/article2510062. ece (accessed 8 October 2015).

Bryce, Derek (2007). 'Repackaging Orientalism: discourses on Egypt and Turkey in British outbound tourism', *Tourist Studies*, 7(2), 165–91.

Bryce, Derek (2009a). 'The generous exclusion of Ottoman-Islamic Europe: British press advocacy of Turkish EU membership', *Culture and Religion*, 10(3), 297–315.

Bryce, Derek (2009b). *Turkey and Western Subjectivity: Orientalist Ontology and the Occlusion of Ottoman Europe*. PhD thesis. Glasgow: Glasgow Caledonian University.

Cabinet Office, Prime Minister's Office, 10 Downing Street and The Rt Hon David Cameron MP (2010). 'PM's Speech in Turkey', Gov.uk, 27 July. Available at: www.gov.uk/government/speeches/pms-speech-in-turkey (accessed 1 July 2015).

Çirakman, Asli (2005). *From the 'Terror of the World' to the 'Sick Man of Europe':* *European Images of Ottoman Empire and Society from the Sixteenth Century to the Nineteenth.* New York: Peter Lang.

Cockburn, Patrick (2012). 'Patrick Cockburn: is Turkey's economic miracle about to fade away?', *Independent,* 22 January. Available at: www.independent.co.uk/ news/world/europe/patrick-cockburn-is-turkeys-economic-miracle-about-to-fade-away-6292806.html (accessed 8 October 2015).

Coleman, Stephen and Ross, Karen (2010). *The Media and the Public: 'Them' and 'Us' in Media Discourse.* Malden, MA: Wiley-Blackwell.

Coughlin, Con (2010). 'Turkey's role in the flotilla affair should worry us all in the West', *Daily Telegraph,* 4 June. Available at: www.telegraph.co.uk/news/uknews/ defence/7802401/Turkeys-role-in-the-Gaza-flotilla-affair-should-worry-us-all-in-the-West.html (accessed 5 October 2015).

Criss, Nur B. (2008). 'Europe and Turkey: Does religion matter?', in Dietrich Jung and Stuart Hall (eds), *Representation: Cultural Representations and Signifying Practices.* London: Sage.

Daily Telegraph (2009). 'Obama reaches out to Muslims with Turkey visit', 8 March, p. 17.

Dede, Alper Y. (2011). 'The Arab uprisings: debating the "Turkish model"', *Insight Turkey,* 13(2), 23–32.

Delanty, Gerard (1995). *Inventing Europe.* London: Palgrave Macmillan.

Devran, Yusuf (2007). 'The portrayal of Turkey in the British media: Orientalism resurfaced', *Insight Turkey,* 9(4), 100–15.

Economist (2011). 'A hard act to follow', 6 August. Available at: www.economist. com/node/21525408 (accessed 2 July 2015).

Eligur, Banu (2010). *The Mobilization of Political Islam in Turkey.* Cambridge: Cambridge University Press.

Findlay, Carter V. (2005). *The Turks in World History.* Oxford: Oxford University Press.

Fletcher, Martin and Erdem, Suna (2010). 'President Gül: Turkey is part of Europe', *The Times,* 2 July. Available at: www.thetimes.co.uk/tto/news/world/europe/ article2583617.ece (accessed 5 October 2015).

Göksel, Oğuzhan (2012). 'Assessing the Turkish model as a guide to the emerging democracies in the Middle East', *Ortadoğu Etütleri,* 4(1), 99–120.

Guardian (2007). 'Islam and democracy', 22 August. Available at: www.theguardian. com/commentisfree/2007/aug/22/turkey.comment (accessed 6 October 2015).

Guardian (2010). 'Turkey: A vital player', 28 July. Available at: www.theguardian. com/commentisfree/2010/jul/28/turkey-david-cameron-gaza (accessed 5 October 2015).

Gürsel, Kadri (2011). 'Who really wants a Muslim democracy?', *Turkish Policy Quarterly,* 10(1), 93–7.

Hall, Stuart (ed.) (1997) *Representation: Cultural Representations and Signifying Practices,* London: Sage

Halpin, Tony (2010). 'Pragmatism, politics and the festering wound of Armenian "genocide"', *The Times*, 5 March. Available at: www.thetimes.co.uk/tto/news/world/europe/article2462885.ece (accessed 8 October 2015).

Hannan, Daniel (2010). 'The EU will regret its dishonest, humiliating treatment of Turkey', *Daily Telegraph*, 28 June. Available at: www.telegraph.co.uk/comment/columnists/danielhannan/7913773/The-EU-will-regret-its-dishonest-humiliating-treatment-of-Turkey.html (accessed 5 October 2015).

Harasym, Sarah and Spivak, Gayatri (1990). *The Post-Colonial Critic: Interviews, Strategies, Dialogues*. London: Routledge.

Harris, Paul, Shabi, Rachel and Beaumont, Peter (2010). 'Gaza flotilla attack: a week that changed Middle East politics', *Observer*, 6 June. Available at: www.theguardian.com/world/2010/jun/06/gaza-flotilla-attack-israel-turkey (accessed 8 October 2015).

Hobson, John M. (2004). *The Eastern Origins of Western Civilisation*. Cambridge: Cambridge University Press.

Huntington, Samuel P. (1993). 'The clash of civilizations?', *Foreign Affairs*, 72(3), 22–49.

İnalcık, H. (1994). *An Economic and Social History of the Ottoman Empire, 1300–1914*. Cambridge: Cambridge University Press.

Independent (2007). 'A surprising source of progressive achievement', 24 July, p. 28.

Kaddorah, Emad Y. (2010). 'The Turkish model: acceptability and apprehension', *Insight Turkey*, 12(4), 113–29.

Karli, Mehmet (2007). 'Secular Turks will settle for nothing less than a truly liberal society', *Guardian*, 31 August. Available at: www.theguardian.com/commentisfree/2007/aug/31/comment.turkey (accessed 5 October 2015).

Kejanlıoğlu, Beybin and Taş, Oğuzhan (2009). 'Türk Basınında AB-Türkiye İlişkilerinin Sunumu: 17 Aralık 2004 Brüksel Zirvesi', *Kültür ve İletişim [Culture and Communication]*, 12(1), 39–64.

Kösebalaban, Hasan (2007). 'The permanent "Other"? Turkey and the question of European identity', *Mediterranean Quarterly*, 18(4), 87–111.

Kylstad, Ingrid (2010). 'Turkey and the EU: A "new" European identity in the making?', LSE 'Europe in Question' Discussion Paper Series No. 27. Available at: www.lse.ac.uk/europeanInstitute/LEQS/LEQSPaper27.pdf (accessed 1 July 2015).

Landry, Donna (2011). 'English brutes, Eastern enlightenment', *The Eighteenth Century: Theory and Interpretation*, 52(1), 11–30.

Lévi-Strauss, Claude (1976). *Structural Anthropology*. Trans. Monique Layton. New York: Basic Books.

Mert, Nuray (2011). 'Democracy a la Turca' or 'Democracy Bon Pour L'Orient'. *Hürriyet Daily News*, 8 July. Available at: www.hurriyetdailynews.com/democracy-a-la-turca-or-democracy-bon-pour-lorient.aspx?pageID=438&n=8216democracy-a-la-turca8217-or-8216democracy-bon-pour-l8217orient8217-2011-08-07 (accessed 2 July 2015).

Miliband, David (2007). 'Turkey is vital to Europe's future', *Daily Telegraph*, 5 September. Available at: www.telegraph.co.uk/comment/personal-view/3642448/Turkey-is-vital-to-Europes-future.html (accessed 5 October 2015).

Musil, Pelin Ayan (2011). 'Turkish democracy as a model for the Middle East?', *The New Presence Prague's Journal of Central European Affairs*, 2(1), 12–19.

Neumann, Iver B. (1996). 'Self and other in international relations', *European Journal of International Relations*, 2(2), 139–74.

Neumann, Iver B. (1999). *Uses of the Other: 'The East' in European Identity Formation*. Minneapolis: University of Minnesota Press.

Neumann, Iver B. and Welsh, Jennifer (1991). 'The other in European self-definition: an addendum to the literature on international society', *Review of International Studies*, 17(4), 327–48.

Noakes, Jeremy and Pridham, Geoffrey (1974). *Documents on Nazism, 1919–1945*. London: Jonathan Cape.

Oktem, Kerem (2005). 'British media perspectives on Turkey's EU accession prospects: Euro-scepticism and Turco-philia'm *Südosteuropa*, 53(4), 587–97.

Paksoy, Alaaddin F. (2012). *Representation of Turkey's EU Bid in the British Media*. PhD thesis. Sheffield: Sheffield University Press.

Pew Research Center (2011). 'The future of the global Muslim population', 27 January. Available at: www.pewforum.org/2011/01/27/the-future-of-the-global-muslim-population/ (accessed 1 July 2015).

Robins, Kevin (1996). 'Interrupting identities: Turkey/Europe', in Stuart Hall and Paul du Gay (eds), *Questions of Cultural Identity*. London: Sage.

Said, Edward (1997). *Covering Islam*. London: Vintage.

Said, Edward (2003). *Orientalism*. London: Penguin Books.

Senior, Antonia (2010). 'Frenemy or enemy, Turkey must be in Europe', *The Times*, 29 July, p. 24.

Spivak, Gayatri C. (1988). 'Can the subaltern speak?', in Cary Nelson and Lawrence Grossberg (eds), *Marxism and the Interpretation of Culture*. Chicago: University of Illinois Press.

Strasser, Sabine (2008). 'Europe's Other', *European Societies*, 10(2), 177–95.

Straw, Jack (2011). 'Europe must embrace this confident Turkey', *The Times*, 14 June. Available at: www.thetimes.co.uk/tto/opinion/columnists/article3060935.ece (accessed 5 October 2015).

Tanör, Bulent (2014). *Osmanlı-Türk Anayasal Gelişmeleri*. İstanbul: Yapı Kredi Yayınları.

Tekin, Beyza Ç. (2008). 'The construction of Turkey's possible EU membership in French political discourse', *Discourse & Society*, 19(7), 727–63.

Telegraph View (2008). 'Turkey's secularism', *Daily Telegraph*, 29 July, p. 19.

Telegraph View (2010). 'Stabilising Turkey', *Daily Telegraph*, 23 February. Available at: www.telegraph.co.uk/comment/telegraph-view/7301577/Stabilising-Turkey.html (accessed 8 October 2015).

Telegraph View (2013). 'A time for reason', *Daily Telegraph*, 10 June. Available at: www.telegraph.co.uk/news/worldnews/europe/turkey/10109387/A-time-for-reason.html (accessed 8 October 2015).

Times, The (2010a). 'Welcome carpet for Turkey', 5 July, p. 2.

Times, The (2010b). 'End of ties with Tel Aviv may push Ankara further eastwards', 1 June, p. 7.

Times, The (2010c). 'US genocide decision threatens to wreck good relations with Turkey', 5 March, p. 31.

Times, The (2013). 'Erdogan and democracy', 13 June, p. 20.

Tisdall, Simon (2010). 'Erdogan needs to raise his game to end impasse in Cyprus', *Guardian*, 20 April. Available at: www.theguardian.com/commentisfree/2010/apr/19/erdogan-cyprus-european-union (accessed 5 October 2015).

Traynor, Ian and Letsch, Costanze (2013). 'Turkey: a country more divided than ever by Erdogan's Gezi Park crackdown', *Guardian*, 21 June. Available at: www.theguardian.com/world/2013/jun/20/turkey-divided-erdogan-protests-crackdown (accessed 5 October 2015).

Turkish Directorate of Religious Affairs (2014). 'Turkish religious life report'. Available at: http://www2.diyanet.gov.tr/StratejiGelistirme/Afisalanlari/dini-hayat.pdf (accessed 26 August 2015).

Whitaker, Brian (2002). 'Islam and the British press after September 11', 20 June. Available at: www.al-bab.com/media/articles/bw020620.htm (accessed 1 July 2015).

Young, Robert (1990). *White Mythologies: Writing History and the West*. New York and London: Routledge.

Žižek, Slavoj (2007). 'Turkey is a thorn in the side of a cosy Western consensus', *Guardian*, 22 August. Available at: www.theguardian.com/commentisfree/2007/oct/23/comment.turkey (accessed 5 October 2015).

10

Covering Iraq

Observations of a Fixer and Journalist

Haider Al-Safi

When journalists get together to talk about the difficulties they face in covering foreign countries, Iraq usually comes up as one of the most troublesome places to cover. Many reporters believe that Iraq is seriously under-reported in Western media. However, several relate that to the fact that it had been almost impossible to cover a number of events, as the situation has become extremely dangerous. The risk of being kidnapped, killed or arrested became evident, and this risk factor was prioritised among journalists. Despite that, some journalists continued reporting from Iraq and managed to walk the fine line between taking the risk and reducing it to a minimum. There are a lot of measures that veteran reporters took or considered, and as a result they have become specialists on Iraq. But what kind of measures should be taken by foreign reporters or journalists to mitigate the risks they might face in reporting Iraq? As an Iraqi citizen and journalist who worked for the foreign media, I was in a position that enabled me to understand the arguments made both by Iraqis and foreign reporters. In this chapter, I will try to explain the many issues I encountered, or situations I witnessed, through my work in Iraq during and after the 2003 Iraq War.

Cultural Differences

In mid-April of 2003, I was entering the Meridian hotel to meet my colleagues from the UK-based newspaper, the *Independent*. A man with big glasses, white with blond hair, Western in appearance, carrying a camera on one shoulder and a bag on the other, was screaming at a relatively young Iraqi man with a trimmed moustache: 'Tell your Baath party comrades to come here now, you are Saddam's dogs, you are cowards'. The young man shouted back while leaving, 'We will come back and I hope you will be around, f***g spy'. This argument was between a French journalist and an Iraqi minder who had been allocated by Saddam's Ministry of Information to monitor foreign journalists visiting Iraq, before the collapse of the regime on 9 April 2003.

This story gives a clear example of a situation journalists should not get into while covering a conflict or when they are sent to a war zone. The French journalist expressed his anger to everyone who gathered around him, that his minder had reported him to the intelligence service, which had meant he would not be able to reach certain areas during the war. This situation made me concerned about the ignorance of this journalist and of others whom I might end up working with. He did not realise how dangerous the situation had become in Iraq, with anarchy on the streets of Baghdad in the absence of law and order. But more importantly, he seemed to be ignoring the fact that Iraqis still keep very strong ties with their tribal roots, their pride and traditions. The minder's anger might turn against this journalist, who in his mind was a 'spy' and a 'Westerner' insulting him in his homeland.

Luckily, I saw this same journalist two years later, alive and well. The journalists representing Western media should have familiarised themselves with Iraqi and Arab culture before arriving, but over time it proved that few of them knew how to tackle sensitive issues, and how to deal with Iraqi culture in particular. In many cases translators, fixers and local journalists played an intermediary role to create the kind of mutual understanding that was required, while Western journalists were actively touring the country chasing stories.

For months, journalists travelled around Iraq from big cities to small villages, driven by the thirst for news. Iraqi people welcomed the journalists, wanting the world to listen to their sufferings and tragedies. Few media personnel were escorted by bodyguards or even thought about their own security, because at that time it was relatively safe. However, the situation was developing rapidly and the coverage often included interviews with angry bereaved families, tribes and crowds who had lost their loved ones. Many of the journalists didn't seem to know how to deal with the cultural sensitivities related to tragic deaths, and hence what to do or what to say in such situations.

Many of the journalists asked bold questions because they wanted a good quote or an interview, without paying attention to how difficult the situation was for their interviewees. In many cases anger was directed towards the journalists themselves, when they asked such questions or acted carelessly. Many Western media workers did not pay attention to the similarities that the crowd could draw between them and the American troops. Both sides spoke English, had an obviously Western appearance, fair skin, blond hair, and were asking for information. Even the dress code of some journalists showed a lack of cultural awareness: I noticed that many were wearing boots and khaki-coloured trousers, which were deceptively similar to some military forces' uniforms.

During the decades of the Saddam regime's rule, one of the biggest fears among the Iraqi public was giving information to strangers – any stranger. Publicly many Iraqi officials claimed that Westerners were 'spies' representing different intelligence services, especially the American Central Intelligence Agency (CIA) and the Israeli intelligence agency, Mossad. After the invasion, this regime collapsed, but these kinds of beliefs had been indoctrinated into the subconscious of the Iraqi people. It became part of the culture to be suspicious of anyone asking questions and seeking information. This was a great challenge for many foreign journalists, considering the amount of time it might take to gain the trust of interviewees. Additionally, some big international news agencies recruited security guards with guns to protect their journalists and premises. These 'guards' behaved in ways that Iraqis found similar to those they had watched in American TV espionage series.

Among veteran journalists there was often a considerable feeling of superiority, but their most counterproductive behaviour was when they did not allow themselves to listen to their local colleagues. Instead of asking for opinions they would give an order – or at least, that was how it sounded. On one occasion back in 2003, we conducted interviews at a funeral tent in Fallujah. There were more than one hundred men in the tent. As soon as we finished the interview my colleague, who is a well-known journalist, asked me if we could leave immediately, which I vetoed. It would have been extremely offensive to do so. We stayed another ten minutes drinking tea and paying condolences to the family. Then we walked out smoothly while expressing our apologies, claiming that we had to leave to conduct another interview with an injured person in the hospital. Although it was not a genuine excuse, it showed that we were keen on meeting another victim, and so enabled us to make an 'unexpected' departure rather than joining them for the post-funeral meal, as is traditional.

When I was exchanging tales and observations with my Iraqi colleagues from different media organisations, I was told many stories about Western journalists who abused their authority and ignored the advice given by the local team they were working with.

There are a lot of cultural taboos that a journalist needs to consider while covering Iraq. For example, it is deemed an insult to cross your legs in a way that shows the soles of your shoes or feet to the person sitting next to you or facing you (UK government, 2007). Also, it is very important to check the religious holidays in the place you are trying to cover, such as Ashora, Eid, and Ramadan (GlobalSecurity.org, 2014). If journalists are not aware of festival times like these their efforts might be wasted, as most interviewees will not respond to interview requests during such periods.

Press Conferences

In 2003, press conferences were given by US-led coalition officials on a daily basis all over the country, though mainly in Baghdad. We were receiving innumerable invitations to attend these events. It was a good way to create a network, but more importantly, to see how influential this group or that party really was. I noticed that many journalists representing international news agencies, freelancers and some from Arabic TV channels, were not interested, and only very few of them were going to those events. On the contrary, when a Western official sent an invitation to the press they would go in a big team. For example, many journalists attended the US army's official briefings. But their numbers declined over a long period of time as the security situation worsened, and the low newsworthiness of the information provided by the spokespeople became evident. I noticed that many veteran journalists were avoiding those conferences, while the less experienced were there on a daily basis. Many of them were taking a huge risk by attending such conferences. Journalists had to queue at the main entrances of the American bases all over Iraq, but mainly in the so-called 'Green Zone' in Baghdad, the fortified administrative centre of the coalition forces. These entrances, including the main entrance to an on-site convention centre, were repeatedly targeted by car bombs, suicide bombers and mortar attacks. This convention centre, where many press conferences took place, was one of the most dangerous places in the Iraqi capital. It was attacked several times. In July 2005, I went there to collect my passport from the British embassy, which was 'temporarily' housed there. I crossed the first checkpoint, the second, and so on, until I was at the main entrance, which was a few hundred metres away from the first gate. Suddenly there was a huge blast, followed by a lot of gunshots, screaming and people running around, injured and shocked. I had thought that place was dangerous from day one, but I never thought that the danger might come that close to me. I was lucky, and escaped the suicide bomber attack and the crossfire afterwards by just a few minutes. I thought about how many times I had been lucky, when I remembered how often I had queued in that dangerous place. It was a place no one wanted to be, according to an American soldier who spent some time manning checkpoints at that entrance (Bexley, 2015). He said that it was a high-priority target because all the high-profile personnel used that entrance to the convention centre.

Was it worth attending these press conferences and taking that risk? This is a question that should be asked by all journalists before heading to any area in a war zone. A local conference in one of the Baghdad hotels might provide a better story and grant more access to different areas, in comparison to an official press conference held by the US army or an embassy official, which would give closely vetted information. What kind of credibility would information provided by Brigadier General Mark Kimmitt, the spokesperson of the coalition forces, really have? Especially when he declared that the propaganda campaign 'was no attempt to manipulate the press' (Ricks, 2006). News value in comparison to risk is the calculation that journalists make with their lives. The low-quality information provided by spokespeople in the Green Zone was not necessarily worth the risk it took to get it; journalists should focus on more newsworthy (although potentially even riskier) stories elsewhere.

On 13 December 2003, Saddam Hussein was arrested. The following day a big crowd of journalists was in the convention centre when the US governor of Iraq, Paul Bremer, announced the ousted dictator's capture. I was watching the news with other colleagues from our hotel room, and I was feeling frustrated because it had been too difficult to get access to the press conference. We still got the news, but I was not happy, as I thought we should have been there. My feelings changed when I saw the crowd of supposedly 'objective' journalists cheering the news: I felt better about not being able to access that 'press conference', in order not to be part of what I considered a staged event and to not be used as an extra in a TV show. What we didn't realise at first, as journalists, local and international, who wanted to cover a significant event, was that officials wanted to make the best out of the busy crowd for their 'Psychological Operation Campaign'.

Military Embedded Journalism

The only embedding I have ever done was with a local Iraqi police patrol, for just a few hours. We were reporting a story about the Iraqi police in Baghdad. I remember a conversation that I overheard between the commander of the area where our patrol was going to take place, and one of his officers. I had returned to his office to collect my sunglasses which I had left on his desk. Before I entered the room, I heard him saying, 'Take them to safe areas where you have more checkpoints, and ask your men to show good manners while those guys are around. You can show them a few places where crimes took place, but don't overdo it. Let them think we are living in Sweden, not in the Wild West.' Then I heard loud laughter, after which I thought I was safe to enter. I claimed I had got lost while looking for the officer and my sunglasses.

The conversation between the two Iraqi officers summarises all embedding procedures: 'Show something but not everything.' I met many Western journalists who were opposed to the idea of being embedded with troops, where you have to rely on their support for matters such as food, safety and protection, but more importantly, where journalists' movement are being controlled.

Some journalists found embedding with the American or British troops to be the only way to reach dangerous areas. A lot of criticism was directed towards embedded journalists (Cockburn, 2010), and questions were asked regarding how is it possible to write something negative about the unit which provides your food and protection. Another reason for hesitation is censorship by the military. Journalists agreed not to reveal operational details, such as the exact location and size of their forces, and stories by embedded reporters were vetted by the military for these details (Baker, 2015). This made the embedded journalists seem to be mouth-pieces for the occupation forces. Also, joining soldiers in their activities could also be dangerous for journalists; according to the Committee to Protect Journalists, seven embedded reporters were killed (CPJ, 2008a). Many embedded media workers were injured or killed while accompanying military forces on duty.

The practice of embedding reporters was adopted for the first time in the US-led war against Iraq in 2003 (BBC News, 2003). Iraqi journalists were often hand picked for embedding by the Coalition Provisional Authorities or the American army, depending on what kind of coverage they had been reporting. It depended on how 'friendly' his/her coverage was towards the USA. The credibility of the Iraqi journalists who were involved in such activities was considered by the public to be 'compromised'. I was told many times by Iraqis that 'it gives the wrong impression to see a journal-ist accompanying American soldiers'. One may ask how likely the public would be to speak to this journalist, especially if he/she was conducting an interview in the presence of an American soldier. Whatever they might say, it would be in the shadow of fearing the journalist's link with the army or with any authority which had paved the way to meet them.

The embedded journalists were able to write about certain stories, but they were missing others happening in different places which were com-pletely unlike the ones they were reporting. In November 2004, many reporters accompanied the US army while it was leading an operation to storm Fallujah. The reporters covered the success of the American army's operation, but they missed the story about how militants took advantage of the absence of US forces in Mosul and captured the second largest city in Iraq for a few hours (Cockburn, 2010).

Many journalists do not favour embedding with troops at all, but in view of the threat of being held hostage during or after the Iraq War (Ignatius, 2010), embedding is not an option to be dismissed out of hand.

Meeting the Militants

Many journalists were obsessed with the idea of meeting those on the other side of the story: the militants who were fighting the US-led coalition. Many tried to interview the militants. Others went further, by getting embedded with the militants themselves during their operations against coalition troops. The idea was very tempting, but the risk was huge. Many journalists were either victims of fraud or were kidnapped, and some of them got killed. A total of fifty-seven journalists were kidnapped between 2003 and 2009, according to the Committee to Protect Journalists (CPJ, 2008b). But shouldn't they have thought of the authenticity of the mediator or the go-between first?

The Authenticity of the Mediator or the Go-Between

The story normally begins with the journalist putting pressure on his/her fixer or driver to arrange a meeting with one of the 'resistance' members. The fixer will use his contacts to find a link with militants in his area, or through his family connections. The meeting will be arranged in a safe house. Many reporters and filmmakers told me that in this way they had met one or more persons, but always masked. They claimed they were fighting the Americans, but there was no way to verify the stories they were telling. There was a driver who orchestrated many such meetings. He told me, after the group that he was working for had left, that all these meetings had been faked. He had asked his cousin, who was studying in the acting department at the Baghdad College of Visual Arts, to play the part of the militant.

Another former officer, who was retired and living on a pension, played the role of an old general formerly of Saddam's guard, supposedly leading the fight against the US army in a Baghdad neighbourhood. The guy made some money and paid his team of fake 'resistance fighters'. Many journalists knew him as someone with 'special' ties with the 'resistance'. I was not sure if he was lying about his fake connections, or if he had truly misled many journalists with these performances in order to make some money. When I expressed my doubts about his story, he got furious, saying, 'Are you crazy? Do you want me to end up like X?' The person he was referring to, X, was a fixer working for a well-known agency. He was assassinated with two members of his family just a week after arranging an interview with a group of Fedayeen Saddam.[1] Other journalists were kidnapped when they went to meet militants.

There are many issues journalists should think of before attempting to meet with militants. If they are asked for money to secure the interview, then it is worth checking if the whole interview is genuine.

Is the Story Worth Taking the Risk?

Many journalists develop feelings of competition and, in some cases, jealousy. Many of them let these feelings override their sense of logic and experience, especially when another colleague from another media outlet secured a scoop. No matter how many stories are available, meeting the enemy will be a priority for those journalists who are competing with each other. I asked one of the journalists, whom I trust and who presumably would have connections with militants because of his Islamic (Sunni) background and tribal connections to Fallujah, about meeting militants. He said, 'Why do you think they should want to meet you?' To which I replied, 'We will give them a chance to express their views and to present their case.'

He smiled, saying, 'You are talking about the 1990s model, those guys have got websites, they can present their case properly, and they don't need to take the risk of being physically present to conduct an interview: if you want to know about their opinions, you can visit their websites.'

Have You Thought about the Background of the Team?

In many cases journalists from a certain ethnicity or background can disappear among the crowd, but many do not. It can be a big deal if you belong to certain countries or to certain religions or sects. In many cases, journalists used fixers from different backgrounds at the same time, such as one Sunni and one Shi'a. This was a good technique to assist in gaining access to both areas.

Journalists were advised to keep a low profile and not to express religious or political views when dealing with such situations. Many journalists were keen to show some sympathy and respect for their interviewees' tragic experiences. Others were overdoing it by pretending to have specific racial or religious links. I came across the story of a foreign correspondent who claimed to be Muslim. He went to pray with the group he was reporting about. It was not that difficult to find out his background with a simple Google search, which revealed that he was an atheist of Jewish background, but luckily they did not discover this during the time he spent with the group.

Do You Have a Sponsor?

Many journalists were moving around the country visiting dangerous areas such as Fallujah, Ramadi, Tikrit, Sadr city and Mosul, but only a few were able to find a sponsor when they got to these areas. Iraq is a tribal society, and even those who live in the city maintain their tribal connections to the regions (GlobalSecurity.org, 2013). There are very few journalists who tried to create connections with the tribal Sheikhs so as to sponsor their movements or interviews in certain areas. Most of them relied on their fixers, but that was not enough to guarantee their safety. A reliable guarantor such as a respected tribal leader or religious figure is an essential thing to secure before taking the decision to go and meet military factions or militias.

Impact of Publishing on Local People

Many journalists published their stories without taking into consideration what would happen to them or their local team members after they had been published. In many cases, a journalist, fixer or driver was threatened because of their involvement in a certain report. These issues need to be discussed with staff. Many journalists think their stories will not be read by the locals because they are going to be published in a foreign language and in a different country. In the age of the internet, this is not the case anymore. Also, many local newspapers might republish stories which editors think suit the Iraqi audience. This is a double-edged sword. If the story did not pay due attention to religious and social sensitivities because it was written for a different audience, that could cause serious trouble. Also, if the translation is poor that might backfire on to the writer. It is always worth checking with the team about the stories reporters would file to their publications. Just a few changes might prevent those reporters putting themselves and their local teams' lives at risk.

Abu Ghraib Prison

When Seymour Hersh uncovered the torture taking place in Abu Ghraib prison in 2004 (Hersh, 2004), many journalists wondered why this story had escaped their attention. In reality, there was less digging about such allegations (Cirillo and Ricchiardi, 2004) in comparison to the many stories which were uncovered and published about Saddam's torture acts. It needed more attention, because the Iraqi victims did not protest very loudly, being scared of the cultural stigma associated with sexual abuse. Nevertheless, those were practices that experienced journalists should have expected during wartime, and should have been investigating.

I remember when I went to a press conference featuring Abu Ghraib prison torture victims in mid-May 2004 – I questioned myself as to who would come forward to speak? Failing to dig for these crimes is one problem, but another is that if it happens victims will not come forward and speak about it. To my surprise, three of those tortured came forward. Two of them were very vocal about their physical torture, but they denied being raped. After the press conference, I asked one of them if he knew any of his fellow inmates who had been victims of rape. He said yes, but added that he will never come forward. He said the victim came from a very big tribe and he had decided to take his revenge, which meant he would fight till he dies. The organiser of the event told me that they had been expecting fourteen torture victims, but only three showed up.

American Soldiers and Mercenaries versus Militants, and the Journalists In-between

One of biggest concerns for journalists in Iraq has become their safety. Iraq became one of the most dangerous places in world to cover. It was the 'deadliest country' for journalists every year from 2003 to 2008 (CPJ, 2003, 2004, 2005, 2006, 2007, 2008c). None of Iraq's regions is considered 100 per cent safe for reporters. Militants and gangs have been ready to take journalists hostage to achieve either political or financial aims. Depending on how big their news organisations are, journalists would choose their own way of conducting their job in Iraq: either to be very visible and lead a high-profile presence, or to maintain a low profile, merging with the Iraqi public.

Many organisations with very big operations in Iraq used private security companies to protect their staff. These companies were very efficient when they were dealing with US soldiers or US security teams, because most of them were former soldiers. But the downside was that many Iraqis confused them with American soldiers. In fact, they were causing more damage to the relationship with the Iraqi public. The *New York Times* newspaper and other news agencies in the same compound decided to put concrete walls around their houses and erect a big gate with a watchtower. Visiting the *New York Times* compound, I was shocked when the guards at the gates were wearing uniforms with a label on the top of the left chest pocket, saying 'NY-Times' (Marlowe, 2005). Many of these big news outlets used armoured vehicles. This was, as a friend who was working for a US-based newspaper told me, to escape being targeted by kidnappers or looters.

However, keeping a low profile was another tactic many journalists used, especially British journalists. It was deemed a better way of dealing with the Iraqi public. But that had its downsides when dealing with American troops. In 2004, I was with another colleague on our way back to Baghdad from Fallujah. We received a call through the Sat-phone from the foreign desk in London. We stopped so that my colleague could take the call, and in the middle of the conversation an American patrol of four Humvees passed near-by. We thought it was too dangerous to stay by the roadside in that area and decided to move. As soon as the car started moving, American soldiers jumped in and surrounded us screaming, 'Out of the car, on your knees.' They took the phone from us and dialled the last number. We tried to speak to them in English, but they were shouting and apparently they were nervous. They let us go after finding out that we were journalists. They said, 'We thought you were Iraqis and you were giving details about the patrol over the phone.' Although my colleague was white British with blonde hair, the patrol still thought that we could be locals helping the militants. In the summer of 2003, a Reuters cameraman was killed by an American sniper after his camera was 'mistaken' for a rocket launcher (Wilson, 2003).

Many journalists started to panic about their daily activity in Iraq. Day by day, the situation grew increasingly dangerous. Many of those who were working for big organisations were held hostage to their security advisors. Many advisors tried to reduce the movements of their clients as much as they could. All over the world journalists are controlled by their editors or publishers, but in Baghdad the journalists were, and still are, under the control of security advisors who may prevent them from covering important stories for sometimes spurious 'security reasons'. Once, the security advisors of a well-known TV network told their staff and reporters that the west wing of the hotel where they were staying in was going to be attacked by mortars. Many asked journalists from other media outlets, who were staying in the east wing of the same hotel, for refuge. The night passed without a single bullet being shot at the hotel. But later, in February 2006, the same hotel was attacked with car bombs. It was the first direct attack against this hotel, which was well-known as one where journalists were staying (Sengupta, 2006).

Freelancers and staff members of small organisations who kept a low profile continued moving around Baghdad to a certain extent. Many of them developed survival tactics. One of the tactics we used in our newspaper was what we called 'ten minutes coverage'. The name explains what our tactic was, more or less. It was basically to go to any incident location and not to spend more than ten minutes there. We assumed that in the best-case scenario any kidnapping operation would take fifteen minutes to stage. When we were going to a given place I would ask the driver to get the car ready on the other side and keep the engine running. We would conduct between two and three interviews, and then dash to another location related to the incident, such as a hospital or a morgue.

Kidnapping became very common in Baghdad. In order to survive, journalists followed certain rules. Many journalists refused to accept private invitations to houses or to political party offices. Once, we were interviewing some refugees from Fallujah when we came across a cleric who was helping distribute food among refugees. He insisted on us having lunch with him. I became uncomfortable when I noticed that three of his assistants disappeared after serving the meal, because this goes against Arabian tribal traditions. I asked my colleagues to leave immediately, pretending that we had got an urgent call from London. He invited us to come again to attend the Eid feast, promising we would meet important men from Fallujah. One year later, it was revealed that this person was responsible for kidnapping Margaret Hassan, senior director of an international non-governmental organisation. He also organised the kidnapping of two Italian journalists (Marlowe, 2009).

When Free Journalism becomes Hotel Journalism

When media members became the target for militant groups, they began to stay inside their hotels and stopped making the effort to move around. Iraqi people started to be hesitant about giving interviews to Western-looking journalists, fearing they would face a dangerous situation or an attack. Also, popular prejudice gave the impression that Western media coverage was biased towards the USA. Journalists ended up becoming prisoners inside their hotels.

Many journalists then started sending their fixers to conduct interviews while they stayed in their rooms or offices. Others started sending drivers out with a phone; they would arrange an interview through the driver's phone, with the help of a translator. This was never mentioned in the articles they were writing or the reports they were broadcasting afterwards.

Robert Fisk, a veteran Middle East correspondent from the *Independent*, criticised these journalists and called their coverage 'hotel journalism' (Fisk, 2005). Some journalists argued they had to adopt this strategy, as the situation was extremely dangerous and they would not survive if they went out. However, Fisk responded by telling me:

> I'm not against journalists [in Iraq] who stay in their hotels. What I do object to is the fact that journalists don't tell their

199

viewers, their listeners or their readers that they are not leaving the hotel, thus giving the impression when they report that American troops have killed forty-two terrorists in north Baghdad that they've gone out and checked it. I simply don't believe it. Indeed, when Iraqis come back with film, there are inevitably women and children among the dead. During the time of Saddam, the BBC always put a health warning on reports: 'This report was monitored by the Iraqi authorities.' Now we also need a health warning.

News coverage has been severely affected by the security situation. Primarily, it has made the journalist's circle of contacts very narrow. If even the rare Westerner, such as Fisk, who ventures out into danger 'can barely grasp what's going on', then others 'sure can't from their hotel rooms' (Cash, 2005).

We did not see many stories from small Iraqi towns. We only saw stories from Baghdad and the other big cities such as Mosul and Anbar (Ponsford, 2005). What is more, news from these places was pretty vague most of the time.

According to Patrick Cockburn (2010) of the *Independent*, 'the British media have never put enough resources into reporting either war to cover them properly. The BBC was the only television company to maintain a permanently staffed office in Baghdad. Most newspapers covered it episodically.'

Some foreign agencies have started to find alternatives to hotel journalism. Reuters and APTN (Associated Press Television News) have become more and more dependent on local Iraqi staff, especially TV crews. This has helped not only in giving the right image about what is going on, but also the right interpretation for the culture of Iraq.

These agencies have begun to train their own staff to deal with the hostility of kidnapping, or how to act if journalists get stuck in crossfire.

The Samarra Bombing Leading Up to the Civil War

In February 2006, the bombing of the Al-Askari shrine in Samarra was one of the events that fuelled the Iraq conflict with sectarian fury (Worth, 2006). It was almost impossible to reach Samarra, but the Al-Arabiya channel's crew managed to feed their report from the outskirts of the town. A prominent journalist, Atwar Bahjat, led the team and got as close as possible to the city.

The decision Atwar took went against the advice of her editor. She was relying on the fact that she originally came from Samarra. Sadly that did not help her; in fact, it gave her a false feeling of confidence. She was kidnapped along with her crew after a few hours, and killed. Their bodies were found the day after (Stack, 2006). The situation was no better in Baghdad. The bombing of the Al-Askari shrine was the beginning of a brutal civil war between two communities, Sunni and Shi'a. It was the time when journalists from different news agencies and media outlets decided to withdraw their operations from Iraq because it was almost impossible to report from any city. It was also the time when a new generation of Iraqi journalists appeared. They started to work directly for the Western media outlets as reporters and correspondents in their own right, gaining by-lines and dominating the airwaves when there was a report about Iraq. Many had previously been fixers or translators, but they proved to be capable of filling the coverage gap created after the news organisations' decision to withdraw their operations from Iraq.

Directly after the bombing, the militia took over the streets of Baghdad. The city became a ghost city. To report in that situation was extremely hard, but there were certain tactics that made it possible to cover events. It was almost impossible to have a high-profile presence. The only way was to reduce your visibility. Local journalists were using equipment which was relatively small, and reduced crew numbers to attract less attention. Journalists were spending much more time on preparing to cover a small story, in order to build trust with their contributors and to avoid kidnapping, which became very common in Baghdad. What made the situation even worse for Western journalists was when the militia realised that they could negotiate with the USA or the UK to gain the release of one of their captured leaders in exchange for a captive Westerner. They kidnapped any Westerner they could, including journalists, soldiers and contractors (Taylor, 2012; Finer and Partlow, 2006; CPJ, 2008b).

Iraq Fatigue

The high level of violence made audiences more familiar with the bad news emanating from Iraq. People started to lose interest in the story because most of the coverage was similar, with almost the same statistics – X amount of people killed, Y number of bombs went off. Media coverage of Iraq dropped dramatically in the USA in 2008 in comparison to 2007 (Ricchiardi, 2008). It was time to set up a different way of covering the story. Journalists and big corporations started covering other, human-interest stories, rather than the bombing stories. Many filmmakers were going to neighbouring countries where large numbers of Iraqis had found refuge. For example, Syria and Jordan were two countries where journalists could have access to Iraqis who had settled there or were waiting for UNHCR reallocation programmes. This helped provide another angle to the war story, giving it a more human face, rather than just the bald statistics. The need to go to Iraq was still an essential part of those stories, but it was more focused on being there for a few days and then leaving after conducting a few interviews. Most of these stories were either covered by big corporates or commissioned to small production companies working within the big news organisations' guidelines. These guidelines included having 'hostile environment and first aid training' (HEFAT) (Kosmides, nd), and buying special insurance when the companies sent reporters to Iraq. Insurance companies were charging huge amounts of money for providing such policies. One condition that most insurance companies required was for the journalists to have undergone the expensive HEFAT training. Freelancers were often unable to afford insurance, because of these twin costs.

Back to Iraq

By 2009 a report to the American Congress claimed that the security situation had improved (US Department of Defense, 2009), but it was still difficult to cover many stories. It was hard to access certain areas and towns, depending on their affiliation with different sects. I was commissioned by a book author to investigate a story that had happened immediately after the 2003 invasion. The story was to find what had happened to a few hundred barrels of explosives. The barrels had been stored in one of the towns on the outskirts of Baghdad, inside an old military industry rig. If it had been 2003 and not 2009, this would have been a one-month task, but it took me six months because of the difficulty in accessing the area. I had to use three fixers, who did not know about each other. The first fixer was able to access the town and to conduct interviews without any trouble because of his tribal connection to that town. He had many cousins who could answer his questions without hesitation. The second fixer was someone who had worked for that military industry rig and could easily get us access to his former colleagues from his previous job. The third fixer had access to what were called at the time the 'Awakening Councils'. They were former insurgents who had changed sides and turned against the militant groups they had once belonged to, in support of the US army. I gathered and cross-referenced the material that I received from each of the fixers. Most of the material was interviews they had conducted, but between the three versions that I received I was able to find out what had happened to those barrels. The information from each of the three fixers complemented each other.

I reported my findings back to the author who had commissioned my services, and he wanted to go with me to Iraq for a week to meet a few of the interviewees whom the fixers had already met. He wanted to get a commission from a big news organisation. Despite having a tempting story, it was hard to find a news company that would take the risk. My colleague wanted to go as a freelancer, but finding insurance was an issue. I had to go to Iraq anyway to visit my family, and I tried to find an insurance policy that would also cover my journalistic activity. To my surprise, I was able to find a policy which covered my trip. There were a few conditions, but they were reasonable. We met all of our interviewees in the hotel, but when one contributor insisted on us meeting him at his farm, we said no, fearing a trap. We arranged to send the fixer who had interviewed him before, with a camera. We interviewed him over the fixer's phone while keeping the camera running. On another occasion, the other fixer told us he could get access to a top leader of Al-Qaeda in Iraq, to which we said no. It was too dangerous, it was against the law and it was difficult to check the authenticity of the interviewee. More importantly, there was no sponsor. We had got our story without needing to take further risks.

The Coverage of ISIS

The coverage of ISIS, has been one of the most problematic issues in the coverage of Iraq, the Middle East and Islam in general. Many Western journalists have tried to use terms like 'fanatical jihadists' or 'extremists', and when they refer to the terror organisation they use the name ISIS or ISIL. The use of these terms was not helpful for many news agencies, including the BBC and Reuters. The BBC was criticised by the Conservative prime minister of Britain for using the term 'Islamic State', and not 'ISIL', because 'it is not an Islamic state' (Dathan, 2015). A more pejorative name, 'Daesh', was introduced from 2014, on advice from Arabic partners, and has been used by Secretary of State John Kerry and French President François Hollande, among others (Yuhas, 2014). On the other hand, the BBC in general insisted on using the term 'militia' (Muir, 2015) when they cover the Shi'a militant groups, which conveys in Iraqi minds a negative concept of lawless military group. Many journalists were prevented from using the term 'militia' in a live broadcast, being interrupted by the Iraqi public and by the forces which were around while covering battles with ISIS. On another occasion Reuters almost froze their activity after a report saying a Reuters staff correspondent had witnessed the execution of an ISIS captive by the Iraqi army (Reuters, 2015). Ned Parker took an editorial decision to publish the story, but it meant that he and other Reuters staff came under the threat of a powerful Shi'a militant group (Gallucci, 2015). He knew, because he had spent a long time covering Iraq, that the government was not powerful enough to confront the Shi'a militants, especially during wartime and with the example of Tikrit in mind (Reuters, 2015). Should he have published that story? I have no answer, but there were certainly a lot of tweaks he could have made that would have helped to make his case. He published the story, but he put himself and his colleagues in a dangerous situation. Mr Parker left the country soon afterwards (NPR, 2015) and could have broken the story afterwards.

Journalists need to assess situations properly before making big editorial decisions. Serious sensitivities could be undermined, and careful discussion is required. Journalists need to bear this in mind when they report on sensitive subjects. There is an essential need to be pragmatic, especially if journalists can afford to change a few terms without jeopardising their editorial integrity. Also, media organisations and correspondents need to be careful about the translation of the terms they are using. Journalists should ask their fixers to read their stories and discuss the content with them whenever they have leisure time before their deadlines. They should ask their advice and welcome criticisms from their team members, especially over issues like cultural differences and the terms that are used. I remember a time when I was in Najaf, when a member of Muqtada Al-Sadr's Mahdi army came to me to say, 'Why do you call us militia? We are an army, that's what we call ourselves, even when you don't say militia you say JAM [Jaysh Al-Mahdi] militia.'[2] I did not have an answer for him, and I still do not have an answer, but not crediting them with the name they had chosen definitely didn't resonate well with the group leaders and members. It is a dilemma that we face all the time, due to the fact that there are a lot of groups which choose potentially controversial names for themselves, such as 'God's Army' in Burma (Associated Press, 2013), and the 'Lord's Resistance Army' in the Congo and south Sudan (Moses, 2013), or more recently the 'Islamic State' (IS). I personally believe the media should not fall into the traps set by these armed groups, and should be more careful when they name them, avoiding giving them the titles they have chosen in order to endorse themselves with their preferred label. Such endorsement might cause a lot of trouble for parts of the wider community with which that group is trying to claim some association or common base.

Conclusion

In summary, the main concern one should bear in mind when visiting Iraq is 'cultural difference'. Do not overdo it, but do not underplay the differences either, as the consequences will be greater than you think. There are many ways of showing respect towards Iraqi culture, which will guarantee access to many stories. Building trust is another issue. Iraqis, as mentioned before, are suspicious of journalists' intentions and their questions. For this reason, journalists need to make an extra effort to build trust with them. Journalists also need to weigh the risks of how far they can go: is the risk worth taking? Can you get a better story by meeting a vendor in the street rather than queuing at a potential target like the Green Zone gate? Many tend to go with what everyone else is covering, but good preparations and up-to-date knowledge about recent events and news from Iraq will help journalists make better judgements about coverage and bring good stories under their radar. Discuss the situation with a colleague who had been there before, but upon arrival try to find another journalist to assess how the situation has developed since then. More importantly, get good updates from fixers and listen to him/her, but also follow the local and regional newspapers, TV and radio stations, which can provide a lot of story ideas.

Notes

1. Saddam Hussein Loyal Forces. A paramilitary group that kept operating after the collapse of the Baath regime in Iraq, reportedly launching attacks on American forces (Lumb, 2003).
2. For more background on what constitutes the Mahdi Army and what it stands for see Cochrane (2009).

References

Associated Press (2013). 'Briefly, Myanmar's "God's Army" twins reunite', *New York Times*, 2 November. Available at: www.nytimes.com/2013/11/03/world/asia/briefly-myanmars-gods-army-twins-reunite.html?_r=1 (accessed 28 May 2015).

Baker, Jonathan (2015). 'Embedded journalism: reporting conflict'. Available at: www.bbc.co.uk/academy/journalism/article/art20130702112133701 (accessed 20 May 2015).

BBC News (2003). 'Iraq war journalism "sanitised"', 6 November. Available at: http://news.bbc.co.uk/1/hi/world/middle_east/3247267.stm (accessed 23 May 2015).

Bexley, Kati (2004). 'Back To Baghdad'. *The St Augustine*. Available at: http://staugustine.com/stories/021504/new_2129536.shtml#.VWuZ9VxVikr. (accessed 14 May 2015).

Cash, Andrew (2005). 'Baghdad's BS Detector *Now Toronto*', 1 December. Available at: https://nowtoronto.com/news/baghdads-bs-detector/ (accessed 20 May 2015).

Cirillo, Melissa and Ricchiardi, Sherry (2004). 'Abu Ghraib time line', *American Journalism Review*, June/July. Available at: http://ajrarchive.org/article.asp?id=3730 (accessed 12 May 2015).

Cochrane, Marisa (2009). *Iraq Report 12: The Fragmentation of the Sadrist Movement*. Washington, DC: Institute for the Study of War. Available at: www.understandingwar.org/sites/default/files/Iraq%20Report%2012%20Sadrist%20Movement%20Fragmentation.pdf (accessed 28 May 2015).

Cockburn, Patrick (2010). 'Embedded journalism: a distorted view of war', *Independent*, 23 November. Available at: www.independent.co.uk/news/media/opinion/embedded-journalism-a-distorted-view-of-war-2141072.html (accessed 23 May 2015).

CPJ (Committee to Protect Journalists) (2003). '42 journalists killed in 2003/motive confirmed'. Available at: https://cpj.org/killed/2003/ (accessed 8 September 2015).

CPJ (Committee to Protect Journalists) (2004). '61 journalists killed in 2004/ motive confirmed'. Available at: https://cpj.org/killed/2004/ (accessed 8 September 2015).

CPJ (Committee to Protect Journalists) (2005). '49 journalists killed in 2005/ motive confirmed'. Available at: https://cpj.org/killed/2005/ (accessed 8 September 2015).

CPJ (Committee to Protect Journalists) (2006). '57 journalists killed in 2006/ motive confirmed'. Available at: https://cpj.org/killed/2006/ (accessed 8 September 2015).

CPJ (Committee to Protect Journalists) (2007). '70 journalists killed in 2007/ motive confirmed'. Available at: https://cpj.org/killed/2007/ (accessed 8 September 2015).

CPJ (Committee to Protect Journalists) (2008a). 'Iraq: journalists in danger', 23 July. Available at: https://cpj.org/reports/2008/07/journalists-killed-in-iraq.php (accessed 26 July 2015).

CPJ (Committee to Protect Journalists) (2008b). 'Iraq: journalists abducted 2003–2009', 23 July. Available at: https://cpj.org/reports/2008/04/abducted.php (accessed 26 July 2015).

CPJ (Committee to Protect Journalists) (2008c). '42 journalists killed in 2007/ motive confirmed'. Available at: https://cpj.org/killed/2008/ (accessed 8 September 2015).

Dathan, Matt (2015). ' "I wish the BBC would stop calling it Islamic State" – David Cameron unleashes frustration at broadcaster', *Independent*, 29 June. Available at: www.independent.co.uk/news/uk/politics/i-wish-the-bbc-would-stop-calling-it-islamic-state–david-cameron-unleashes-frustration-on-broadcaster-10351885.html (accessed 26 July 2015).

Finer, Jonathan and Partlow, Joshua (2006). 'Missing soldiers found dead in Iraq', *Washington Post*, 21 June. Available at: www.washingtonpost.com/wp-dyn/content/article/2006/06/20/AR2006062000242.html (accessed 26 July 2015).

Fisk, Robert (2005). 'Hotel journalism gives American troops a Free hand as the press shelters indoors', *Independent*, 17 January. Available at: www.independent.co.uk/voices/commentators/fisk/hotel-journalism-gives-american-troops-a-free-hand-as-the-press-shelters-indoors-5344745.html (accessed 27 May 2015).

Gallucci, Maria (2015). 'Death threats over Tikrit coverage force Reuters' Baghdad bureau chief to flee Iraq; latest sign violence against journalists is rising', *International Business Times*, 11 April. Available at: www.ibtimes.com/death-threats-over-tikrit-coverage-force-reuters-baghdad-bureau-chief-flee-iraq-1878490 (accessed 28 May 2015).

GlobalSecurity.org (2013). 'Operation Iraqi Freedom, civil military operations, cultural issues in Iraq'. Available at: www.globalsecurity.org/military/library/report/call/call_04-13_chap02-c.htm (accessed 24 March 2015).

Hersh, Seymour M. (2004). 'Torture at Abu Ghraib', *New Yorker*, 10 May. Available at: www.newyorker.com/magazine/2004/05/10/torture-at-abu-ghraib (accessed 10 May 2015).

Ignatius, David (2010). 'The dangers of embedded journalism, in war and politics', *Washington Post*, 2 May. Available at: www.washingtonpost.com/wp-dyn/content/article/2010/04/30/AR2010043001100.html (accessed 23 May 2015).

Kosmides, Michael (nd). 'Inside BBC journalism: reporters and reporting', BBC World Service. Available at: www.bbc.co.uk/worldservice/specials/1715_reporters/page6.shtml (accessed 25 May 2015).

Lumb, Patrick (2003). 'The Fedayeen: Saddam's loyal forces', BBC News, 24 March. Available at: http://news.bbc.co.uk/1/hi/world/middle_east/2881889.stm (accessed 20 May 2015).

Marlowe, Lara (2005). 'Democracy in hiding', *Irish Times*, 15 January. Available at: www.irishtimes.com/news/democracy-in-hiding-1.406699 (accessed 24 May 2015).

Marlowe, Lara (2009). 'Hassan family appeals to Iraqis for help in finding sister's body', *Irish Times*, 2 June. Available at: www.irishtimes.com/news/hassan-family-appeals-to-iraqis-for-help-in-finding-sister-s-body-1.775090 (accessed 24 May 2015).

Moses, Kara (2013). 'Lord's Resistance Army funded by elephant poaching, report finds', *Guardian*, 4 June. Available at: www.theguardian.com/environment/2013/jun/04/lords-resistance-army-funded-elephant-poaching (accessed 28 May 2015).

Muir, Jim (2015). 'Ramadi battle: Shia militias near IS-held Iraqi city. Analysis', BBC News, 18 May. Available at: www.bbc.co.uk/news/world-middle-east-32777138 (accessed 28 May 2015).

NPR (National Public Radio) (2015). 'An American journalist explains why he had to flee Iraq', 16 April. Available at: www.npr.org/sections/parallels/2015/04/16/399816144/an-american-journalist-explains-why-he-had-to-flee-iraq (accessed 28 May 2015).

Ponsford, Dominic (2005). 'Carroll: we must keep reporting from Iraq', *Press Gazette*, 26 October. Available at: http://ns337646.ip-5-196-77.eu/node/32403 (accessed 20 May 2015).

Reuters (2015). 'Special report: after Iraqi forces take Tikrit, a Wave of looting and lynching', 4 April. Available at: http://in.reuters.com/article/2015/04/03/uk-mideast-crisis-iraq-tikrit-specialrep-idINKBN0MU1DR20150403 (accessed 28 May 2015).

Ricchiardi, Sherry (2008). 'Whatever happened to Iraq?', *American Journalism Review*, June/July. Available at: http://ajrarchive.org/Article.asp?id=4515 (accessed 26 May 2015).

Ricks, Thomas (2006). *Fiasco*: The American Military Adventure in Iraq. United States. Penguin.

Sengupta, Kim (2006). 'How to stay alive in a war zone', *Independent*, 19 February. http://www.independent.co.uk/news/media/how-to-stay-alive-in-a-war-zone-5335452.html (accessed 20 May 2015).

Stack, Megan K. (2006). 'I have seen death', *LA Times*, 15 March. Available at: http://articles.latimes.com/2006/mar/15/world/fg-bahjat15 (accessed 20 May 2015).

Taylor, Richard Norton (2012). 'Shia militia ready to return body of kidnapped Briton Alan McMenemy', *Guardian*, 5 January. Available at: www.theguardian.com/world/2012/jan/05/militia-to-return-body-of-alan-mcenemy (accessed 26 May 2015).

UK government (2007). 'Iraq: cultural appreciation booklet'. Available at: www.gov.uk/government/uploads/system/uploads/attachment_data/file/16869/iraq_cultural_appreciation_booklet.pdf (accessed 30 March 2015).

US Department of Defense (2009). 'Measuring stability and security in Iraq, report to congress'. Available at: www.defense.gov/pubs/pdfs/Measuring_Stability_and_Security_in_Iraq_March_2009.pdf (accessed 22 May 2015).

Wilson, Jamie (2003). 'US troops "crazy" in killing of cameraman', *Guardian*, 19 August. Available at: www.theguardian.com/media/2003/aug/19/iraqandthemedia.iraq (accessed 24 May 2015).

Worth, Robert (2006). 'Blast destroys shrine in Iraq, setting off sectarian fury', *New York Times*, 22 February. Available at: www.nytimes.com/2006/02/22/international/middleeast/22cnd-iraq.html?_r=0 (accessed 23 May 2015).

Yuhas, Alan (2014). 'US general rebrands ISIS 'Daesh' after requests from regional partners', *Guardian*, 19 December. Available at: www.theguardian.com/world/2014/dec/19/us-general-rebrands-isis (accessed 28 May 2015).

11

Reflections and Observations on Covering the Middle East

Syria, Yemen and Saudi Arabia

Lina Sinjab

Covering the Middle East as an Arab journalist is never easy. It is hard to operate independently in the Arab world, especially when one is covering his/her own country for an international organisation. Syria has been particularly difficult. Having worked for the BBC helped me acquire international journalism standards and apply them in my own country. It also gave me some sort of protection, this Security Protection from all parties after a point in the Syrian conflict was no longer available.

During the years of the Arab revolts, I extensively covered the uprisings in both Syria and Yemen. But as protest movements turned into civil war, I had to cover the conflicts from outside the countries' borders. Saudi Arabia is another place I visited to look at the situation in Yemen, when Saudi-led airstrikes on the Houthis started before I managed to get into Sanaa. This has given me the chance to look at Saudi policies, both from a government perspective and how Saudi society perceives government policies, and also how outsiders perceive Saudis.

In this chapter, I will present a reflection on working in these countries as a journalist. I will try to explore similarities and differences in countries run by dictatorships and monarchies that are trying to remain in power; how the protest movements were perceived and handled; and the emergence of citizen journalists reporting on the conflict in Syria, who were the ears and eyes for the world in a place where government and, later on, armed groups censored the flow of information.

Censorship: Living, Thinking and Reporting in Fear

Dictatorial regimes are excellent at blocking the flow of information and controlling media organisations so they can control the dissemination of news, in order to serve their interest. In Syria, the Ministry of Information is the body that controls press cards for local journalists and those working for international media, as well as monitoring and controlling output for local news. This particular ministry shows how the sectarian line has been manipulated by the Assad regime. For years, the minister assigned this job has been of the Alawite sect. There have been only two Sunni ministers, who took this job during the days of Assad junior, including the current minister, Omran Al-Zobi, who comes from Deraa, where the protest movement started in March 2011. Like any other state establishment, the show is really run by the security apparatus, which gives the green or red light when it wants. But what's interesting about this ministry is the divide in the workers there; the ones who are most powerful are not only Alawites, but they actually hold official jobs with the security branch. It is not clear how the system really operates but with the few cases I have been in touch with directly, it was evident that they were assigned by security to be at the Ministry of Information.

One junior employee at the ministry is capable of blocking any international journalist from entering the country by simply reporting him/her to the security apparatus. This also applies to how local journalists are allowed to operate. Syrian journalists have no immunity and are hardly able to operate independently and professionally. The term freedom of expression rarely surfaced in Syria before the protest movement began. The more loyal journalists are, in broadcasting or publishing lines dictated by the security apparatus, the more access and advantage they can have.

But these advantages and immunities are not everlasting. With this type of regime, you can be powerful one day, and the next morning you can be sidelined or even imprisoned, if not killed. When your phonecalls are not answered and you are not invited to press conferences, you know immediately that you are on the black list. And it can get worse. The standards are not how professional you are, but how loyal you are to the regime.

'The more famous and successful one gets, with closer access to the regime, the more they expect you to be loyal to them', Ibrahim Hamidi tells me (email communication, 2015). Hamidi is a prominent Syrian journalist who for years was the bureau chief of Saudi newspaper *Al-Hayat*, a major pan-Arab newspaper.[1] Mr Hamidi is considered by his peers as one of the most well-informed journalists on Syria, and he had rare access to the inner circles of the Assad regime, which made his writing insightful and exclusive in providing insights into the regime's thinking. But this leverage of fame and knowledge didn't not protect him. 'When I started in the nineties and was not famous, I had more freedom and courage in my writing.' Mr Hamidi paid a high price and spent six months in solitary confinement in 2003. 'It was simply for trying to do my job and be a professional journalist. This was the result of an accumulation of the regime's dissatisfaction with my work. The way I covered peace talks and I interviewed prominent opposition figures, such as Riyad Al-Turk upon his release, was enough for the regime to imprison me.' Despite the fact that many believe Mr Hamidi is close to the regime and sometimes his writing serves the regime's interests, he had to leave Syria after the uprising began, as there was no margin left for any professional journalism.

I was privileged to work for BBC World and broadcast in English, which meant I was not under the government's and the rebels' daily surveillance. Like any other journalist, one needs to have connections with all sides to get access to the story. But in Syria, I knew I shouldn't be too close to anyone so I didn't jeopardise my journalism. Yet, I had to maintain a certain number of links to maintain access to stories. I had the connections but not close ties. Nevertheless, I had my share of punishment even before the uprising began. One article on women's rights caused a call-in and a cup of coffee; which in Syrian terms it means summoning and scolding. In 2010, I interviewed Syria's first lady, Mrs Asma Al-Assad, following a conference she called on opening up to non-governmental organisations. At the time, any such organisations operating in Syria were the ones blessed by the first lady's office. To balance my story, I interviewed women's groups who were defending women's rights and were not able to register. I didn't even tackle the issue of human rights in Syria, which were undergoing huge violations, yet that was enough for a threat from the government. Bushra Kanafani, who was then in charge of foreign media at the Ministry of Foreign Affairs, called me in and literally said: 'Who the hell you think you are to question her highness's success? With a stroke of my pen you can disappear!' I continued reporting at that time, but I wasn't invited to any events by the Ministry of Foreign Affairs, or at the presidential palace, for a few months.

The situation has changed drastically with the beginning of the uprising in March 2011. The regime was keen on imposing a blackout on information. During the first few months there were still some international and Arab media operating in Syria. Reuters correspondent Khaled Oweis, who bravely covered the developments, breaking all the taboos the regime imposes on the media, was given two hours to leave the country during the second week of the uprising. On the same day, I was arrested with my cameraman in Douma, a suburb of Damascus, where huge protests against the regime took place. Things started deteriorating after that, with more bloodshed, and more crackdowns on freedom of expression. No journalists were able independently to report on the ground. Foreign media were blocked from coming in, except in a few cases later on, and were only allowed to go to areas specified by the government to control what they saw. Local journalists were threatened and imprisoned, and many were killed. The Committee to Protect Journalists has documented more than eighty-five journalists killed between 2011 and 2015 (CPJ, 2015). Only a few of them were foreigners. Since then, the media world has largely relied on 'citizen journalists' who risk their lives to tell the story. I left Syria in March 2013.

Dictatorship with Freedom of Expression in Yemen

This wasn't the case at all in Yemen. When I visited the capital Sanaa to cover the first protest in February 2011, I was surprised how open the opposition were in speaking their minds or meeting publicly. I was coming from a background of fear in Syria, and when I met with anyone I would make sure I lowered my voice and looked around to see if someone was following or listening. But when I asked them if they were worried, they would laugh and say, we have freedom here, but we still want a change.

Yemeni President Ali Abdullah Saleh ruled Yemen for more than thirty years. Many believe he is still the ruler, although he has been out of office for over four years now. He was accused of corruption, and dragging the country into poverty and division that made it easier for him to rule. He was described as 'dancing on the heads of snakes' in the way he managed to create a balance between the tribes, controlling them for decades.

Saleh comes from the Zaidi tribe, which adopts a religion closer to Shi'a Islam. Though their practices are not religious per se, Saleh knew very well how to create a balance between different tribes. Throughout his rule, he received support from the Saudi kingdom across the border – it didn't pump in enough money to nourish the country, but it did keep it safe enough in order to protect its own backyard. The Houthis, an offshoot of the Zaidi tribe residing in Saada in northern Yemen, on a stretch of the southern border with Saudi Arabia, were for a long time a common enemy to both Saleh and Saudi Arabia. In 2009, the Houthis launched an attack at the border of Saudi Arabia and the Saudis fired back. But the balance of power changed after Saleh was ousted from power in 2011. Later on, he created new alliances so he would not be the only loser in the equation.

Unlike Syria, there was no media blackout in Yemen during its uprising. Instead there was a ping-pong show between Saleh and the opposition. Every Friday, at 60 Street leading to Change Square, the opposition would march chanting for democratic change, and at the same time Saleh would appear at 70 Street and address his own supporters in a defiant attempt to remain in power. No opposition members were imprisoned for their political views, nor journalists disappeared for reporting independently. In fact, in one incident a journalist criticised Saleh in an article and the president answered back in another article. Minders from the Ministry of Information used to take journalists to opposition houses and shake hands with them. And in the hot late afternoons, when the time arrives for chewing Kat, you can find members of the opposition sitting in same *majles* of Kat chewing with government ministers, discussing politics and agreeing and disagreeing on the situation. When I met President Saleh in the spring of 2011 in his presidential palace, he appeared very confident that he wouldn't be thrown out. 'We adhere to people's demands and ballot boxes' he told me in an interview for the BBC.[2] 'The world is listening to the minorities and ignoring the demands of the majority' claiming that the majority wants him to remain in power. Similar messages were heard repeatedly by Syria's President Bashar Al-Assad. But in Yemen, the

Gulf Cooperation Countries backed by the EU managed to strike a deal to get the president out of office and have his deputy Abed Rabbo Mansour Hadi replace him. Saleh only agreed to this after an attempt to assassinate him, after which he was flown to Saudi Arabia to be treated for severe burns to his face and hands.

Nearly four years on, Yemen has descended into a civil war where divides are not only along political lines but, like Syria and Iraq, along sectarian ones. The Houthis came from Saada in the north of the country, near the border with Saudi Arabia. They invaded the capital, Sanaa, and took control. Later on, they stretched out further south and are now trying to capture the whole country, flouting the Saudi-brokered political deal that ended Saleh's reign. The Saudis see the Houthis as proxies to the Shi'a clerical rulers of Iran and have started an air bombing campaign against them.

Censorship and Stereotyping in Saudi Arabia

Censorship takes a different shape in Saudi Arabia. It is not a country where you can get a tourist visa, and then leave and write a piece. Every permit to enter has to be approved and strictly kept to the requested details of the mission. Media access is very rare, and only given at the invitation of the government when they wish to get a message across. Saudi Arabia is heavily involved in developments in the region, especially following the Arab Revolts. The king granted 36 billion dollars in benefits for social systems to appease citizens when the protest movements started in the Arab world, as a measure to stop any potential social unrest. But the kingdom itself is facing troubles in Qutaif with its Shi'a minority. They are sidelined, and not treated as equals in relation to their fellow Sunni citizens. Some protests took place there that were not highlighted in the news, but this is not the only trouble the richest country in the Arab world is facing. The radical Islamic teaching and practices by its religious clerics are believed to be the ones producing and exporting extremist ideologies. After the appearance of ISIS, the West, shocked by its brutal practices, formed a coalition led by the United States to fight the extremist group both in Syria and Iraq, especially after the beheading of American and British citizens there. But the same countries that are fighting ISIS for its practices didn't condemn similar practices, such as beheading, conducted by the state of

Saudi Arabia. Nearly nineteen cases of public beheading were reported during the year of 2014.

In 2015, as Saudi Arabia launched its war against the Houthis in Yemen, I had the chance to visit Saudi Arabia. Following the start of 'Decisive Storm' – the airstrike campaign against the Houthis – Saudi Arabia allowed many journalists to visit the country and organised tours and daily military briefings to update the news on the operation. It was a clear effort to assert the government's position on a 'violation' in their back yard: Yemen. Many said it was an uncalculated decision that had no clear strategy.

Talking to Prince Turki Al-Faisal in an interview for BBC Arabic, the prince gave a very calculated diplomatic answer on Saudi Arabia's involvement in the region. He said their action in Yemen came in accordance with the legitimate Yemeni government's request, a line you repeatedly hear from the government. However, the understanding was that Saudi Arabia's involvement in Yemen is not only due to the sensitive situation at its border, but is to send a message to the Iranian regime to stop what Saudi Arabia believes to be meddling in the region. Prince Turki Al-Faisal played down the conflict with Iran, saying they are ready to cooperate if the Iranians are ready to do so.

But the reality is different. The tension is rising between Sunni-majority Saudi Arabia and Shi'a-majority Iran. The nuclear deal with Iran that was signed with the United States and the EU in June 2015 is widely seen in the Gulf region as a green light to Iran to continue its involvement in the region. Therefore, Saudi Arabia, the West's ally in the region, is asserting its power through proxy wars as in Syria, or directly as in Yemen.

Saudi Arabia doesn't feel like a pariah state for visiting journalists (as Syria feels) – minders accompanying foreign journalists in Saudi Arabia don't act like security watchdogs as is the case in Syria – yet it is still hard to hear a voice opposing the regime line.

Interviews with people on the street in Riyadh or Jeddah speak the government's mind. Opposition voices are silenced when they tackle different views on religion, like the case of Raif Badawi, the blogger sentenced to 1,000 lashes for challenging religious views.

However, there is still a sense of stereotyping when it comes to how Saudi Arabia is seen and covered by outsiders. When asked about the influence of Saudi extremist Wahhabis in the region, people reject the accusation and say Wahhabism represents one segment of the society and it doesn't mean that the whole society subscribes to their ideology. A prominent female TV presenter, Muna AbuSulayman, who presents the popular TV show *Softly Speaking* on Saudi-funded Arab channel MBC, provides a surprisingly different image of Saudi women than what is usually seen. In a report on the rights of women in Saudi she told me the situation is not as bad as it is represented in the Western media. Ms AbuSulayman believes the world fixates their view on a mainstream narrative of oppressed Saudi women who are covered in black from head to toe, but she and many like her are not. In fact, the view was even echoed by a covered Saudi woman in her veil who was getting ready to go and do her PhD in Britain. While the world focuses on women in Saudi Arabia being deprived of their rights to drive, they are fighting a more important battle to secure rights in society and family law.

The battle for Saudi Arabia as a kingdom, however, is more challenging. Radical Islam that is nourished at home is exporting a transnational extremist ideology that Saudi Arabia says it is fighting in its own land and abroad. The fear is that unless society revolts against hard-line religious preaching and practices, it is hard to see the kingdom's efforts in combating terrorism being successful any time soon.

Arab Autumn: Worsening Reporting Conditions

At the beginning of the uprising in Syria, a pro-government journalist told me[3] 'the Egyptians have regretted giving up power in response to the people's demand after they saw how *we* stayed in control'. He continued by adding that 'the methods that the Syrian regime is using have made other leaders in the region learn not to give up. Now the Egyptian military and security are cooperating with *us*' (emphasis added). By referring to the regime with the words 'we' and 'us', he identified himself with the circle of power.

This loyal journalist conveyed to me what was hard to believe or verify at the time. Four years on, looking at how things drastically deteriorated in Syria, his words ring true. The regime has managed to stay in power and turn the myth of extremism and terrorism that was completely unfounded at the beginning of the uprising into a self-fulfilling prophecy.

The crackdown on journalists intensified in Syria, where it became almost impossible to work independently. I had to leave in 2013 after several arrest experiences and a nearly year-long travel ban, when I was not allowed to leave the country.

While the regime prevented foreign journalists from entering Syria when the protests were peaceful, they are now allowing more frequent visas for journalists to come to areas under their control to see the effects of the war. The narratives of 'fighting Islamic terrorism', and 'protecting minorities' have prevailed in Western media coverage, as this was the story they could access when visiting regime-controlled areas. In rebel-held territories, things got worse, with a high number of kidnappings of foreign journalists and aid workers. The media refrained almost completely from getting into northern Syria after the rise and expansion of ISIS, which executed a number of journalists and aid workers.

Consequently, this meant that the narrative of ordinary Syrians, the call for freedom and change, and even the daily suffering of Syrians from government barrel bombs and air bombardment have dropped off the news agenda. With the exception of a limited number of foreign journalists having rare access to the north, we rely largely on citizen journalists who are risking their lives to keep the stream of news coming out, when and if international agencies find an important line to cover. Without those unknown soldiers, the world wouldn't have seen evidence of the chemical attack that took place in August 2015, killing at least 1,500 people in Eastern Ghouta in the suburbs of Damascus, most of whom were children.

Nowadays, the news coming out of Syria mainly focuses on fighting ISIS. Their executions of Westerners pushed the United States into forming a coalition to fight the group in June 2014, and airstrikes targeted Iraq and Syria shortly after. For Syria's regime, this is the best enemy they can have. The international agenda has shifted from ousting the regime, to engaging with it to fight terrorism.

The Assad regime is known to be very good at time games. Mr Lakhdar Brahimi, who succeeded Kofi Annan as a UN Arab envoy for Syria, said, following the failure of Geneva talks in 2014, 'The regime was never willing to negotiate. They always acted as they were going to win in a few weeks.' Although the official regime narrative always claimed it was engaging in a political solution and negotiations, their words said one thing but their actions said differently. It was clear during the Geneva talks in 2014, where world powers gathered to support negotiations endorsed by a UN resolution. And as a sign of goodwill, the regime was asked to lift the siege on Homs, which had been besieged for nearly two years by that time. A deal only took place to allow civilians out of Homs three months later, and only after rebels captured Iranian soldiers, meaning that Iran's ambassador to Damascus was in Homs to facilitate the deal. This says a lot about Syria's struggle. While 'Friends of Syria', a group formed by eleven members of the international community, failed to keep a consistent and united position on supporting the opposition, Iran and Russia, Syria's main allies, have been consistent and firm on their position assisting Assad's regime. Each state is doing so for its own strategic interests.

The bottom line is that ordinary Syrians feel left out of the equation. Their supposed allies have taken action not to ease their sufferings, but to fight an enemy taking Islam as a flag which feeds into the West's Islamophobia. This is causing an increasing sense of grievance in Syria. This is hardly being reported or reflected in the media, as the focus now is mainly on the battle against ISIS.

In Yemen, and following the Houthis taking over the capital Sanaa, the situation has also deteriorated for journalists. The Houthis started targeting journalists who they consider loyal to President Abd Rabbo Mansour Hadi; and the Saudis on their part have included journalists in the embargo they imposed on the country. It has been difficult to get access to report on developments since the Saudi-led airstrikes began. Once again, the world relied on brave local journalists to report the story and bring images of Yemeni devastation to the television screens. After months of trying, I managed to travel to in Sanaa in summer 2015. It was a scene of a failed state but also the failed hopes of Yemenis who dreamed of change.

Reporting as an Arab woman in Sanaa has always been surprisingly easy. The society has high level of respect for women, such that even walking in the streets with my jeans and hair uncovered has never been a problem. People show a lot of respect for women and the same applies to the government and politicians. During my time there, I was surprised by the strong outspoken women I met in 2011 who were part of the protest movement.

Samia Haddad, one of the leading women activists who took to the streets and lobbied for political and democratic change in 2011, has moved from being a democracy activist to a displaced Yemeni who has nearly lost hope.

I followed Samia and her fellow activists in the months of the uprising in 2011 when they were all filled with hope and energy, that their country, Yemen, which already suffered poverty, underdevelopment and corruption was about to ride a wave of change.

She was among the few people I met in 2011 who is still in Sanaa and believes that Yemen combines elements of all the wars that are happening in the Middle East at the moment. 'We have two divided governments, one outside and one inside like Syria, we have the Sunni/Shi'a divide like Iraq and we have a south/north divide like Sudan.'[4] For many Yemenis, the revolution has been hijacked by the Muslim Brotherhood's Islah party and Abd Rabbo Mansour Hadi, who took power after ousting former President Ali Abdalla Saleh, was and still is too weak to rule. He fled with his government to Riyadh to escape the Houthis' advance. People like Samia, who are critical of the Houthis taking over Sanaa, are also angry at Saudi Arabia's actions: 'Saudi Arabia has always been helpful to Yemen, now they are spending millions of dollars to bomb us! Wouldn't have been more helpful if they have used this money to develop Yemen?'[5]

The main game-changer behind the scenes is not the Houthis, according to Samia. It is former President Ali Abdullah Saleh, who wasn't happy being out of the game after being the leader for more than thirty years: 'He still holds many of the cards. He still controls a lot of the military, about 80 per cent are in his hands and he can control them as he wants, and his alliance with the Houthis, he's just using them.'[6]

Many people I met on the streets in the capital told me the same. I interviewed former President Saleh when he was in office in 2011, just before he was ousted. Now his men are the ones who are trained and organised on the ground. The Houthis are new to power, they are chaotic and lack experience. A government official told me an illiterate sentry at the ministry he works for has become a deputy minister. 'They come from the countryside and know nothing about ruling an establishment.'[7] Their acting leader, Mohammad Ali Al-Houthi, now sits in the presidential palace. I met him in the same building I met Saleh four years ago. When asked about their connection with Saleh he denied any alliance. 'Saleh is not in power now but after the Saudi invasion, everyone is standing together to fight the Saudis'[8] he told me.

Another Arab State where spring turned into autumn and dictatorship still holds on at the expense of the country and the people. For Arab journalists, I still believe it is spring despite the crackdown and the difficulties. So many new talents are emerging. We may have a long way still to go before we have free and independent media in the Arab world, but the journey has started.

Notes

1. See Ibrahim, 1997. Also see *Al-Hayat* website in Arabic: www.alhayat.com/.
2. On 24 April 2011, available from: www.bbc.com/news/world-middle-east-13181324. There is also a longer version in Arabic: www.youtube.com/watch?v=-ihjwY8E_mE.
3. Comments made and given clearance to publish with promise of anonymity in June 2011.
4. Interview recorded in Yemen in June 2015. It hasn't been published on the BBC.
5. Samia Haddad, interviewed in Yemen in June 2015; interview not published on the BBC.
6. Samia Haddad, interviewed in Yemen in June 2015; interview not published on the BBC.
7. Interview conducted during my last trip to Yemen in June 2015, broadcast on BBC Arabic, no link available.
8. Interview conducted during my last trip to Yemen in June 2015, broadcast on BBC Arabic, no link available.

References

CPJ (Committee to Protect Journalists) (2015). '85 journalists killed in Syria since 1992/motive confirmed'. Available at: https://cpj.org/killed/mideast/syria/ (accessed 12 August 2015).

Ibrahim, Youssef (1997). 'Al-Hayat: a journalistic Noah's Ark', *New York Times*. Available at: www.nytimes.com/1997/01/15/world/al-hayat-a-journalistic-noah-s-ark.html (accessed 15 August 2015).

Index

Index